ANDREW S

The Vegetarian Guide to Britain & Europe

- **Britain's top 100 places to eat**
- **Package holidays for vegetarians at home and abroad**
- **Recommended European restaurants, lodgings and holiday ideas**

SIMON & SCHUSTER

LONDON·SYDNEY·NEW YORK·TOKYO·SINGAPORE·TORONTO

First published in Great Britain by
Simon & Schuster Ltd in 1992
A Paramount Communications Company

Simon & Schuster Ltd
West Garden Place
Kendal Street
London W2 2AQ

Simon & Schuster of Australia Pty Ltd
Sydney

A CIP catalogue record for this book is
available from the British Library
ISBN 0-671-65313-X

Typeset in Sabon 10/12 by Goodfellow & Egan
Printed and bound in Great Britain by
Billing & Sons Ltd, Worcester

For Gerry and Joshua
– fellow travellers –

Contents

Acknowledgements

With many thanks for ideas, information, help and encouragement to:
Sarah Brown, author of *The Best of Vegetarian Britain* and many cookery books; Matthew Collins, of BBC2's *The Travel Show*; Margaret Greenwood, author of the *Footloose Guide to Spain* and other guidebooks; Roby Harly, of the Israeli Ministry of Tourism; Leah Leneman, author of *Vegan Cooking* and several other books for vegans; Leon Lewis, author of *Vegetarian Dinner Parties*; Maria Salvenmoser, of Kitzbühel, Austria; and most of all, to my patient, helpful constant companion Geraldine Dunham.

Introduction

All over Europe an interesting thing is happening to vegetarian food. More and more restaurants, guesthouses and hotels which are *not* vegetarian are offering good-quality meals without any meat or fish. At the same time, the mediocre cooking offered in some traditional vegetarian restaurants (often too heavy in Britain, or too austere in Europe) has started to seem unacceptable. Vegetarian eating is everywhere becoming not just ethical and healthy, but creative, imaginative and delicious. At last we may be witnessing the emergence of a real life-loving, cruelty-free haute cuisine in which asceticism and self-righteousness have absolutely no part to play.

Curiously, considering its dubious reputation for food, Britain leads the way in this trend. In the last two years, Britain has seen a tremendous improvement in both the number and quality of restaurants offering vegetarian meals. A new type of diner is sitting down at the table, one who is happy to eat either meat or meatless dishes – as long as the food is good. This is raising the expectations of vegetarians and therefore, one hopes, generating yet more improvement. As cooks and diners both find their way abroad, these changes are beginning to have their effect in other countries as well.

Maybe the word vegetarian will fade away from menus altogether eventually, as meatless dishes become increasingly normal. However, things have not yet reached that stage. Vegetarians heading even for a night out – and certainly for a holiday – still have to think carefully where to eat and where to stay.

Who's listed in the Guide

In this first edition of *The Vegetarian Guide*, the selection represents a personal choice. It has been my objective to find the best, the most interesting and the most useful of restaurants and accommodation throughout Britain and Europe. I have stretched Europe's borders a little to include Israel, an excellent country for vegetarians.

Every place listed caters for vegetarians as part of its normal service, reaching a standard of cooking which is well above the average. No establishment has been included which can only offer a main course of omelette or salad.

Numerous other establishments which do serve meatless food have *not* been included because they were not of a sufficiently high standard. Of course, the number of places is vast, so some may have been overlooked: down any backstreet which I passed unknowingly, there may be a new restaurant, or one which I did not hear about – let me know (see page 217) if you think certain addresses deserve to be included in the next edition.

A uniform standard cannot be applied to the whole of Europe – there are too many variations from country to country. The quality of vegetarian cookery in Britain and Ireland is generally the highest, with France second. In Italy, many meat-free dishes are available in excellent restaurants which do not claim to cater for vegetarians. German establishments on the whole do not reach a high standard. But while Britain and Germany both have thousands of vegetarian establishments, France has a mere handful – and this illustrates the problem: German places have been listed which would not be included if they were British or French. Most countries still have so few good-quality suitable restaurants and hotels that to be too choosy might leave nothing at all. Indeed, certain countries do not make an appearance in this edition for that very reason: I found nothing there worth mentioning.

Inclusive holidays

When it comes to package holidays, obviously vegetarians cannot choose just anything from the glossy pages of brochures displayed in travel agencies. Anyone keen to avoid meat needs to be cautious about which destination to choose, and which company to book with. The mainstream tourism industry deals in mass markets and majority tastes. It flies planesful of people to huge modern hotels in predictable places where the greatest attractions are hot sunny weather and cheap wine. Something called 'international' food is provided – easily recognisable, popular dishes with just a pinch of local character. A better option, and it's increasingly available, is to travel with a smaller tour operator who understands vegetarian requirements and makes a feature of catering for them. Some even have completely vegetarian programmes. I have looked in detail at what they can offer: see Chapter 2.

What *is* a vegetarian

The varieties of diets referred to as vegetarian are extremely diverse, but by contrast the reasons for being vegetarian are very few. The basic principle is the avoidance of all meat and meat products. Most also avoid fish. Some try to eliminate from their diet all cheeses containing animal rennet (a coagulant obtained from the stomachs of calves). Most Western vegetarians do eat eggs, while most from Asian countries do not. In Britain, vegans – who eat no animal products at all – form a considerable minority. In other countries, people who try to eat only raw food, only organic food, or even those who eat fish but not meat, also come under the 'vegetarian' umbrella. The macrobiotic diet is something quite different, based on quasi-scientific philosophical principles of balancing 'yin' (female) and 'yang' (male) influences in the diet, but it does cause many of its adherents to become almost completely vegetarian.

The four usual reasons for giving up meat can be described as ethical, religious, political, or for improved health. The ethical or moral approach is the most common in Britain, and stems from a concern for the welfare of animals, together with a belief that human beings are not superior to others, and that it is wrong to use force to humiliate other species. This is not entirely the same as having religious motives – some Christians (Adventists, for example) assert that Christ was a vegetarian and that they should follow suit; many Jews adopt a vegetarian diet, especially when travelling, partly because it is an easy way to keep kosher; Hindus, who make up a large proportion of Britain's vegetarians, are specifically proscribed from eating any meat or eggs. The political viewpoint is based on the idea that the large-scale raising of animals for meat is a wasteful use of farmland, thus contributing to poverty and malnutrition in many countries. The desire for better health (numerous studies do show the advantages of a meat-free diet) is by far the commonest reason in most European countries, and is often combined with various other health-promoting practises, such as avoiding alcohol and caffeine.

This guide has been written for those who, whatever their reasons, eat no meat or fish, but do eat all milk products and eggs.

Other Guides

The Vegetarian Guide to Britain and Europe complements my other book, *The Vegetarian Traveller* (Grafton, £4.99), which gives full information about what food is eaten in each country and how to make the best of it as a vegetarian. Vocabulary lists and names of dishes to look out for are included for all countries in Europe and the Mediterranean area.

The International Vegetarian Travel Guide (Vegetarian Society, £3.99) sets out to list all vegetarian facilities throughout the whole world, from Argentina to Zimbabwe. These are included irrespective of how good they are, and range from cafeterias in community centres to dining rooms in luxury hotels. This can be useful. Unfortunately, owing to the size of the task, many errors creep in and it is also difficult to keep the information up to date – so before travelling to any listed establishment, always phone to ensure that it is still in existence.

Prices

Prices quoted were correct as we went to press but should be taken only as an approximate guide.

Getting the facts

To the best of my knowledge all information in The Vegetarian Guide To Britain And Europe is true and accurate at the time of going to press. Similarly, all comment on hotels, restaurants, and other businesses is made solely on the basis of personal opinion, either my own or that of informants.

CONTRIBUTE!

Please let me know if you spot anything out of date or inaccurate in this guide. If you stay in any hotel, eat in any restaurant, or travel with any tour operator really deserving to be recommended, send full details for inclusion in the next edition. Use the questionnaire on p. 217. Senders of contributions used will be entitled to a free copy of the next edition.

READING AN ENTRY

Every establishment in the guide is recommended – those with stars are outstanding. All can provide a full vegetarian meal without advance notice. It is not necessary for them to describe the dishes as 'vegetarian'.

Entries list the following information:

Name of village or town (county)
Name of establishment, address and phone number
What kind of place is it – hotel, restaurant, guesthouse? Is it 100% vegetarian? For places with accommodation, the proprietors' names are given.

After a description of the premises and the food, I give these details:
For restaurants – price of a meal; price of wine; hours of opening.
For hotels and guesthouses – when open; how many rooms; prices for food and for accommodation; price of wine; whether credit cards accepted.

The Stars

★★★★ a meal of the highest standard in an entirely vegetarian establishment
no 4-star award made

★★★ a vegetarian meal of the highest standard
The PARK HOTEL Kenmare, Ireland
The LYGON ARMS Broadway, Great Britain

★★a magnificent example of a vegetarian meal
BALLYMALOE HOUSE Shanagarry, Ireland
CASHEL PALACE Cashel, Ireland
CHEWTON GLEN New Milton, Great Britain
La COMÉDIE Cagnes-sur-Mer, France
DROMOLAND CASTLE Newmarket-on-Fergus, Ireland
FRITHS London, Great Britain
HOPE END Ledbury, Great Britain
L'HORIZON St Brelade, Great Britain
Le JARDIN GOURMAND Auxerre, France
LEITH'S London, Great Britain
LONGUEVILLE MANOR St Saviour, Great Britain
Le MIMOSA St Guiraud, France
MOORINGS Wells Next The Sea, Great Britain
La VENDÉE Geneva, Switzerland

★vegetarian meal reaching an unusually high standard
ALASTAIR LITTLE London, Great Britain
ARBUTUS LODGE Cork, Ireland
Le BEFFROI Caromb, France
La CANTINETTA DI RIGNANA Greve in Chianti, Italy
La COMBE Les Eyzies, France
CORSE LAWN HOUSE Corse Lawn, Great Britain
DRIMCONG HOUSE Moycullen, Ireland
EN KAMONIM near Parod, Israel

L'ESCARGOT London, Great Britain
Le FAUROU Belvès, France
FLITWICK MANOR Flitwick, Great Britain
GARBO'S Kings Lynn, Great Britain
HASSLER-VILLA MEDICI Rome, Italy
JOIA Milan, Italy
LUPTON TOWER Kirkby Lonsdale, Great Britain
MIJANOU London, Great Britain
Les MILLÉSIMES Gevrey-Chambertin, France
La NEYRETTE St Disdier-en-Dévoluy, France
The OLD RECTORY Wicklow, Ireland
PAULIAC Ribérac, France
Le POUSSIN Brockenhurst, Great Britain
QUAYLES Cardiff, Great Britain
QUINCE & MEDLAR Cockermouth, Great Britain
RESTAURANT 44 Belfast, Ireland
RISON St Clar, France
SOUTH LODGE Lower Beeding, Great Britain
The STANNARY Mary Tavy, Great Britain
STON EASTON PARK Ston Easton, Great Britain
SUTHERLAND'S London, Great Britain
THAT CAFÉ Manchester, Great Britain

. . .

See also: The LANESBOROUGH London, Great Britain

Package Holidays

Why travel with a big holiday company which doesn't know what a vegetarian eats and just treats you as a nuisance? Instead, book with a firm which welcomes vegetarians and can cater for them properly. Here is a selection of inclusive vegetarian holidays currently on the market.
Prices quoted should be taken as an approximate guide only – most refer to 1991 season.

In the UK

Totally (or mainly) Vegetarian

AUNTIES *56 Coleshill Terrace, Llanelli, Dyfed, tel. (0554) 770077*
What Aunties offer is bed, breakfast and evening meal for vegetarians in friendly, efficient guesthouses around the country. Overnight stops or longer stays are equally available. All the places have been personally checked and a good, reliable standard established. This is a useful service, because travellers wanting to stay in an unfamiliar area may be either overwhelmed by a choice of vegetarian guesthouses without knowing which of them are good, or stumped by a complete absence of vegetarian addresses. Some of the guesthouses are booked through Aunties, while others have to be contacted directly. Prices are astonishingly low. Perhaps especially useful are those close to London. Aunties will prepare a touring itinerary to fit in with your travel plans, arranging vegetarian accommodation en route.
Typically about £15 per person for bed and breakfast.
London breaks: £105 per person per week.

BICYCLE BEANO *59 Birchill Rd, Clehonger, Hereford, tel. (0981) 251087*
Cycling on one-week planned itineraries with a group of up to 30 people through the pretty parts of Britain. Each person can go at

their own pace, and the group meets up for lunch, tea, and in the evening. Pubs and cafés, places of interest, possible detours, are shown on route maps provided. Distances covered vary from 25 to 60 miles per day, with nights spent either under canvas or in simple indoor accommodation. All food is hearty wholemeal vegetarian. Bike provided, or use your own.
£200 per person – includes accommodation, breakfast, tea and evening meal.

GARTH CASTLE *Maryse Vogelaar, Garth Castle, Keltneyburn, Nr Aberfeldy, PH15 2LG, Scotland, tel. (08873) 519*
This extraordinary 1000-year-old stone castle at the end of a mile and a half of track in the middle of nowhere is Maryse's home. Coming from her native Holland, she bought it eight years ago, but started opening the castle to visitors only a year ago because 'it took seven years to clean out all the negative energy from the place'. Certainly it had a blood-curdling history when it belonged to Alexander Stuart, 'The Wolf of Badenoch'. Now it's a magical, special place which can take up to fifteen guests. From spring to late autumn, a guide from the Scottish Wildlife Trust is based here. It's a perfect base for hill walking, and there's also riding, golf, and watersports all close at hand. Alternatively, just come, relax, do your thing, and enjoy the birds, waterfalls, and surrounding country. Everyone eats together and helps with such everyday jobs as making beds, baking bread and tending the fire, and, for those who want them, there are courses in painting, cookery, leylines and dowsing, among others. Several guests bring musical instruments; if you have one, bring it along. It's full board, 100% vegetarian, with minimum stays of a week. Visitors are advised to bring a warm woolly – to wear indoors.
£195 per person per week full board, excluding any courses taken.

HEAD FOR THE HILLS *Garth, Builth, Powys, tel. (05912) 388*
Small groups of walkers literally take to the hills under the guidance of Laurence Golding, the idea being to move through the land and its features without encountering any sign of the twentieth century. Laurence sees it as not just a holiday, but a kind of mental 'cure' for the state of mind induced by modern disregard for nature. He describes walking as 'a meditation'. People are urged to put away their watches, and simply walk at their own pace. The walks follow ancient footpaths, which – unlike modern roads – are moulded to the form of the land. Perhaps the only paradox in these trips is that

all luggage is taken on to the next stop by Landrover! It hauls a horsebox within which there's a larder, library, and everything necessary to ensure pleasant stopovers. Accommodation is under canvas in farmers' fields, and tasty vegetarian food is provided. The walks, lasting four to nine nights, are all over the country, for example Wiltshire, Welsh valleys, Yorkshire dales, and Pembrokeshire coast.
Full-board prices range from £112 for four nights, to £225 for nine nights. Reductions for people on low incomes.

MELINDWR HOLIDAY COURSES *Melindwr, Hen Goginan, Aberystwyth, Dyfed, tel. (097084) 350*
Stay in Shelagh Hourahane's friendly house, in the country some seven miles from Aberystwyth, and learn about Welsh culture and countryside as well as taking part in short courses combining photography, writing, local mythology, Welsh language, bird-watching and personal development, all aimed at giving an understanding of oneself in relation to the local environment. All the courses include plenty of opportunity to walk and explore the surrounding country. Bring waterproofs and stout walking shoes. Sheelagh is an artist and art-historian, and her early nineteenth-century house was once the home of the 'captain' of one of the local lead mines, which used to be a feature of this region, though now many have been re-landscaped. The accommodation is in comfortable rooms, usually sharing. All meals are vegetarian, and organic whenever possible.
Example courses/prices: 'Autumn Celebration' –
£175 for one week; 'Landscape and Green Photography' – £105; 'Naming the Place' – £105.

NORTH MYMMS COACHES – *see* Abroad *below*.

SUNRA *Grimstone Manor, near Yelverton, Devon, tel. (0822) 854358*
Yoga and meditation weekend retreats at Grimstone Manor on the edge of Dartmoor. This is a peaceful and rigorous break, but not austere: the house, in twenty acres, has its own heated pool, 'jakuzzi' (as Sunra call it), and sauna. Guests can also ride, windsurf and play golf.
Weekend cost: £113.50.

VEGETARIAN HOLIDAYS *Susan and Brian Burnett, Nant Yr Hafod Cottage, Llandegla, Clwyd, tel. (097888) 442*
Easy-going, relaxed walking in North Wales learning from Brian about local wildlife, with lodgings in Brian and Susan's own home, a former walkers' hostel standing by Offa's Dyke path. Accommodation is simple, with shared rooms, and the two- or three-course meals too are very simple, wholesome and vegetarian. From 1992, boating holidays on similar lines.
£50–£60 for a weekend, £120–£150 for a week.

VEGETARIAN SOCIETY COOKERY SCHOOL *Parkdale, Dunham Rd, Altrincham, Cheshire, tel. (061) 928 0793*
Take a break and learn something useful! Throughout the year, the Vegetarian Society runs residential cookery courses lasting one week or a weekend at its headquarters in Altrincham, ten miles south of Manchester. The town itself has history and character, and there's plenty to see in the surrounding area. The courses give you the Society's widely-recognised Cordon Vert qualification.
One week residential course: £239.
Weekend residential course: £135.

VEGI VENTURES – *see* Abroad *below*.
Nigel Walker's extensive programme includes activity holidays in Scotland, the Lake District, and other areas of Britain.

Non-Vegetarian

FURTHER AFIELD *Warcarr, Greenhead, Northumberland, tel. (0697747) 358*
Individually tailored walks or cycle rides on peaceful back routes in the wide open landscapes of Northumberland. You don't travel in a group – everything is worked out just to suit you. The idea could hardly be simpler or more appealing. First make your own way to Northumberland, where you can be collected from station or airport, or if you are driving your car will be safely parked. The route – based on your own interests as explained on the booking form – consists of anything from six to fifteen miles a day for walkers, or fifteen to 45 miles a day for cyclists. But if you want to cut a day short, for any reason at all or even for no reason, you will be collected by car and driven on to your next overnight stop. Your luggage, in any case, is always carried on ahead to the village hotels, guesthouses and pubs where you'll spend each night and have

breakfast in the morning. Other meals are not included in the quoted price, but all accommodation has been chosen on the basis that good vegetarian food is always available.
One week's walking – £190; cycling – £245.

TRUSTHOUSE FORTE LEISURE BREAKS UK *Reservations: (0345) 500 400 or (081) 567 3444*
All Trusthouse Forte hotels offer vegetarian food – although exactly what they offer is a matter of individual hotel policy, and you would have to check first before booking. THF is a major international hotel chain, with 245 hotels in Britain, 40 on the Continent, and nearly 500 in the USA. THF in Britain offer a broad selection of full holidays, 'anytime breaks', short breaks, special interest weekends and so on, with accommodation at their hotels. These are mostly smart, high-quality modern places in the three- or four-star range. It's refreshing to hear a spokesman for Crest (one of the THF brand names) taking the view that 'conventional food and drink is not necessarily required by every guest'.
Short holidays from about £32 per person per night for half-board. ABTA bonded.

Abroad

Totally (or mainly) Vegetarian

ANDREW SANGER'S VEGETARIAN TRAVELLERS
60 Crewys Road, London NW2 2AD, tel. (081) 201 9054
This is my own travel company, through which inclusive travel and half-board accommodation can be booked at a small selection of hotels and guesthouses in Europe (and Israel). Currently, they include a luxury country house hotel in Ireland, two friendly rural guesthouses in the Dordogne, a charming hotel on the Spanish island of Menorca, and a village guesthouse in Galilee. English is spoken at all establishments, and all provide a good-quality vegetarian menu. The basic holiday is one or two weeks with half-board, but we're flexible and can usually make arrangements to suit exactly what you require.
Two weeks in the Dordogne – from £250 per person (includes half-board and Channel crossings). Flights CAA-bonded.

ATSITSA – *see* Skyros Centre, below.

Canterbury Travel Vegetarian Holidays
248 Streatfield Rd, Kenton, Harrow, Middlesex, tel. (081) 206 0411
Canterbury Travel put together a number of small travel programmes of different types, including this one for vegetarians. It's been going for several years, but has been contracting rather than expanding because, as Mrs Collins, of Canterbury Travel, explains, 'The demand for these holidays really isn't very large.' Currently they are offering just two hotels, both in Austria. The hotels are both friendly, well-equipped comfortable places in attractive mountain-and-lake countryside within easy reach of Salzburg, and can provide vegetarians with well planned four- and five-course meals of a good standard. Non-vegetarian fellow travellers are equally welcome. You can fly, drive, or go by train.
From around £350 per person for one week, with air travel; from around £370 per person for 2 weeks, if travelling in own car.
ABTA bonded.

Cortijo Romero *24 Grange Avenue, Chapeltown, Leeds LS7 4EJ, tel. (0532) 374015*
Inclusive self-discovery/personal development holidays at a beautiful country house in Andalusia, southern Spain.
For more details, *see* Spain, p. 138.
From about £305 for one-week course including return flight and full board.

North Mymms Coaches *P.O. Box 152, Potters Bar, Herts EN6 3NR, tel. (0707) 371866*
This small but well-established coach tour operator has taken to organising occasional inclusive trips for vegetarians, though meat-eating companions can often be catered for by special request. Destinations will vary from year to year, but currently include an August week at a family-run village hotel in the Austrian Alps. Western France and Holland are also planned. They have UK holidays as well, with a September week in North Devon.
Austria week £239 pp, Devon £195 pp, both inclusive of all travel and half-board.

Skyros Centre, Skyros Institute, Atsitsa
92 Prince of Wales Road, London NW5 3NE, tel. (071) 284 3065
All on the Greek island of Skyros, these are three personal development centres ideal for an unusual holiday – from which you

could return a different person. The Skyros Centre is in the island's tiny capital, Skyros village. The Centre runs personal development courses and 'the opportunity to get to know oneself and others in an honest and open way'. Accommodation is in simple village rooms, and there's plenty of time to enjoy the sun, sea, and Greek island atmosphere. The Skyros Institute provides training courses for professionals in holistic health techniques, such as massage, yoga, Alexander technique, sexual counselling, etc. Students receive a certificate (denoting only that they attended the courses), or, in certain cases, credits towards a professional qualification. Apart from the courses, there's plenty of leisure time. Atsitsa is more purely holiday-orientated; it's situated among Mediterranean pines by the sea, nine miles from Skyros village. There's a friendly community atmosphere, and lots of group activities: dance, aerobics, yoga, T'ai Chi, massage, theatre, and more. The food is mainly organic and predominantly vegetarian. *See also:* Greece, p. 90.
Two weeks £385–£595 includes accommodation and full-board at Atsitsa or half-board at Skyros Centre. Flights not included.

VEGI VENTURES *17 Lilian Road, Burnham on Crouch, Essex CM0 8DS, tel. (0621) 784285*
This is the leading, most successful proponent of totally vegetarian package holidays abroad. They are rather like vegetarian chalet parties, but with lots of freedom to do whatever you want. Guided groups of around ten to twenty people, under the personal supervision of chef Nigel Walker or a member of his staff, travel to such diverse destinations as Portugal, Norway, Paris, Berlin, or stay within Britain. Activity holidays are a major feature, and range from sailing off the Essex coast to skiing in Norway and to windsurfing in the Mediterranean. There are multi-activity weeks in Scotland. Accommodation is generally in comfortable villas. The food is of good quality at every meal, and reflects local traditions. Local organic produce is used wherever possible. Vegans are happily catered for.
Some example prices: a weekend in Britain's West Country – £94 half-board; Portuguese fortnight – £589 per person, including return flights and full-board accommodation.

Non-Vegetarian

BORDERLINE HOLIDAYS *Les Sorbiers, rue Ramond, 65120 Barèges, France, tel. (010 33 62) 92 68 95*
A range of skiing, walking and other activity holidays based at the Pyrenean mountain resort village of Barèges. Proprietors are Peter Derbyshire and Jude Lock, and accommodation is in their clean, attractively modernised hotel. Inclusive walking (six days – £225), mountain cycling (seven days – £285), flower discovery (seven days – £269) and skiing (one week from £229, two weeks from £358) are all on offer – with vegetarian or non-vegetarian meals as preferred. The food's good; as Pete and Jude say, 'Don't come to lose weight!' For more detail, *see:* France, p. 37.
Prices as above, plus £139 for return flights to Lourdes airport and transfer to Barèges; half-board accommodation without activities also available; from £140 for one week, £260 for two weeks.

EL AL (KIBBUTZ HOTELS PACKAGE) *El Al Israel Airline, 188 Regent St, London W1, tel. (071) 439 2429*
El Al provides a number of inclusive package deals to Israel, with scheduled flights to Tel Aviv. The eight-day 'Arrive & Drive Israel' deal includes a hire car, and B&B accommodation in five-star kibbutz hotels. The breakfast is along typical Israeli lines – abundant, healthy, with salads, yoghurts and cheeses, breads, etc. For other meals, allow £20–£30 per day. Evening meals are always available in the kibbutz guest dining room, and there are always vegetarian dishes on the menu.
'Arrive & Drive Israel'; £405 pp for eight days, includes scheduled flights, Hertz car with unlimited mileage, and B&B.
CAA and ABTA bonded.

INNTRAVEL *The Old Station, Helmsley, York YO6 4BZ, tel. (0439) 71111*
This small and friendly family-run travel company (proprietors: Richard and Linda Hearn) specialises in inclusive holidays at small and friendly family-run country hotels! Most are in the French countryside, though others are in Belgium, Switzerland, Norway, Italy and Ireland. The business comes in various guises, such as Winter Inn (short breaks out of season), Across Country (skiing), and Inn Active (walking, cycling, riding and other interests). They are extremely flexible, with masses of ideas, like farm weekends, riding weekends, 'unknown' cities, cookery courses at French

hotel-restaurants, breaks close to Channel ports, three-centre breaks along the Loire, and so on.

Generally, except for the 'active' breaks, you travel in your own car, though they also do some fly-drive deals. The 'active' holidays are not terribly arduous either, all luggage being carried for you, and accommodation being, as always, in unpretentious and charming little hotels noted for good food. If that doesn't sound like a typical vegetarian holiday, it must be admitted that the Hearns never set out to cater for vegetarians. However, they offer a personal service, and make an effort to ensure that every client is satisfied, and it seems that a surprising number of their customers have requested vegetarian food. As a result, the Hearns have discovered which hotels can best cope with this request. Specify that you are vegetarian when booking, and Inn Active will advise which destinations and hotels would be suitable.

A weekend break with two nights' dinner, bed & breakfast, plus Sunday lunch, all Channel crossing costs, plus maps and insurance would come to £66 each in a party of four.

ISRAEL HOLIDAYS LTD *PO Box 2045, Herzliya B, 46120 Israel*

This company puts together personalised packages in Israel, including vegetarian holidays if required.

Wide range of prices, not including travel to Israel.

SUSI MADRON'S CYCLING FOR SOFTIES *22 Lloyd St, Manchester M2 5WA, tel. (061) 834 6800*

This friendly and low-key 'activity' specialist puts together lovely cycling tours in many areas of rural France. You go from one pleasant small country hotel to the next, with a good dinner included in the price. Normally, such hotels would rarely have much idea what to give vegetarians, but those featured in Susi Madron's brochure have been given some information on the matter. Few companies have done more to encourage French hotels to cater for vegetarians. Susi Madron provides the hotels with lists of what vegetarians eat, and in recent years has taken the imaginative step of inviting French hotel chefs to come on vegetarian cookery courses in Britain (supervised by Sarah Brown). However, be warned that only a small proportion accept the invitation, and I am informed that even some of those who come don't seem to learn a great deal. Some, though, have really taken their lessons to heart and are now offering vegetarian main dish or even a vegetarian

menu at their hotels. At least Susi Madron has impressed upon them that vegetarians exist and are an important part of the holiday market.
Example prices including all transportation and half-board: ten-day tour in Beaujolais from £552 per person; one-week tour in the Dordogne from £460 per person.
CAA bonded (only for holidays including air travel).

VFB HOLIDAYS LTD *Normandy House, High St, Cheltenham, Glos, tel. (0242) 526338*
This much-acclaimed little company specialises in 'the real' France (the letters stand for Vacances Franco-Brittaniques). Their brochures are a delightful collection of photos and ideas in which francophiles can revel blissfully. Attractive small hotels in country areas ('Auberges' brochure) are a particularly strong point with VFB, but they also have Paris breaks, as well as activity ('Canal boats' brochure) and self-catering ('Cottages' brochure). The holidays, though packaged to a degree, are flexible and appeal to independently-minded travellers. Holidays are a minimum of three nights. One bonus for vegetarians is that VFB are willing to advise vegetarians on suitable destinations, and have made a point of discovering which of their hotels have a good, co-operative attitude to providing vegetarian meals.
Prices very variable, example: £350 per person for nine nights, including ferry crossings with car, plus half-board.
AITO and CAA bonded.

WORLD WINE TOURS LTD *4 Dorchester Rd, Drayton St Leonard, Oxfordshire, tel. (0865) 891919*
This small company run by a husband and wife team (Liz and Martin Holliss) specialises solely in quality wine tours 'for those with a lively interest in fine wine'. A tour operator specialising in wine-tasting and wine appreciation might seem an unlikely choice for vegetarians. That's not because vegetarians do not enjoy high-quality wines, but because . . . surely, on such holidays, there are a lot of restaurant meals loaded with meat? Indeed there are – unless clients specify that they are vegetarian, in which case they are assured that all meals will be prepared in accordance with their wishes.

World Wine Tours organise travel in groups of up to 30, under the leadership of a Master of Wine (the UK wine trade's highest qualification). The tours last from four to eight days, and this year include Alsace, Australia, Bordeaux, Burgundy, Champagne, Germany, Languedoc, Loire, Madeira, Portugal, Rhône valley, Tuscany and Umbria. Martin Holliss explains that it is easy to accommodate vegetarians because, owing to the size of the groups, set meals are arranged in advance with restaurateurs. Although most clients are fond of traditional gourmet food, there have also been many vegetarian wine-lovers, and they have always been happy with their meals on a World Wine Tours holiday. The company also offers the chance for individuals or small groups to stay as paying guests in exclusive private châteaux all over France, to self-cater in Tuscany, and to cruise in luxury barge-hotels on the French canals.

Inclusive prices range from about £500 to £1300 per person.
CAA bonded (flights only).

Benelux

Belgium, Netherlands, Luxembourg

Dialling code from abroad: 010 32 to Belgium, 010 31 to Netherlands, 010 352 to Luxembourg
Currency: Belgium and Luxembourg – Belgian Francs (BF), just under 60 to the £; Netherlands – Guilders (Fl, Hfl, f or fl), about 3.3 = £1

For over 30 years, Amsterdam has been firmly established as one of Europe's capitals of youth culture and alternative lifestyles. That perhaps explains why Holland has such a large vegetarian movement and some good eating places offering meatless meals. It doesn't explain why vegetarianism is equally popular in Belgium. In many ways, though, in spite of a sometimes acrimonious language split, these two small countries – together with the little duchy of Luxembourg – comprise a single cultural unit. In Holland and northern Belgium, the principal language is Flemish, while in southern Belgium and Luxembourg, French is spoken. Vegetarians are rather more numerous in the Flemish areas, while in the Walloon (French) districts many establishments espouse a macrobiotic philosophy. In both, organic and even bio-dynamic produce is much used.

As a holiday destination, the whole of the Benelux region contains a surprising variety. Although this corner of northern Europe is notoriously flat, densely-populated, highly-industrialised, there are also light and airy expanses of neat open country cut across by waterways, very appealing and undemanding for cyclists, as well as the thickly wooded hills of the Ardennes. There are interesting, cultured cities and towns – Brussels, Amsterdam, Luxembourg, Bruges – ideal for browsing among the museums, bookshops, bars and streets of Flemish architecture, and of course, sampling the local cuisine.

Package Holidays

Inntravel, The Old Station, Helmsley, York YO6 4BZ, tel. (0439) 71111, see p. 15.

North Mymms Coaches, PO Box 152, Potters Bar, Herts EN6 3NR, tel. (0707) 371866, see p. 13.

Recommended Hotels and Restaurants

Belgium

Bruxelles/Brussels

LE PARADOXE *329 Chaussée d'Ixelles, 1050 Bruxelles, tel. (02) 649 89 81*
Restaurant. Mainly vegetarian.
Some come to eat, some to listen, and most come to enjoy both at what the proprietors call *Dîners Musicaux*, Musical Dinners. Quite apart from the fact there is also a bar and a shop here, this is really much more than a restaurant, and even issues its own monthly programme (on recycled paper) of forthcoming live music and dance events. There's something on every weekend. These range from Moroccan dance to jazz to a full flamenco session to samba to classical performances – and often accompanied by the appropriate cuisine. For example, a Portuguese band played while we tucked in to Portuguese specialities! Wonderful. On weekdays there's live piano music every evening. With simple wood décor and white-painted brick walls, there are several different rooms, two with so many plants that you might think you've wandered into a greenhouse. Appropriately, the food embraces cooking from many countries, ranging from traditional filling country dishes to the finesse of French nouvelle cuisine. And it's all high-quality vegetarian except for some fish dishes. Staff are smart, efficient, and helpful.
Allow 380BF for three-course meal. Wine: organic from 620BF/bottle. Open 12–2, 7–10 (10.30 Fri and Sat), closed Sun.

Gent/Gand/Ghent

PANDA *Oudburg 38, 9000 Gent, tel. (091) 25 07 86*
Restaurant. Mainly vegetarian
Modern, stylish, with lots of greenery and a curious pleasing effect created by cloths draping the ceilings, Panda is a good-quality vegetarian restaurant (some fish) adjoining an attractive food store. It's right beside the river which flows through the middle of this interesting old city. Staff will help you through the menu, which is in Flemish. Almost everything on it is organic. Cooking combines western and eastern influences, with particular emphasis on things Japanese – seitan, tofu, miso, as well as, surprisingly, sake as an aperitif. The organic wines include some interesting examples,

including several clarets and a champagne (they have healthier drinks too!). The 'Menu of the Day' is a very enjoyable three courses, of say breaded pleurotte mushrooms, steamed tofu, and lemon gâteau.
Menu of the Day: 385BF. Organic wine only: from 480BF/bottle. Open 12–2, 6.30–9.30, closed Sun.

DE WAREMPEL *Zandberg 8, 9000 Gent, tel. (091) 24 30 62*
Restaurant. Mainly vegetarian.
In a seventeenth-century house with a quiet atmosphere, this city centre restaurant has a fish menu and a vegetarian menu of local and ethnic dishes. The cooking is good, dishes are seasonal in character, and the choice is different every day. The sort of thing you might have is a goatcheese quiche with tomato sabayon to start, a main course of chicory with nut stuffing and a cream sauce, with home-made cakes and ices to finish.
Main courses: about BF220. Complete meal: about BF600. Wine: from BF295/bottle. Tue–Sat noon–2, Fri–Sat 6–10.

Louvain/Leuven

LEUKMIEKE *Vlamingenstraat 55, 3000 Leuven, tel. (016) 22 97 05*
Restaurant. 100% vegetarian.
Youthful, friendly, popular place by the park in the centre of this likeable university town. Good wholesome standard vegetarian dishes are offered at very reasonable prices. The 'dish of the day' is generally a meal in itself – for example, five different vegetables plus brown rice.
Daily dish: 230BF, or allow 350BF for three courses. Wine: from 280BF/litre, organic 300BF/bottle. Mon–Fri 12–2, 6–8.30.

Netherlands or Holland

Amersfoort

SALON DE NIEUWE GANG *Hof 9, 3811 CJ Amersfoort, tel. (033) 620023*
Restaurant.
One of the best restaurants in town, modern and stylish, situated in a historic building. Vegetarians can have a four-course set meal of a high standard, using mainly organic ingredients.

Set meal: fl 37.50. Organic wine only: fl 18.75/bottle.
Weekdays 5.30–11, weekend 11.30–11, closed Wed.

Amsterdam

DE BOLHOED *Prinsengracht 62, 1015 DX Amsterdam,*
tel (020) 261803
Restaurant. Mainly vegetarian.
Two rooms, a warm sixties-style atmosphere, non-stop music (sometimes live), and exhibitions of paintings, provide the setting for good, imaginative snacks and meals. It's a welcome change that they offer a daily three-course *vegan* meal. Plentiful use is made of soya products, but there are also several Greek/Middle Eastern dishes. Finish from a large selection of cakes and pastries. Almost everything is organic.
Around fl 25 for three courses. Organic wine: fl 24.50/bottle.
Open 12–10.

KLAVERKONING *Koningsstraat 29, 1011 ET Amsterdam,*
tel. (020) 26 10 85
Restaurant.
In an interesting old building in the heart of the city, this restaurant has a range of 'international' dishes using mainly organic produce. They do have a good selection of suitable vegetarian options, though seem to be under the impression that snails are a vegetable! Approach with care.
Three-course meal: fl 32.50. Wine: from fl 19/bottle.
Tues–Sat 5.30–11.30.

KOSMOS *Prins Hendrikkade 142, 1011 AT Amsterdam,*
tel. (020) 23 06 86
Restaurant. 100% vegetarian.
Coffee shop, bar, restaurant, De Kosmos is in the city centre about 200 metres from the main railway station. It has a cleanly modern style, and there are art exhibitions in the restaurant. The food is uncomplicated but well made, and is good value for money: salads, soups, pasta, rice dishes, with cake or yoghurt (for example) to finish.
Allow fl 22.50 for three courses. Wine: from fl 6/bottle,
or organic from fl 4/glass. Open 9am–midnight, closed Sat.

De Waaghals *Frans Halstraat 29, 1072 BK Amsterdam, tel. (020) 6779609*
Restaurant. 100% vegetarian.
On the edge of the city centre – close to the Rijksmuseum – this is an untouristy backstreet in a part of town with a feel of genuine Amsterdam. The restaurant – its name means The Daredevil – has big front windows, tiled floor and plenty of wood. It is relaxed and friendly, with a very mixed clientele, and everyone feels at home here. They offer a choice of set meals as well as *à la carte* eating. The approach to cooking is intelligent and imaginative; each month they present a menu from a different country, in addition to their normal dishes which change every week (and are constantly improving). The food is presented in the Flemish manner, with four or five things all on the plate together. The sort of thing you might have is, for example, a starter of salad or soup or Flemish cheese croquettes; a main dish of vegetable pie with salad, or stuffed pepper with mushroom risotto, beans, and salad, or possibly something Middle Eastern like cheese borekas and tabouleh. Desserts include pancakes filled with fruit, all sorts of flans and cakes, sorbets, ice creams, and a lovely apple and fig crumble. Almost all the produce is organic.
Four courses: fl 22.50 or fl 27.50. Organic wine: fl 11.50/carafe. Tue–Sun 5.30–10.

Berg En Terblijt

Huis Aan De Rots *Geulhemmerweg 32, 6325 PK Berg en Terblijt, tel. (04406) 41912*
Hotel-restaurant.
Proprietors: Guido and Willie Nijssen. English spoken.
Not far from Maastricht (a pleasant town in the far south of Holland, accessible on direct flights from London), this modern little hotel can be found in open country, beside a river among wooded hills. Most guests seem to be aged in their 30s, and there's a good atmosphere. The restaurant menu offers traditional Dutch food but also includes several complete vegetarian meals, and there's a set meal for hotel occupants, for example chervil soup, stir-fried veg with rice and seaweed, and a peach-and-grapefruit ice. Organic wine includes champagne.
Closed Feb. Ten rooms (one with own bathroom). B&B fl 35 pp, half-board fl 64.50 pp. Organic wine from fl 20.50/bottle. Credit cards accepted.

Burgwerd

De Goede Ierde *Doniaweg 1, 8742 KR Burgwerd, tel. (05157) 2752*
Guesthouse. Mainly vegetarian.
Proprietor: Riet van Russum. English spoken.
Small and friendly family guesthouse in an old farmhouse at a village in Friesland province. There's an open fire and a homely atmosphere; simple meals are prepared using fresh produce from their own garden.
Open daily 10–10, closed Nov–Mar. Five rooms.
Room only: fl 17.50. Camping also available. Breakfast: fl 5 to fl 9. Lunch: fl 7.50. Dinner: fl 14.50. Wine: from fl 18.75/bottle, fl 3.50/glass. Reservation advisable for restaurant. No credit cards.

Bussum

'T Klinkertje *Herenstraat 17, Bussum, tel. (02159) 33211*
Restaurant. 100% vegetarian.
Small, homely, with informal and friendly service, this generous and inexpensive eating house offers a great variety of dishes: French, Indian, Tunisian, Spanish, Italian. Typical starters include

soup or pâté; main dishes cheese pie or stuffed pepper; ice cream or pastries for dessert.
Four-course menu fl 27.50; six-course fl 36.50.
Wine from fl 15/carafe. Open 5–10, closed Mon.

Den Haag/The Hague

De Dageraad *Hoolkade 4, 2514 BH Den Haag,*
tel. (070) 364 56 66
Restaurant. 100% vegetarian.
Warm and friendly city-centre eating place with a tempting and varied selection of set meals. There's a Nut Meal, a French Meal, an Indonesian Meal, a Seasonal Meal, and others. Two people together can order a cheese fondue. Most expensive and best is the three-course Menu of the Month. For example: avocado and tomato with herb sauce; stuffed pepper with walnuts, roquefort, mushrooms in cream sauce; endive salad with orange and pepper dressing; pineapple with cream.
Three-course set meals from fl 26 (main dish only: fl 18.50).
Organic wine only: from fl 19.50/bottle. Daily 5–9pm.

Hortas *Prins Hendrikstraat 53, 2518 HJ Den Haag,*
tel. (070) 3456736
Restaurant. 100% vegetarian.
In a fine building in the old heart of the city, this simple restaurant offers a selection of interesting dishes from Indonesia, India, Mexico and the Mediterranean as well as cheap snacks.
Three-course set menu: fl 25. Organic wine only: from fl 22/bottle.
Open 5–8.45, closed Mon.

Driebergen

Lembas *Hoofdstraat 153–155, 3971 KJ Driebergen,*
tel. (03438) 18637
Restaurant. 100% vegetarian.
Warm and friendly, located in a small village, this restaurant is committed to using organic and bio-dynamic ingredients only. They make extensive use of cheese and soya products to 'convert' a range of familiar European dishes into vegetarian versions. Lots of tasty desserts and an extensive range of hot and cold drinks, including wines by the glass.
Allow about fl 20 or 30 for three courses. Organic wine only:
from fl 18/bottle. Open Tue–Sat, 12.30–3, 5–8.30.

Eindhoven

IRIS *Voorterweg 168, 5611 TT Eindhoven, tel. (040) 123466*
Restaurant. 100% vegetarian.
City centre restaurant offering tasty, very varied meals, mainly using organic ingredients. Some classic vegetarian fare, some more ambitious dishes, salad buffet, quite a few Mexican specials, and an unusual vegetarian cheese fondue. Wide selection of drinks, too. Pleasant terrace in summer. The proprietor is the publisher of the Iris guides (in Dutch) listing vegetarian establishments – the Benelux countries in one volume, France, Spain and Portugal in another.
Allow around fl 25 for meal; special four-course menus around fl 37. Organic wine from fl 13/half-litre. Open 5.30–8pm, closed Sat and Mon.

Groningen

BRUSSELS LOF *Akerkstraat 24, 9712 BG Groningen, tel. (050) 127603*
Restaurant. 100% vegetarian.
Located close to the centre of town, Brussels Lof (the name means salad chicory) is convivial and welcoming, stylish, and offering a high standard of cooking on an extensive, imaginative menu with French and Italian influences. Main course specialities are fondue, and mushroom dishes.
Three-course meal: fl 25. Wine: from fl 20/bottle, fl 22.50 for organic. Open daily from 5.30pm.

Leiden

SPLINTER *Noordeinde 30, 2311 CE Leiden, tel. (071) 149519*
Restaurant.
Well-known and well-liked town centre eating place, bright attractive interior and modern music. There are a large number of hot and cold vegetarian dishes such as moussaka or stuffed pancakes, and tasty desserts.
Two-course daily vegetarian set meal: fl 10.75; or allow about fl 21 for three courses à la carte. *Organic wine: from fl 3.25/glass. Open 5–9.30 pm, closed Mon.*

De Trommelaar *Apothekersdijk 22, 2312 DD Leiden, tel. (071) 130055*
Restaurant. Mainly vegetarian.
There's a choice of separate fish and vegetarian menus at this simple, agreeable, inexpensive eating house committed to using wholesome organic produce. It's well placed in the centre of town, and has a summer garden/terrace.
Allow around fl 20 for three courses. Organic wine only.
5.30–8.30, closed Sun.

Rotterdam

Bla Bla *Piethensplein 35, 3024 RJ Rotterdam, tel. (010) 4774448*
Restaurant. 100% vegetarian.
In one of the few nice historical parts of the city, just outside the centre (five minutes' drive from the station), you'll find in this small pink-fronted building a cheerful bar-restaurant with a choice of five set meals. They're inspired by a multitude of influences – Greek, Indian, Italian, Mexican, African and English – but are all the same price; or you can eat *à la carte*. A typical meal would be soup, salad or fried feta; a main course of vegetable pie or goat's cheese pastry; finishing with cake and ice cream.
Three-course set meal: fl 21. Wine: from fl 24/litre.
Open 5–10 (till midnight Fri and Sat; closed Mon).

Schoorl

'T Strooie Huys *Burg. Peecklaan 11, 1871 BA Schoorl, tel. (032) 2209-1260*
Guesthouse and restaurant. 100% vegetarian.
Proprietor: P.P. Bleeker. English spoken.
Pleasant, light, attractive, this modest family guesthouse is near the sand dunes which border the sea on this northern coast. It's close, too, to the town centre of this small resort, and makes a good spot for a decent simple meal or lodgings.
Closed Jan, Thirteen rooms (two with bath/shower).
B&B: fl 32.50 per person. Half-board: fl 47.50. Table d'hôte: fl 19.50.
Organic wine only: from fl 17.50/bottle. No credit cards.

France

Dialling code from abroad: 010 33. For Paris numbers, dial an additional code prefix: 1. Currency: Francs (F or FF) – about 9.80F = £1

Not only does France lead the world in the art of cooking, but it has an unrivalled variety of holiday interest, ranging from the most chic and sophisticated resorts to the most simple and rustic villages, or from long-distance footpaths to all-night entertainment, with the world's most luxurious accommodation, and also thousands of more homely inexpensive hotels, as well as a huge number of campsites (11,000). There are exceptional historical and artistic treasures to enjoy, and superb beaches on two oceans.

Yet for vegetarians its scope is limited in places by the lack of suitable facilities. They are not by any means completely absent though, and a close study of the recommended restaurants and guesthouses (below) shows that France can make a good choice for a totally vegetarian holiday. Some of the establishments listed reach a high standard. However, many others were of such a poor standard that I decided not to include them. A common fault was that, perhaps reacting against the usual French approach, they took too austere an attitude towards food.

Some of the best places are run by foreigners – mostly English, Belgian and Dutch. French vegetarians are rare indeed; those who do exist are often deeply preoccupied with their own health, and many have never even encountered the principle of giving up meat to avoid killing animals; one French vegetarian to whom I explained this idea considered it startlingly altruistic. French vegetarian establishments often offer therapies and health courses of various kinds. Far more popular than vegetarianism in France is the macrobiotic diet, again usually taken up as an aid to greater physical fitness and mental health.

Vegetarian restaurants generally use the traditional three- or four-course meal structure, but replace the main meat course with a

substantial grain and vegetable dish. Even if they offer a much lower standard of cooking than 'ordinary' restaurants, at least you can have confidence that no meat products have been used.

Organic produce (*biologique* or *bio*) is widely available, and much in demand by non-vegetarians (see box).

ORGANIC FOOD AND WINE

Organic foods in France are now very widely available, with even the most conservative of diners being fully aware of the advantages in health and taste (two very French preoccupations) of food which has not been tampered with. Many – perhaps most – country markets all over France now have at least one stall specialising in *Produits de Culture Biologique* (organic produce). This is a minority interest, but not marginal. Restaurants of all types are happy to proclaim that their ingredients are organic simply for the implication of full flavour.

Likewise, organic wines are produced by numerous vineyards in all the main grape-growing areas. However, in general, organic wines do *not* taste discernably different from non-organic wines of the same standard and region; but it makes for more enjoyable drinking to know that chemical manufacturers have not slipped anything poisonous into one's glass.

For wine-lovers travelling independently, a tour of France's organic vineyards makes a rewarding excursion. Two useful books are *The Organic Wine Guide*, by Charlotte Mitchell and Iain Wright (Mainstream Publishing) and, simply giving addresses without comment, *Les Bonnes Adresses du Vin Biologique*, by Jean-Marc Carite (Editions d'Utovie, Bats 40320, France).

A recommended route round some of the best of organic winemakers in France might be along these lines . . .

CHAMPAGNE – Yves Ruffin, 6 boulevard Jules Ferry, Avenay Val d'Or 51160 (tel. 26 52 32 49): white and rosé Champagne, and non-bubbly Côteaux Champenois red

ALSACE – Pierre Frick, 5 rue de Baer, Pfaffenheim 68250 (tel. 89 49 62 99): Appellation Contrôlée of several different grape varieties

BURGUNDY – Pierrette & Jean-Claude Rateau, Chemin des Mariages, Beaune 21200 (tel. 80 22 52 54): Appellations Contrôlées Beaune Premier Cru/Puligny Montrachet/Haute Côtes de Beaune/Côtes de Beaune/Beaune Clos de Mariages; Alain Verdet, Arcenant 21700 (tel. 80 61 08 10): Appellations Contrôlées Hautes-Côtes de Nuits/Aligoté/Cremant de Bourgogne

BEAUJOLAIS – Christian Ducroix, Thulon 69430 (tel. 74 69 20 47): Appellations Contrôlées Beaujolais Primeur/Beaujolais Villages/Cru Régnié

RHÔNE VALLEY – Daniel Combe, Vignobles de la Jasse, Violes 84150 (tel. 90 70 93 47): Appellation Contrôlée Côtes du Rhône; Cave Coopérative 'La Vigneronne', Villedieu 84110 (tel. 90 36 23 11): a cave coopérative which has gone over to organic production of Appellation Contrôlée Côtes du Rhône

PROVENCE – François Dutheil de la Rochère, Château Ste Anne, Ste Anne d'Évenos 83330 (tel. 94 90 35 40): Appellations Contrôlées Côtes de Provence/Bandol

LANGUEDOC & ROUSSILLON – Simone Couderc, 32 rue du Conseil Général, Neffies 34320 (tel. 67 24 62 28): Appellation Contrôlée Côteaux de Languedoc; Jean-Claude Beirieu, Roquetaillade 11300 (tel. 68 31 60 71): Appellation Contrôlée Blanquette de Limoux (a very old-established sparkling wine); Erenest Bissa,

Domaine de l'Île, Esperanza 11260 (tel. 68 74 07 97): Appellation Contrôlée Limoux; Tim Sparham (who is English, but has been a wine maker in France for some eighteen years), Domaine des Palats, Fonjoncouse 11360 (tel. 68 44 05 76): Appellation Contrôlée Corbières
BORDEAUX REGION – Château Barrail des Graves, St Sulpice de Faleyrens 33330 (tel. 57 74 94 77): St Émilion Appellation Contrôlée; Château Jacques Blanc, St Étienne de Lisse 33330 (tel. 57 40 18 01): St Émilion Grand Cru; Château de Prade, Belves-de-Castillon 33350 (tel 56 40 19 73): Appellations Contrôlées Bordeaux Supérieur/Côtes de Castillon
MONBAZILLAC & BERGERAC (Dordogne) – Château le Barradis (Serge & Christian Labasse-Gazzini), Sigoules 24240 (tel. 53 58 30 01): Appellations Contrôlées Monbazillac (sweet)/Bergerac
LOIRE VALLEY – Guy Bossard, La Bretonnière 44430 (tel. 40 06 40 91): Appellation Contrôlée Muscadet; Nicole & Christian Dauny, Champtin, Crézancy en Sancerre 18300 (tel. 48 79 05 75): Appellation Contrôlée Sancerre

Package Holidays and Information

Susi Madron's Cycling for Softies, 22 Lloyd St, Manchester M2 5WA, tel. (061) 834 6800, see p. 16
Vegi Ventures, 17 Lilian Road, Burnham on Crouch, Essex CM0 8DS, tel. (0621) 784285, see p. 14
Inntravel, The Old Station, Helmsley, York YO6 4BZ, tel. (0439) 71111, see p. 15
World Wine Tours, 4 Dorchester Rd, Drayton St Leonard, Oxfordshire, tel. (0865) 891919, see p. 17
North Mymms Coaches, P.O. Box 152, Potters Bar, Herts EN6 3NR, tel. (0707) 371866, see p. 13
Borderline, Les Sorbiers, rue Ramond, 65120 Barèges, France, tel. (010 33 62) 92 68 95, see p. 15
VFB, Normandy House, High St, Cheltenham, Glos, tel. (0242) 526338, see p. 17
Andrew Sanger's Vegetarian Travellers, 60 Crewys Road, London NW2 2AD, tel. (081) 201 9054, see p. 12
Self-catering – many companies specialise in inclusive holidays with cottage accommodation in rural France, including Gîtes de France (tel. 071 493 3480), Meon (tel. 0730 68411), VFB (tel. 0242 580187), Bowhills (tel. 0489 878567), Vacances en Campagne (tel. 07987 411). Inclusive camping holidays are another good option in

this land of first-class sites; good companies include Eurocamp (tel. 0565 3844), Canvas Holidays (tel. 0992 553535), Sunsites (tel. 0565 55644), Select Site Reservations (tel. 0873 890770).

For more travel and holiday information contact the French Government Tourist Office, 178 Piccadilly, London W1V OAL, enclosing SAE.

In France: you may find it useful to contact the Alliance Végétarienne, one of the larger national vegetarian organisations. They are based at Villa Florès, Alvignac 46500 (tel. 65 33 63 33). Their quarterly journal is La Feuille. In health food shops you will find Le Lien, a journal with several useful small-ads for guesthouses and restaurants.

Recommended Accommodation, Holiday Centres and Restaurants

When touring, or choosing a holiday, it's sometimes useful to understand certain French terms. *Chambres d'hôte*: like a B&B; *Table d'hôte*: a set meal at a place with accommodation; *Pension*: accommodation with meals, at an inclusive price (at such places, *pension* or *pension complète* refers to full-board, *demi-pension* to half-board); *Hôtel*: most French hotels are small, family-run affairs, offering a full dinner and a light breakfast; their accommodation is generally charged per room, not per person; *Menu*: a set meal at a fixed price; *la Carte*: what is called in English a menu, or a bill of fare; the *carte des vins* is the wine list. *Végétarien* means vegetarian; *végétalien* means vegan. *Macrobiotique* (macrobiotic) and *biologique* (organic) are words you'll often see at vegetarian establishments.

SELF-SERVICE RESTAURANTS

Vegetarians on the move, if not seeking a high standard of cooking, are often glad to discover one of the large self-service cafeterias which exist in most medium-to-large French towns. Here you'll find salads, cold dishes, chips, fruit, plain full-fat yoghurt, desserts; to drink there's mineral water, beers, wines, fruit juice, coffee, usually decaffeinated coffee as well, and herb teas (*tisanes*). One of the largest and most popular self-service chains is Flunch: it has currently 110 branches. Major supermarkets like Casino, Auchan, Carrefour and Euromarché also frequently have self-service restaurants where vegetarians can find a reasonable if unconventional meal at a budget price.

In the listings below, I have described both *Chambres d'hôte* and *Pensions* as Guesthouses. Note that restaurants almost without exception accept credit cards, but guesthouses (*pensions*, *chambres d'hôte*) often do not. The most widely accepted are Visa and Access, known in France as Carte Bleu and Masters respectively.

Albi (Tarn)

LE TOURNESOL *11 rue de l'Ort en Salvy, Albi 81000, tel. 63 38 38 14*
Restaurant. 100% vegetarian.
Named in honour of the South-West's most dramatic crop, the sunflower – vast fields of their huge golden heads are a feature of the region in early summer – this likeable unpretentious restaurant proves that if the cooking is good enough it's possible to run a totally vegetarian establishment in an ordinary provincial French town. Albi, after all, is no capital of vegetarianism, yet this restaurant is a popular and busy place. Proprietors Sally and Jacques Pignet (Sally is English) provide a short *carte* which changes daily. Two courses should be enough for a good meal, but I had a starter of vegetable pâté and salad, followed by aubergine gratin (having been tempted by diced tofu with Chinese vegetables), and a dessert of delicious peach and almond tart. Another of Sally's desserts is apple crumble – considered very exotic in Albi. Everything is made on the premises, with fresh, mainly organic ingredients. You can eat in the bright, cheerful interior at pine tables, or on one of the outdoor terraces. The location is good, in a backstreet close to the town's centre and its famous sights: the rather overpowering cathedral, and the permanent exhibition of the work of Toulouse-Lautrec.
Allow about 60F for three-course meal. Vegan dish daily. Organic wine: 17F/half-litre. Open lunch Tues–Sat 12–2, dinner Fri–Sat only, 7.15–9.45.

Amiens (Somme)

LA SOUPE A CAILLOUX *16 rue des Bondes, Amiens 80000, tel. 22 91 92 70*
Restaurant.
At this likeable, popular eating place adjacent to the town's magnificent Gothic cathedral, vegetarians are able to enjoy a good meal of generous mixed salad followed by, for example, a carrot

gratin or wholegrain galettes with aubergines and roquefort cheese.
Allow 85F for full meal. Wine: from 49F/bottle.
Daily (exc Mon) 12–2, 7.30–10.30.

Aspres-sur-Buëch (Haute-Alpes)

Le Moulin *Aspres-sur-Buëch 05140, tel. 92 58 65 09*
Farm guesthouse.
Proprietors: Alain and Agnes Marcellin. English spoken.
The Marcellins are nice, friendly people, and their three-hectare (seven-acre) organic farm in the Provençal Alps is a haven of tranquillity and good, healthy living. They do not use any synthetic products, whether food or not: even the materials with which they renovated and decorated this fourteenth-century mill were of the old-fashioned organic variety, and all their clothes, bedding, etc are of natural materials. This makes for an exceptionally congenial environment. Bedrooms are beamed, plain and simple with white walls, wooden or quarry tile floors laid with rugs, and the furniture, even where new, is made of solid wood in traditional local style. However there is central heating, and woodstoves for extra heat – this area is under snow for part of the winter. Among the rooms is one large bedroom which can be used either by a family, or as a children's room.

All guests eat together in the beamed dining/living room. A lot of things are served which are not available in shops: on their little farm the Marcellins have 25 different sorts of vegetables, as well as soft fruits, nuts, hens, and goats for milk and cheese; they also grow wheat and spelt (an ancient form of wheat) which they either cook as a grain or grind into flour for bakery. Alain and Agnes are concerned to maintain a traditional French approach to food – that is, to use high-quality local ingredients, skilfully prepared. As well as milk and cheese, they make their own bread, ice-cream, and conserves. They take the refreshing view too that most French dishes can be easily adapted to suit vegetarians; for example, they use mushrooms to replace snails. All their menus are basically vegetarian, but they do offer meat occasionally. Meals are 90% organic, much of the produce being their own. The food is very simple and unpretentious, but full of flavour and well-prepared. My dinner was soup *au pistou* (ie. with basil, garlic and olive oil); grated raw beetroot with chickpeas and lettuce; sesame pastry filled with delicious goats' cheese; baked tomatoes with herbs; finally, Gâteau Marcellin. Despite the name, this tart of eggs, fruit and

almonds, was not invented by Alain and Agnes! There's more home-made organic produce at breakfast, with a choice of drinks, bread, cheese, fruit in season, and interesting granola (lightly grilled muesli of their own wheat flakes, sesame seeds, raisins and honey) served with goats' milk. In summer Le Moulin makes a good base for excursions into the mountains – Alain and Agnes can advise on routes and sights – and in winter is only fifteen minutes from small-scale ski resorts.
Open all year. Four double rooms, one family room.
Price: 160F per person for dinner, bed and breakfast (that is the only arrangement possible); most guests stay two weeks, but overnight visitors are equally welcome. Wine: local organic, included in price. No credit cards.

Auxerre (Yonne)

★★LE JARDIN GOURMAND *56 boulevard Vauban, Auxerre 89000, tel. 86 51 53 52*
Restaurant.
Two Gault-Millau 'toques' and two Michelin 'knives and forks' testify to the high esteem in which this wonderful restaurant is held. Gault-Millau, incidentally, singled out the vegetables here for special praise, describing the way they had been prepared as 'miraculous' and 'among the most beautiful in France'! You can eat in the stylish rooms with Louis XVI furniture indoors, or on the terrace. Owner-chef Pierre Boussereau doesn't see why every meal should contain meat, and offers at least two vegetarian main dishes every day. Based very much on vegetables (not grains), these tend to be strikingly imaginative, yet in essence simple, and eating here is all about delicacy and finesse. What you will find on the *carte* is unpredictable – it depends on what is at its best on that day. We enjoyed a salad which included an exquisite tomato sorbet; a hot and cold dish with melon sorbet in a melon sauce; fritters of courgette flowers; and an orange mousse.
À la carte: allow about 200F. The set menu at 120F can be vegetarian with advance notice – you will need to reserve in any case to eat here. Wine: from 90F/bottle for a modest Chablis; good selection of local wines (Chablis is only twenty km away).
Daily 12–2, 7.30–9.30.

Barèges (Hautes Pyrénées)

Borderline Holidays *Les Sorbiers, rue Ramond, Barèges 65120, tel. 62 92 68 95 fax. 62 92 66 93*
Hotel.
For brochure call 0272 778015 in UK. English proprietors: Peter Derbyshire and Jude Lock. Jude is vegetarian.
Les Sorbiers is, in effect, a *pension* in the main street of this bustling little mountain resort town. Theoretically, travellers knocking at the door could ask for a bed and dinner – they would not be turned away, assuming there were vacant rooms. However, in practice almost all bookings are made through Peter and Jude's UK trading operation, Borderline Holidays, which puts together half-board holidays from Britain. Flights to Lourdes airport can be booked, with inclusive transfer to Barèges. Car hire can be arranged. Guided walking tours of different lengths are organised for those who want them. These are serious excursions into the high mountains of the National Park, staying mainly at staffed refuges (which, incidentally, have very good catering despite their remoteness). They also organise a seven-day mountain bike tour across the high mountains into Spain. In winter, of course, there is skiing (both downhill and cross-country). All these activities are optional, and have to be paid for separately. Clients are equally welcome to do nothing at all.

Many people come in spring to see the flowers, which are spectacular here and of special interest to botanists.

On average, one third of guests are vegetarian, and at the time of my visit, the cook was herself vegetarian. At dinner, everyone sits together in a simple, functional dining room. There's a different meal every night for two weeks. A typical meal would be: start with fresh tomatoes grilled with local goats' cheese; a main course of stuffed aubergines with baked potatoes and mixed vegetables; and a dessert of, say, profiteroles. There's curry one day a week. Breakfast is juice, bread, muesli, conserves, tea/coffee. English tea is available. The atmosphere at Les Sorbiers is friendly, relaxed and informal, yet efficient and orderly. There's a little bar where guests can help themselves to drinks, music and guidebooks and get to know each other. Bedrooms are pleasant, in pale colours, with modern pine furniture.

Open May–Oct and Christmas–Easter. Nine rooms, all with shower (some with WC – cost £15 extra per week).
Half-board prices per person: low season £140 one week, £260 two weeks; high season £155 one week, £295 two weeks.
Flight Gatwick–Lourdes; £139 rtn, incl. transfer to Barèges.
Travel insurance available. Wine: ranges from 17F/litre local ordinaire, to 40F/bottle good Madiran.

Beaulieu-sur-Dordogne (Corrèze)

L'ESPERANCE *Barennac-Sioniac 19120, tel. 55 91 08 54*
Guesthouse. 100% vegetarian.
Proprietors: Jacques and Geneviève Deretz. English spoken.

Jacques Deretz has been vegetarian since birth, having been brought up in an Adventist family. At his quiet and remote guesthouse the food is normally cooked without any animal products, though eggs, cheese, etc will be made available if required. There's a set meal for lunch and dinner, changed every day for a month. The food is plain and simple, healthy, quite well-prepared, and could be, for example, oat galettes with vegetables, or tomatoes provençales with artichokes. Desserts are on the heavy side, and include coconut pudding or crêpes. No wine is served. Breakfast is bread, margarine, jam and hot drinks. Cooking classes are given, and Jacques Deretz is also a qualified naturopath, practising iridology (making diagnoses from studying the eyes), massage, aromatherapy, shiatsu, thalassotherapy, etc. The place, and the atmosphere, would be too austere for some tastes, stark-feeling, without luxury. The bedrooms are of one-star hotel standard. But it is welcoming and restful, and the setting is superb. Barennac, where L'Espérance is situated, is a hamlet in utterly tranquil rolling countryside of woods and fields near the village of Sioniac, a few kilometres from the extremely picturesque riverside town of Beaulieu.

Closed Nov, Dec & Jan. Seventeen double rooms.
Full board, per night, in simple room: single 220F, double 360F.
Full board in room with own shower and toilet; single 270F, double 410F. Deduct 20F per person for half-board.
No credit cards.

Bellegarde-en-Diois (Drôme)

LE GÎTE *Bellegarde-en-Diois 26470, tel. 75 21 40 74*
Hotel-restaurant. 100% vegetarian.
Proprietors: technically owned by Monsieur Knotter, who is Dutch, but in reality is run by an association (of which he is a member) of some fifteen friends – Dutch, German, Swedish and French, all vegetarian and macrobiotic – who live together at Bellegarde (surprisingly, their common language is Dutch).
English spoken.

'We just want this to be an ordinary village hotel-restaurant, except that the food has no meat in it,' I was told at Le Gîte, and they have more or less succeeded in this objective. Indeed, francophiles will be delighted to learn that it is a member (one-star) of the Logis de France federation (a group of about 5000 small, unpretentious independent family-run hotels, mainly in country districts, which represents among the most appealing accommodation in France. To be selected for membership, a hotel must be clean and welcoming and have a good reasonably-priced restaurant). Le Gîte has been a vegetarian hotel for thirteen years, and had previously been a famous meat restaurant ('when we first took over and started cooking our kind of food, it was like selling umbrellas in the Sahara'). It stands by a stream – on the other side of which the hotel has its own private garden (mainly lawn, ideal for children) – on the little-used main road of this quiet village up in the Provençal Alps. Most guests are French and, apart from the food, they find nothing unusual about the place.

The bedrooms are simple, wallpapered and carpeted, with functional furniture; they are clean and well-maintained. There's an annexe up the road, in which the rooms are larger (and there's a two-room family suite), with their own entrances. In a large dining room generously-sized tables are nicely set out, with white paper tablecloths at dinner. Locals occasionally pop in for a drink at a small bar in the dining room.

The meals are different each day for two weeks, and textured soya protein is used in some dishes for the satisfaction of diners who want the illusion of meat. There's a set five-course *menu* each day, or one can eat from an extensive range of dishes *à la carte*. These include a simple brown rice and vegetables (39F) and a profuse Assiette Macrobiotique (65F). There are also omelettes and pizzas, but here, by a curious irony, these are ordered mainly by meat eaters unwilling to try anything more interesting. I chose the set meal, which started with a good tomato salad with a dressing of olive oil, lemon juice and herbs; cauliflower fritters (a little bland) with a spicy sauce followed; then a tasty main course of 'Hungarian goulash' (which was never like this in Hungary!), in fact a thick stew with cubes of soya protein, served with brown rice; there was a selection of middle-priced French cheeses; and finally a decidedly un-French dessert of *pommes au granola* – apple compote in layers with granola. Service was friendly, polite and professional. Gentle flute music played in the background. Breakfast for overnight guests is white or brown bread, jam or honey, and choice of hot drinks; people staying *en pension* (full board) can have a larger breakfast including muesli or porridge, yoghurt, and fruit. Diois, by the way, is pronounced *dee-wah*.

Open all year. Eight double rooms, one triple, two family rooms (six rooms have shower/WC; one has shower only; others have washbasin and bidet). Prices: rooms from 112F–340F; five-course menu 70F; breakfast 24F; full board 185F (simple room) or 220F (room with own shower/WC) per person; half-board 135F or 170F. Children under six half price. Wine: mostly good local Côte du Rhône at 19.10F/litre for non-organic, 35.70F/bottle for organic. Vegans catered for. Credit cards accepted.

Belvès (Dordogne)

★LE FAUROU *Orliac, 24170 Belvès, tel. 53 29 13 14*
Guesthouse. 100% vegetarian.
English proprietors: Cherith and Peter Beglan.
Superbly situated between two valleys in a lush, quiet corner ten km south of the river Dordogne, this lovely old farmhouse has been run as a comfortable and welcoming vegetarian guesthouse since 1988. However, the Beglans (their French-sounding name is in fact Irish)

have been here a lot longer than that: they are old Dordogne habitués, living in the region for over seventeen years. Rooms are light and attractive, and there are six hectares (fifteen acres) of private grounds with orchards, meadows and magnificent views. It makes an excellent base from which to explore the whole of this fascinating and beautiful region. The Beglans also put on occasional special 'activity' breaks with tuition; for example, excursions in hot-air balloons, quilting, and painting courses. The setting would appeal strongly to birdwatchers, flower-lovers and walkers.

Cherith cooks wholesome, well prepared and delicious meals, which are eaten with everyone sitting together around one large table. We had, for example, an excellent soup made of new carrots; a mushroom and avocado 'salad' and tabouleh with mint instead of parsley; a superb nut roast stuffed with prunes (prunes, by the way, are a delicious speciality of the south-west) and served with buttered haricots with sage; a green salad with walnut oil (another local speciality); a good cheeseboard, including local cheeses; and freshly gathered ripe strawberries with fromage frais. Much of the produce comes from their own expanding and increasingly organic kitchen garden. Two good organic wines (an A. C. Cahors and Vin de Pays de l'Aude) were served freely at the table. Breakfasts of coffee or tea, with breads, muesli and other cereals, home-made jams, juice, fruit and yoghurt, are generous and reminiscent of home. Indeed in some ways life is rather English here – BBC Radio 4 was on as we had breakfast – and our bill was in sterling. Le

Faurou combines – in just the right proportions – a friendly vegetarian guesthouse, the gorgeous countryside of rural France, and something of an English country house hotel.
Five double rooms (three with own bathroom).
B&B: £15 without bath, £17 with bath (under tens, £10 unless sharing with parents). Most guests book by the week.
Dinner: £7 inc. wine. No credit cards.

Boussac (Creuse)

Le Prieuré *St Pierre le Bost, Boussac 23600, tel. 55 65 16 16*
Guesthouse. 100% vegetarian (but see below).
Proprietor: Cécile Surply. English not spoken 'but we'll manage'.
In the extreme north east of the Limousin, almost in the Loire valley region, this is a pleasing guesthouse in a twelfth-century former priory surrounded by trees. It's about seven km from Boussac in the direction of Préveranges. On arriving at St Pierre, the house is about 700 metres from the crossroads. Though sufficiently modernised to be comfortable, it retains a great sense of history, enhanced by antique furnishings. Cécile Surply has been vegetarian for eighteen years, and although she says she now appreciates the ethical value of not killing animals, her motivation is still based on the French 'diététique' quest for health. Guests are in general *en pension* – staying on full-board – and are fed according to certain rules and principles about diet.

Meals are simple, organic, and their nutritious content carefully balanced. Nevertheless, the cooking is good, and can be adjusted to suit individual needs and preferences. Dinner consisted of melon, green salad, lentils and carrots cooked together and served with millet, and a milk pudding made of soya milk. The bread was home made. There is no wine – only springwater, and in any case drinking while eating is (in keeping with a popular dietetic theory) discouraged. In contrast to this regime, Cécile is also prepared to provide a more lavish five-course gastronomic meal (including apéritif and organic wines), usually only for people who come in just for a meal, or are staying just one night. Although she normally serves vegetarian food, Cécile will provide fish or even meat at one of these special dinners if it's for a group among whom some of the people are not vegetarian. Breakfasts are buffet style, with bread, hot drinks, cereals and fruit.
Open all year. All guests must book in advance. Three rooms (each suitable for up to three people), all with shower/WC. Full board:

260F per person per night (230F per person if sharing a room); half board: 200F (150F if sharing). The 'gastronomic' meal is 140F all included. No credit cards.

Cagnes-sur-Mer (Alpes-Maritimes)

★★LA COMÉDIE *85 Montée de la Bourgade, Haut-de-Cagnes 06800, tel. 93 73 44 64*
Restaurant.
This high-quality restaurant in the picturesque old upper part of Cagnes, close to the château, is comfortable and elegant, with stylish blue and grey décor and white tablecloths. The restaurant is not vegetarian, but the chef is, and always has at least one complete vegetarian menu on offer. This is cooking far, far away from the austere 'dietetic' approach of some other establishments. Dishes are imaginative, with, for example, lovely fruit and vegetable salads, artichoke mousses, soya and vegetable main courses with delicate sauces, an excellent flaky pastry wrapped around warm goats' cheese (with ginger), and delicious desserts. The wine list is excellent and extensive.
130F menu (three courses). Wine: cheapest is 118F/bottle for a good Côtes de Provence. Daily 12–2, 7.30–10.30 (closed Mon in winter).

LE GRAIN SAUVAGE *22 avenue de la Gaude, Cagnes-sur-Mer 06800, tel. 93 73 10 00*
Restaurant. 100% vegetarian.
This is a health-food shop and simple restaurant, with white walls and plain wooden tables, serving a choice of two main dishes each day: either a wholegrain with vegetables and usually tofu, or a vegetable gratin with flan. Cooking is of reasonable home-cooking standard. The food is almost entirely organic.
64F for three-course menu. Wine: from 18F/litre organic. Lunchtime: Tue–Sat 12–2; evenings: Fri–Sat only, 7.30–9.30.

Caromb (Vaucluse)

★LE BEFFROI *Caromb 84330, tel 90 62 45 63*
Hotel-restaurant.
The ebullient Monsieur Lahontan's picturesque two-star Logis near the ancient belfry in the old part of Caromb, near Carpentras, combines rusticity with civilised comforts. He features several

acclaimed menus, including one for vegetarians: courgettes stuffed with olive paté, with tomato coulis; or aubergine stuffed with a *confiture* of onions. A nice honey sorbet was served between courses.
Closed Weds in winter, and in February. Ten rooms.
Prices: rooms from 145F; four-course menu 100F; breakfast 35F; half-board 220–300F. Credit cards accepted.

Chaveignes (Indre-et-Loire)

Château De La Vrillaye *Chaveignes 37120, tel. 47 95 32 25. Fax 47 95 31 91*
Guesthouse.
English proprietor: John Hadman.
A splendid nineteenth-century château with Renaissance-style exterior, built in white stone on the site of its sixteenth-century predecessor, Vrillaye is reached at the end of a long driveway lined with handsome lime trees. This is John Hadman's home, and he is gradually restoring the interior. Much work, however, remains to be done. The stately château stands reflected in its 'bassin' (a shallow pool in the large front courtyard), and to either side are eighteenth-century dependencies and an impressive seventeenth-century dovecote. All round are some 24 acres of woods and parkland, as well as a walled organic vegetable garden (and hens) producing much of the château's food.

Vrillaye is south-west of Tours, near Chinon and Richelieu – the location is really ideal for seeing many of the most handsome towns and famous châteaux of the Loire valley. You could also join one of the relaxed and interesting summer courses which are put on at the château; these are in painting, musical appreciation, and architecture (this last includes visits to local châteaux and gardens). The majority of the guests are English, but not many of them are vegetarian, even though John enjoys catering for vegetarians and can provide very acceptable wholefood meatless meals (and sometimes he puts on 'vegetarian fortnights'). The cooking is good, often imaginative, without being over-complicated; ingredients are all marvellously fresh, and flavours are preserved by a great use of steaming. Each evening there's a set five-course dinner. Although John takes note of people's food preferences, there is no written menu and what will actually be served remains a surprise.

Our meal started with huge courgette slices fried in garlic and olive oil, served with sliced tomatoes on top, with lightly melting Roquefort cheese on top of that; a grilled dish of steamed veg-

etables mixed with slices of cheese, accompanied by a salad selection (not quite a typical *crudités*) then a cheese course. Dessert was baked banana with honey, served with real fresh ice cream (not home made, but bought from a local *pâtissier*). After-dinner coffee, tea or herb tea is included in the price. Perhaps cheese played too big a part in this meal, but John points out that no dinner is 'typical' – it varies constantly. Guests eat all together around a big round table in the grand dining room, in an agreeable dinner-party atmosphere at which good local wine flows freely (you're paying for it though, even if at a most reasonable price). Afterwards, relax in the large, comfortable sitting room or the library. Breakfasts are good, with fruit in season; fruit juice; cereal (muesli is available); and croissants, toast or bread. Bedrooms range in standard from stylish and spacious doubles to simple dormitory accommodation.

Open all year. Seventeen rooms, all double or triple (nine with shower/WC). Overnight prices vary according to the type of room chosen. B&B: single 150F–330F; two persons 210F–450F. Lunch: from 20F for snack up to 160F for full five-course meal. Dinner: 160F for five-course set meal. Wine: a charge of 50F per bottle of decent Chinon or Vouvray – you drink as much as you like at dinner, and John estimates what the charge should be (this system seems to work quite well). Half-board rates (minimum three nights): 240F–360F per night per person. Credit cards accepted. Reservation essential; dinner must be ordered in advance.

Dijon (Côte d'Or)

Le Potimarron *ave de l'Ouche, Dijon 21000, tel. 80 43 38 07*
Restaurant.
Dijon is the historic capital of the great Duchy of Burgundy, famous throughout the world for food and wine. It's a pity vegetarians are poorly catered for in this heartland of gastronomy. But at a little distance from the centre of town, one possibility is this small restaurant which offers a curious *carte* of meat and macrobiotic dishes, including many which are vegetarian.
Allow about 70F. Mon–Sat for lunch and dinner.

Domfront (Orne)

Maison Jonquille *25 rue Maréchal Joffre, Domfront 61700, tel. 33 30 19 95*
Guesthouse. 100% vegetarian.
Welsh proprietor: Chris Gwilliam.
In this old Normandy house, three simple but comfortable bedrooms and a dining room have been set aside for guests. Chris and her husband Diarmuid have a separate dining room and lounge of their own. The atmosphere is relaxed and easy-going. Families are very welcome (Chris has a small child of her own), and meals are of a high standard. The sort of thing you might expect to eat is a starter of bean pâté or a spiced lentil and coconut soup; main course of spinach and watercress roulade or hazelnut and courgette bake; and dessert of orange and cointreau pancake or home-made ice cream. No smoking is allowed in the house.
Open Feb–Dec. Three rooms, sharing a bathroom (two are family rooms). Bed and breakfast – 85F per person, or 260F–275F for family with up to four children if sharing a room. Evening meal: 50F for three courses. Much reduced meal prices for children. No credit cards.

Les Eyzies (Dordogne)

⋆**La Combe** *24620 Les Eyzies, tel. 53 06 94 68 (between Les Eyzies and Le Bugue)*
Farm-guesthouse/Restaurant.
Belgian (Flemish) proprietor: Françoise Wagnon. English spoken.
Unmistakable red teapot signs lead the way along country lanes to this farm guesthouse in the heart of the Dordogne. It has the

disorganised and untidy feel of a hippy settlement, though in fact is run fairly efficiently by Françoise and her daughter Orphée. Françoise is a formidable character, as well as an excellent cook. She came from Gent in the early 1980s, and has been living here since, with cows, goats, sheep, hens, ducks, and vegetable patch. Almost everything served in the dining room is made from the products of her 20-hectare (50-acre) organic farm, including the milk and cheeses. Considering how chaotic the place seems, it's incongruous that guests are turning up in smart Volvos and Saabs from all over France, Holland, Britain, Germany and, especially, from Belgium. Some are initially disappointed; one woman explained to me that she had expected it to be a castle (because there are many in the Dordogne), but that three things redeemed it: the bed is comfortable, there's a lot to do and see in the area, and the food is extremely good. Bedrooms are in various of the stone buildings, and they vary in style and size. They are mostly simple, quite tasteful, with firm low beds, basic furnishings, and their own shower and toilet. Some rooms have a balcony. Alternatively, well-equipped ready-erected tents can be hired, and there are also a few caravans, apartments, and a cottage available.

Most guests are particularly enthusiastic about the food; I met regulars who have been coming for a fortnight every year for six years, who cited the cooking as their main reason. About half the guests are vegetarian, as is Françoise herself. Meat-eaters and vegetarians alike sit together at big dark wooden tables in the large dining room. The food is served with several different items on the plate together (presumably this saves on washing-up!). On my plate were a potato dish similar to gratin dauphinois but with layers of cheese; a single succulent slice of celeriac, boiled, seasoned and baked; slices of fennel with their lacy tops; French beans; radishes tasting as radishes should; and sliced, dressed cucumber with slivers of seaweed. Everything was wonderfully good. The cheese course consisted of lettuce with slices of home-made goats' and cows' cheese. To finish there was a chocolate walnut cake (made with as much ground walnut as flour, and raised by beating the eggs with honey) which was a touch too heavy and dry. Breakfast is home-made bread, coffee, muesli, fruit juice and fruit, home-made jams and honey. There's nothing laid on at La Combe in the way of activities or entertainments (though there is a pond suitable for swimming), but there's a vast amount to see in the immediate area, including the dramatic caves with prehistoric wall-paintings at nearby Les Eyzies.

Open all year. Seven double rooms (five with own bathroom). Full-board in room with own shower/WC. 1505F per person per week. Half-board: 1260F per person per week. Wine: from 26F/litre for local organic. Less than a week by arrangement. Book well in advance. No credit cards.

Fouras (Charente-Maritime)

GÎTE DE FRANCE *48 boulevard Allard, Fouras 17450, tel. 46 84 08 25*
Guesthouse. Mainly vegetarian.
Proprietor: Jacqueline Malinverny.
As the name makes clear, this guesthouse is in the Gîtes de France organisation, which ensures certain standards of comfort and cuisine for holiday accommodation (it has three *épis*, the organisation's equivalent of stars). In fact, Jacqueline Malinverny is a great believer in *la cuisine française*, though without the meat. Her spacious house, 150 metres from the Atlantic, on the edge of a well-placed seaside village – it's on a green, calm peninsula – draws the same contented clients year after year. The whole house, including the bedrooms, is furnished with country-style antiques. She takes guests on a half-board basis only. Jacqueline herself is vegetarian, but serves macrobiotic food too. Meals are all freshly prepared, they are presented and served with elegance, and almost everything is organic. Since 'you won't be given the same thing twice', she asks me *not* to mention any typical dishes! However, you may find a starter of soup or crudités, a main course of perhaps vegetable escalope, followed by cheeses. Desserts include all sorts of cakes, puddings and pastries. Breakfasts too have plenty of choice and are generous. In winter, Jacqueline gives cookery classes.
Open all year. Five double/triple rooms, all with shower/WC. Half-board: 250F per person per night, or 220F per person if two sharing. Wine: from 60F/bottle organic. No credit cards.

Gagnac-sur-Cère (Lot)

LAVAUR HAUTE – CENTRE HARMONIE VITALE
Gagnac-sur-Cère 46130, tel. 65 33 85 83
Guesthouse. 100% vegetarian.
Proprietor: Jean-Marie Hertay. A little English spoken.
To find this marvellous countryside retreat leave Gagnac (on the Cère river near Bretenoux) and take the back lane signposted Laval

de Cère. The Centre attracts people for all sorts of different reasons. Some come for the healthy food and environment, some for the atmosphere of spirituality, some simply for a restful holiday in these lovely wooded hills. Lavaur Haute is a hamlet of solid old stone farmhouses, most of which has become the Centre Harmonie Vitale. It's way off the beaten track, down a long shaded country lane on a ridge above the Cère. You can camp, stay in a small unisex dormitory, or have a small private bedroom, but all guests are on full-board.

There's home-made wholemeal bread, while fruit and vegetables are produced in the Centre's own organic garden. You may help in the garden if you wish, or go for walks or to a nearby lake for swimming. At the Centre there's massage, T'ai Chi, rebirth through breathing, and gestalt therapy, but no obligation to take part in these activities. Shoes may not be worn indoors. The interior is attractive, full of character, with bare stone walls and varnished wooden floors. The food is ultra simple and wholesome, with lunch of, for example, fruit, yoghurt and nuts, or dinner of salad, soup, vegetables and rice. Neither wine nor coffee are served. Breakfast is bread, jam, tahini, butter, and herb teas or grain coffee. As a guest told me, 'The Centre offers delicious calm and rest, unspoiled nature, and a symphony of birdsong in the morning. There's nothing else to entertain you here.'

Open April–Sept only. Maximum twenty guests.
Price per person for full board: in small bedroom 140–160F;
in dormitory or camping 100–120F. Prices are per night,
but bookings should be for one week minimum. No credit cards.

Gevrey-Chambertin (Côte d'Or)

★LES MILLÉSIMES *25 rue de l'Église, tel. 80 51 84 24*
Restaurant.

This high-quality restaurant (Michelin rosette, Gault-Millau toques) high up in the midst of a famous wine village is the cellar – beautifully done up – of an old winegrower's house. It's pricey, and certainly not vegetarian, but presented us at less than an hour's notice with a very acceptable five-course meal: tomato consommé; vegetable terrine with green salad; artichoke mousseline (with a meaty garnish which was quickly whisked away when we objected); excellent cheese selection (over 30 varieties); and substantial desserts. Presentation and preparation were both meticulous, yet flavour was sometimes lacking.

Our meal: 200F each. Wine: from 220F/bottle. Open daily for lunch and dinner (until 9pm), except Tue, and Wed lunch. Recommended hotel in the same village – LES GRANDS CRUS, tel 80 34 34 15, opposite the twelfth-century church: comfortable, well-kept rooms, and a delightful garden where you can have breakfast.

Grenoble (Isère)

AU P'TIT POIDS *4 place de Gordes, Grenoble 38000, tel. 76 51 58 39*
Restaurant.
Bright, cheerful, on a South American theme and specialising in dishes from that part of the world, this restaurant has a small but useful and enjoyable choice of vegetarian options on its *carte* (vegetarians will not be able to order the fixed-price menu). Start with one of the mixed salads – you could order the Sud-Americain, but ask for it 'sans thon' (without tuna) – and follow with either tacos or perico (made with eggs, tomatoes and onions and served with beans and rice).
Allow about 80F for three courses. Wine: from 29F/litre. Daily (exc Sun) 12–1.30, 7–10.30.

Gréoux-les-Bains (Alpes-de-Haute-Provence)

MAISON VERTE *7 Cité Paradis, route de Valensole, Gréoux-les-Bains 04800, tel. 92 74 21 20*
Guesthouse. 100% vegetarian.
Proprietor: Jacqueline Feldman. English spoken.
At one time, Jacqueline's pleasant house in its garden on the edge of Gréoux was known as a restaurant, but she now runs it entirely as a *pension*. It's a calm, agreeable location, and Jacqueline is a welcoming host. She has been vegetarian since birth – or rather, as she points out, since before she was born, as her parents (her father a refugee from Hungary) were also vegetarian. Rooms are simple but well-equipped and comfortable, and have a little kitchen corner (when the guesthouse is closed for the winter, it's possible to rent a room on a self-catering basis). Food is likewise simple but good, with meals of, for example, vegetable pâté or crudités to start, main course of perhaps croquettes, tofu and vegetables, and scrumptious desserts of tarts and cakes. Cheese is available on request. Breakfast is French style, with wholemeal bread and butter with coffee, tea or herb tea. There are croissants on Sundays.

Open March–November. Four double rooms, four singles (all with shower/WC). 215F per person per night full board, 185F per person half-board. Wine: from 25F/bottle for local vin de pays, *with good organic wine at 60F/bottle.*
Credit cards accepted.

Lalinde (Dordogne)

LA FORGE *Lalinde 24150, tel 53 24 92 24*
Hotel-restaurant.
An agreeable two-star Logis de France hotel close to the river Dordogne, prettily old-fashioned, in the shade of plane trees. Some of the rooms are in an annexe in gardens on the banks of the Dordogne. One of chef-patron Monsieur Gouzot's menus is fully vegetarian: main course tarte of cèpes with pine nuts; 35 varieties of cheese; interesting desserts. Good local wines, too.
Closed Sun evenings in winter, from Christmas to the end of January, and for a week in October. 21 double rooms.
Prices: rooms from 235F; breakfast 30F; menus from 60F; half-board 230F. Credit cards accepted.

Marseille (Bouche-du-Rhône)

AUBERGE IN *25 rue de Chevalier-Roze, Marseille 13002, tel. 91 90 51 59*
Restaurant. 100% vegetarian.
This reliable and well-known eating place in the heart of Marseille provides a reasonably comfortable and attractive environment for a decent lunch or dinner at a modest price. You could start with, for example, vegetable pâté or blinis, and have a main course of wholegrain with vegetables. The *plat du jour* is a meal in itself, with crudités, grain, cooked vegetables, and perhaps vegetable tart. There's a big choice of tempting desserts, one of the best being Gâteau Norvégien, a rich layered sponge cake with fruit juice.
50F menu (three courses plus drink). Wine: from 30F/litre organic.
Daily (exc Sun) 12–2, 7–10. Metro: Colbert or Vieux Port.

COUNTRY LIFE *14 rue Venture, Marseille 13001, tel. 91 54 16 44*
Restaurant. 100% vegetarian
In a spacious, comfortable setting located in the Canebière district between rue St Ferreol and rue Paradis, this buffet-style restaurant

(attached to a health shop) is open for weekday lunches only. It offers healthy, well-balanced main dishes, light pastries or sorbets, and herb teas.
Around 50F. Mon–Fri, 11.30–2.30. Metro: Estrangin.

Molezon (Lozère)

See Ste Croix Vallée Française

Montpellier (Herault)

Tripti-Kulai *20 rue Jacques Coeur, Montpellier 34000, tel. 67 66 30 51*
Restaurant. 100% vegetarian.
In a backstreet close to Place Comédie, which is the heart of this agreeable city, this was until recently an Auberge In. Anyone who wished its cooking could be a little more interesting and tasty should pay another visit now. The new owner-chef is Padmasini Juellet, who works with two other cooks – one English, the other Japanese – to create copious salads and vegetarian hot dishes using 'recipes from the entire world'. What you'll find depends on which day you happen to come – there could be tapenade (like an olive pâté), vegetable terrine, aubergine 'caviar' – and it is planned to introduce Indian days and Japanese days. There's a big range of delicious *à la carte* dishes, as well as set three-course meals which typically start with a choice of soup, pâté or crudités, followed by a main course grain-and-vegetable dish, and finish with fromage blanc, fruit salad or some more filling pud. The name, or so they told me, is Bengali for satisfaction, but I'd have been even more satisfied if I could have had a glass of wine with my meal.
60F for three-course menu. No wine (they suggest organic fruit juice instead). Daily (exc Sun) 12–3, 7–9.30.

Paris

There are half-a-dozen vegetarian eating places in the city, and several others which provide a vegetarian choice, though most of their customers are tourists (English, American, Dutch, German) rather than locals. In addition there are big self-service cafeterias, brasseries and cheese restaurants all over the city in which it's often possible to get a good meatless meal. Typical brasserie food includes mixed salads, fried eggs, omelettes, chips.

AQUARIUS *54 rue Ste Croix de la Bretonnerie, 75004, tel. (1) 48 87 48 71*
Restaurant. 100% vegetarian.
Uninteresting but useful, serving mainly salads and omelettes, with some galettes. Simple café-style interior, reasonable cooking, popular with regulars. Sometimes art exhibitions, and music.
Three-course menu (inc drink) 60F. Wine: from 15F/litre.
Daily 12–10. Metro: Hôtel-de-Ville.

AQUARIUS 2 *40 rue de Gergovie, 75014, tel. (1) 45 41 36 88*
Restaurant. 100% vegetarian.
In some ways similar to the other, more central Aquarius above, with wooden tables and simple décor in three rooms, and with exhibitions of paintings. But the cooking is better at this branch. The chef here is Richard Leith, author of *La Nouvelle Cuisine Végétarienne* (Hachette), who prepares a wide variety of dishes for a diverse *carte*. Some are familiar foreign favourites, acceptably done (moussaka, lasagne), some use seitan etc to imitate French meat dishes, some are British vegetarian classics like nut roast with sauce and roast potatoes. Desserts are English- and French-style cakes and pastries, and good ice creams.
Three-course menu (inc drink) 60F. Wine 15F/litre.
Open 12–2.15, 7–10.30. Metro: Pernety.

BOL EN BOIS *35 rue Pascal, 75013, tel. (1) 47 07 27 24*
Restaurant.
One of the earliest macrobiotic eating places, founded over twenty years ago, this rather austere restaurant, shop and library is still serving good-quality dishes based mainly around soya in all its various forms. Some fish makes an appearance.
Dish of the day 50F. Mon–Sat, 12–2, 7–9.30.
Metro: Censier Daubenton.

COUNTRY LIFE *6 rue Daunou, 75002, tel. (1) 42 97 48 51*
Restaurant. 100% vegetarian.
A large, light, air-conditioned two-floor restaurant, with plenty of plants. You help yourself to buffet-style vegan lunches, with a large selection of salads and a choice of two or three tasty hot dishes of whole grains with vegetables.
Allow around 55F. No wine. Mon–Fri, 11.30–2.30. Metro: Opéra.

Aux Délices D'aphrodite *4 rue de Candolle, 75005, tel. (1) 43 31 40 39*
Restaurant.
Greek restaurant with Greek island theme, blue and white decor, and a small selection of well-prepared vegetarian dishes such as aubergines stuffed with vegetables and pine kernels.
Allow 120F for complete meal. Wine: from about 45F for half-bottle. Open daily exc Mon, 12–2.30, 7–11.30.
Metro: Censier-Daubenton.

Downtown *29 quai de la Tournelle, 75004, tel. (1) 46 33 66 66*
Restaurant.
A pleasant Seine-side (Left Bank) restaurant with simple modern white decor and potted greenery outside. It's not vegetarian, but has several imaginative meatless macrobiotic-style dishes, including aubergine 'caviar', soya 'steak' and vegetable terrine.
Allow about 130F for three courses. Wine: from 65F/bottle.
Daily 12–2, 7.45–12. Metro: Pont Marie or Maubert-Mutualité.

La Fermette D'olivier *40 rue du Faubourg Montmartre, 75009, tel. (1) 47 70 06 88*
Restaurant. Mainly vegetarian.
Pretty, floral, little macrobiotic restaurant with a daily Zen Plate (four grains, veg stew, optional fish, veg fritters, and salad vegetables) as well as a more traditional *carte* with palatable vegetarian dishes.
63F for Zen Plate, dessert and non-alcoholic drink.
Wine: from 24F/litre organic. Mon–Fri 12–4, 6–10.
Metro: Montmartre or Pelletier.

Galerie 8 *8 rue Rochebrune, 75011, tel (1) 47 00 62 44*
Restaurant.
A macrobiotic restaurant, with some well-prepared dishes of North African inspiration, such as cous-cous, as well as brown rice and veg. Wide range of dishes and of prices.
Lunch, allow 60F; dinner, allow 100F.
Wine: from 60F/bottle organic. Tues–Sat 12–2.30, 7.30–10.
Metro: St Ambroise.

Au Grain De Folie *24 rue de la Vieuville, 75018, tel. (1) 42 58 15 57*
Restaurant. Mainly vegetarian.
This useful little Montmartre vegetarian restaurant (some fish makes a rare appearance) is well-placed and well-known. Owner Marie-Cécile Dubuis provides a good quality menu of salads, vegetable tarts and pies, a range of meatless dishes from around the world, and an 'Exotic Fruit Crumble' to finish.
Full meal just under 100F. Wine: from 38F/bottle.
Daily 12.30–3.15, 7–11. Metro: Abbesses (rue de la Vieuville is opposite the station).

Grand Appetit *9 rue de la Cerisaie, 75004, tel. (1) 40 27 04 95*
Restaurant.
Macrobiotic shop with a light, modern restaurant serving a main dish of brown rice with one other grain, plus (for example) tofu and cooked vegetables, and salad.
Allow 75F. No wine. Organic beer from 14F.
Daily exc Sat, 12–2.30 and (in summer only) 7–9. Metro: Bastille.

Le Grenier De Notre Dame *18 rue de la Bûcherie, 75005, tel. (1) 43 29 98 29*
Restaurant. Mainly vegetarian.
This very popular two-storey macrobiotic restaurant not far from the river, in the Latin Quarter, offers a varied selection of good *à la carte* vegetarian and fish dishes, as well as a cheap set vegetarian meal. The main dishes are substantial grains and vegetables. Both floors are usually crowded, and you may have to share a table. Service is friendly, but sometimes disorganised because of the number of customers.
Three-course menu 60F. Wine: from 57F/bottle organic.
Daily 12–2, 7.30–11.30. Metro: Maubert-Mutualité.

Le Jardin *100 rue du Bac, 75007, tel. (1) 42 22 17 91*
Restaurant.
This unusual eating place (plus shop) with its verandah, garden and greenery, proposes what it calls a 'balanced' style of eating, which however, is non-vegetarian, although there are several meat-free dishes. It's mainly aimed at dieters – calorie counts are shown on the menu. However, there's nothing restrained about the food, which includes vegetable gratins, flans, potato-dishes and egg

dishes. Pastries and cakes to finish. Changes are anticipated, however, especially in the lunchtime menu.
Three-course meal 70F. Wine: from 60F/bottle.
Mon–Sat 12–2.30, 7.30–10. Metro: Rue du Bac.

LACOUR *3 rue Villedo, 75001, tel. (1) 42 96 08 33*
Restaurant. 100% vegetarian.
One of the best bargains in Paris, even if it could do with a lick of paint. This long-established little family-style Restaurant Végétarien serves decent lunchtime set-meals at unbelievably low prices. Typical dishes are rice mixed with vegetables, or quiche with vegetables.
Three-courses for 30F or (more copious) 35F – and another 4F for a jug of delicious coffee. Wine: from 35F/bottle. Daily 12–2.15. Metro: Pyramides or Palais Royal.

LA MACROBIOTHÈQUE *17 rue de Savoie, 75006, tel. (1) 43 25 04 96*
Restaurant.
In a smartish part of the Left Bank, this well-known and old-established little macrobiotic restaurant (and shop) serves a wide selection of interesting dishes like soya croquettes, as well as sensible wholesome dishes like rice and veg.
Lunch menu 41F, dinner menu 70F. No wine.
Mon–Sat 12–2, 7–10. Metro: St Michel.

NATURALIA *107 rue Caulaincourt, 75018, tel. (1) 42 62 33 68*
Restaurant.
In the basement, behind a health food shop, this lunchtime restaurant serves good vegetarian dishes daily, plus meat on Thursdays, fish on Fridays.
39F for dish of the day; full meal about 70F. Mon–Fri 11.30–3.30. Metro: Clichy.

PICCOLO TEATRO *6 rue des Ecouffes, 75004, tel. (1) 42 72 17 7*
Restaurant. 100% vegetarian.
Small and friendly unpretentious café-style restaurant currently completely vegetarian, with dishes such as vegetable gratins, salads, and carrot caviar. Everything is organic.
Weekday lunchtime: menus at 49F and 70F. All other times, allow 50F–80F for a meal à la carte. *Wine: from 45F/litre organic. Daily (exc Mon) 12–3, 7–12. Metro: St Paul or Hôtel de Ville.*

RAYONS DE SANTÉ *8 place Charles Dullin, 75018, tel. (1) 42 59 64 81*
Restaurant. 100% vegetarian.
This bright and cheerful Montmartre restaurant, bookshop and health food shop is run by a charming couple, originally from Hungary. It steers a course between the dietetic and gastronomic, catering for 'experienced' vegetarians and non-vegetarians alike. The daily *carte* covers a wide range, with a simple whole-grain and vegetable meal, or tofu sausages, omelettes, soya ragout, ricotta ravioli, and vegetarian cous-cous among several interesting dishes which can be eaten in the simple interior or at pavement tables.
40F 'formula' pays for a starter and main dish, plus 10–15F for a dessert. No wine. 12–3, 6.30–9.30, closed Fri evening and all day Sat. Metro: Anvers or Abbesses.

LA VOIE LACTÉE *34 rue du Cardinal Lemoine and 3 rue des Ecoles, 75005, tel. (1) 46 34 02 35*
Restaurant.
This address was formerly the home of Auberge-In, one of the first vegetarian restaurants in Paris. However, it's now a simple Turkish restaurant-snackbar, not connected with the previous establishment. The name means The Milky Way, but that doesn't refer to the cuisine. Main dishes are simple, but tasty, and include several vegetarian possibilities (ask for a meze végétarien, for example) as well as a vegetarian dish of the day.
Lunchtime menus: 42F for main dish plus dessert;
65F for three courses. Dinner: à la carte *only.*
Wine: from about 70F/bottle. Mon–Sat, 12–2.30, 7–12.
Metro: Cardinal Lemoine.

PAULIAC (Dordogne) – *See Ribérac*

Pontigny (Yonne)

LE MOULIN DE PONTIGNY *20 rue Paul Desjardins, Pontigny 89230, tel. 86 47 44 98*
Restaurant.
At a former mill, in a comfortable country-style dining room with beams and a big fireplace, few diners are vegetarian. So few, indeed, that owner-chef Hubert Rilliot has given up his vegetarian menu. He previously had a restaurant in Auxerre where for many years he offered a meat-free meal daily. He will still cater for vegetarians (it

will help if you mention this when reserving a table), albeit not with much flair – your meal will probably consist of salad followed by a plate of vegetables.

Three-course menu 50F. Wine: a good selection of Burgundies from 95F/bottle (Chablis is 15km away). Open 11.30–1.30, 7–9 (closed Mon evening and Tues, except Jul and Aug, when closed Tue evening only).

Port-Ste-Marie (Lot-et-Garonne)

Le Marchon *Bazens 47130, tel. 53 87 22 26*
Guesthouse. 100% vegetarian.
Dutch proprietors: Maria and Henk van Straaten. English spoken.
Take the road from Port-Ste-Marie, a riverside town on the Garonne's north bank, for some four km through the fields towards Bazens, and you'll see signs to Le Marchon, a peaceful, welcoming country guesthouse standing among cedar, lime and oak trees. Tables grapes, apples and vegetables are grown here, all organically, on 8½ hectares (25 acres) of hillside. The main building is a large attractive old farmhouse. Outside there's a big oval swimming pool (nude swimming OK), and beautiful views of the rolling Gascon hills. Nearby is an organic canning factory (because there are so many organic farmers in the area), and a little noise can be heard from this in certain parts of the garden. Bedrooms vary: most have a timber floor with handmade rugs, plain walls, and simple furnishing including a firm bed.

Meals are of good home-cooking standard, tasty, filling and wholesome classic vegetarian fare. Ingredients are organic. A typical three-course dinner starts with a big mixed salad or soup, or sometimes fruit salad; the main course will be millet or rice, with vegetables and tofu in sauce; to finish, there are sometimes cheeses, but usually desserts of, say, fruit compote or crêpes. Breakfasts are of organic home-made bread, organic home-made jam, muesli, home-made yoghurt, fresh organic fruit juice in season (the home-made grape juice is rich, sweet and delicious), and various hot drinks. In the warmer months, eating is mostly out of doors at a large round table on a shady terrace. Alternatively, the spacious dining/living room has a blazing log fire, scattered tables on a distinctive black-and-white tile floor, and a piano for guests to play.

Sculptures around the room are by Henk, who teaches sculpture, and can do clay or stone portraits. Maria is a qualified nurse, can assist with diets, can give massage and also supervise a 'sound bath'

with Tibetan bells. Other full-time residents are Luc (Belgian) and Lisa (Danish). Bikes can be hired, and maps supplied. Train travellers can be picked up from Agen for a small fee.
Open all year, six double rooms (three with own bath or shower and WC). Full board price in high season, in room without shower; 190F per person. Add 20F per person for room with shower. Subtract 20% for low season booking, and deduct a further 40F per person for half-board. Most guests choose half-board and the average length of stay is ten days, though one-night stopovers are also welcome. Wine: 25F/bottle for organic Bordeaux. No credit cards.

Ribérac (Dordogne)

★PAULIAC CHAMBRE D'HÔTE *Celles, 24600 Ribérac, tel. 53 91 97 45*
Guesthouse-restaurant.
English proprietors: John and Jane Edwards.
For further information in the UK, tel. (091) 284 1627.
It feels like a privilege to stay in a hamlet which is not even marked on the detailed yellow Michelin map of the region. Pauliac, a few kilometres from Ribérac, consists of just five houses at the end of a narrow lane lined with wildflowers, looking out across rolling north Dordogne farmland. On one of them the sign 'Carruthers' hangs half-hidden, in token of the fact that the real owner of this big restored farmhouse is Jane's father, Bill Carruthers. At the back is a delightful terraced garden with a simple fountain and a couple of shaded tables. John and Jane have been running the place as a *pension* for a couple of years, catering mainly to meat-eaters, although they are always trying to attract more vegetarians. Almost all guests are English. Most of the house is still in the process of improvement. Our bedroom had basic furnishing, was a bit tacky, and suffered from the rather odd combination of bare stone and pink flock wallpaper. The dining room is large and beamed, with a massive old fireplace, and is one of the few rooms in the house which really looks finished.

Jane goes to some trouble over the food: there's a set meat meal and a set vegetarian meal, although she does discuss preferences before cooking. We had a good sorrel soup, followed by huge artichokes with mushrooms on the side; the main course was a 'blue cheese soufflé' which was light and eggy but didn't taste of blue cheese at all; an unusual selection of side vegetables included

little spinach tartlets, and a tasty sauce of onion, milk and nutmeg. Anyone choosing the cheeseboard helps themselves freely from a high-quality selection. The walnut tart dessert was well made and filling. I didn't like their coffee, however. Pauliac is well placed for outings to some of the Dordogne's greatest 'sights'. Périgueux, the département's capital, is about 50km away. Guests can be collected from railway stations or airports for a small fee.
Open all year. Six double rooms (four with shower/WC); from 120F to 185F. Breakfast 15F. Dinner: four courses 80F, five courses 95F. Wine: good ordinaire at 20F/litre. No credit cards.

Rouen (Seine-Maritime)

Apple Paille *7 rue Rollon, Rouen 76000, tel. 35 98 39 30*
Restaurant.
The name is a sort of joke, since 'Paille' is pronounced like the English 'pie'. However, the interesting thing here is neither apple pies nor *paille* (straw), but galettes. There's always at least one vegetarian main dish at this quiet little eating place in the middle of old Rouen. On the day I visited, there were wholewheat galettes with tofu and mixed vegetables. Start with salads, and finish with a choice of desserts.
50F menu. Wine: from 32F/litre. Daily (exc Sun) 12–2, 7–10.30.

St Christol-lès-Alès (Gard)

Le Mas Perdu *Boujac 30380, tel. 66 60 76 80*
Guesthouse. 100% vegetarian.
Proprietors: Le Mas Perdu belongs to an association called Santé et Vie, but the house is the home of the Garcia family, who form part of the association. English spoken.
'Mas' is the southern word for a building out in the country, and 'perdu' means lost, so the name of this *pension vegetarienne* is apt. At the traffic lights in St Christol-lès-Alès (*lès* means near), turn right if coming from Alès or left if coming from Montpellier. Follow signs for Boujac Tennis Club or to Auberge du Serre d'Avène. When you reach the Auberge, you'll see small signs along a rough track to Le Mas Perdu. It's a handsome restored stone farmhouse draped in greenery, standing in extensive private grounds. Three hectares (say eight acres) of the land is cultivated with organic vegetables, and horses are used to work the grounds. Other areas are ideal for relaxing in the shade of trees. There's a

pleasant, friendly atmosphere, with cicadas providing a soporific background. As well as people on holiday, there are others staying here to learn organic farming techniques, and also a number of young people with problems (eg heavy drugs) who are trying to return to a healthy, normal life. The Garcia family who run the place are Adventists, but there's no overtly religious dimension to the activities of the house.

It's the habit of the house to have a big breakfast and a late lunch. In the enticing organic vegetable garden the produce looked superb. Disappointingly, the standard of cooking does not always make the best of these fine ingredients. To some extent it is restrained by high principles – no spices, for example. My meal started well enough with delicious raw tomatoes dressed with fresh herbs, but the vegetable tart (pastry overcooked) and aubergines (undercooked) in tomato sauce (overcooked) were not so good. There was no cheese course, and dessert was a bowl of custard. No wine is served, and no coffee or tea. Meals are eaten by all guests sitting together at a single table in a large beamed dining/living room with big fireplace and quarry tile floor, or at a long table outside beneath the shade of a tree. For breakfast there's fruit, herb tea, bread and butter, and muesli. Bedrooms are simple, with plain white walls and plain tiled floors, though most have their own shower/WC.

Open all year, seven rooms, all suitable for one, two or three people (five rooms with shower/WC). 160F full board per person in room with shower/WC. Vegan and other diets catered for. No wine. Credit cards acceptable.

St Clar (Gers)

★HOTEL RISON *pl de la Lomagne, St Clar 32380, tel. 62 66 40 21*
Hotel-restaurant.
English proprietors: Elwyn Edwards and Steve Moore.

Until its two English owners took over, this was a typical little hotel-restaurant of rural Gascony, specialising above all in local gastronomy. Gascon cuisine revolves around the goose, whose fat is used for much of the cooking, and whose liver, when suitably bloated as a result of force-feeding, is one of the greatest French delicacies – foie gras. The new owners did not change any of this, and the Rison's menus are a catalogue of goose and duck dishes of the rustic south-west. However, one change they did introduce, causing local newspapers to run amazed reports, was a daily five-course vegetarian menu. Local people have flocked in to try it, because any new gastronomic experience is of interest to them. Not only is the cooking good and copious, but prices are wonderfully low. The sort of thing you will be offered is an hors d'oeuvres of *tourin végétarien* (a *tourin* is a milky soup poured over bread), followed by an *assiette de crudités*, then a main course of hot vegetarian terrine, then a green salad, and either cheese or dessert to finish. Gascon desserts are pretty scrumptious, too, and make good use of another local product – Armagnac. Croustade is a lovely apple and Armagnac tart. Gascony also makes several wines, which vary considerably in quality. Without doubt the best of them (and best bargain) is the rich red from Madiran.

This is very much a *restaurant avec chambres*, in other words, the accommodation takes second place to the cooking. Rooms are simple, but adequately comfortable and moderately priced. The little town of St Clar is a *bastide* (medieval fortified 'new town' built during the wars between France and England) with two handsome arcaded main squares. In one of the squares there's a thirteenth-century covered market which every Thursday throughout the summer months houses one of the most important garlic markets in France. The town's well placed for exploring rural Gascony, and is easily accessible by autoroute coming from either Bordeaux or Toulouse. The hotel stands on the edge of town, surrounded by open countryside.

Open daily Jul/Aug; rest of year closed Sun pm and all day Mon. Eight rooms (two with bath/shower). Room only: 120F for two persons, 100F for one. Breakfast: 20F. Half-board: 140F per person. Dinner only (five-course vegetarian menu): 75F. Wine from 22F/litre. No credit cards.

St Disdier-en-Dévoluy (Hautes Alpes)

★LA NEYRETTE *St Disdier-en-Dévoluy 05250, tel. 92 58 81 17*
Hotel-restaurant. English spoken (not very well).

It is very pleasing indeed to discover a two-star Logis de France hotel (in other words, my ideal hotel) at which the proprietors are vegetarian and offer a full vegetarian menu which changes daily. La Neyrette, just outside St Disdier on the road to Corps, is well-placed and welcoming. Rooms are comfortable, carpeted, of the usual two-star standard. Owners Monsieur and Madame Muzard (she does the cooking) offer a traditional meat menu as well, and most of their clients take that option. The vegetarian meal started with salade de chèvre chaud (a small salad with warmed goats' cheese – delicious), or one could have crudités; the choice for main course included galettes with vegetables (some from their own garden), or tourton au pommes de terre, a local speciality of flaky pastry filled with potato and caraway. A cheese course was followed by a choice which included fresh fruit salad or another local speciality, an open tart with nuts. Milk and milk products come mainly from neighbouring farms. Breakfast is a traditional French style bread with café-au-lait, but cereals are available.

Open all year (except 20–30 Apr, 1 Nov–15 Dec). Twelve rooms (eight double, four family rooms), all with shower or bath and WC. Vegetarian menu: 80F for four courses. Wine: from 32F/bottle. Room only: 190F for single, 230F for two. Breakfast: 23F. Half-board: 280F for single, 420F for two. Full-board: 350F for single, 560F for two. Credit cards accepted.

St Guiraud (Herault)

★★LE MIMOSA *St Guiraud 34150, tel. 67 96 67 96*
Restaurant.

This first class gastronomic restaurant, in a beautifully restored building at a small, quiet vineyard village in the Languedoc back country, is unusual in at least two ways. Firstly, it is one of very few English-run restaurants to receive acclaim in the French food guides – Michelin give it one 'knife-and-fork', and, far more important, the Gault-Millau guide has awarded it one toque (chef's hat, their symbol of excellence). Secondly, it is one of very few such highly reputed mainstream French restaurants to offer a vegetarian menu. Proprietors Bridget and David Pugh met when she was a Royal Ballet dancer, and he a violinist at the Royal Opera House. Later, they moved here after ten years as leading members of the Norwegian National Opera and Ballet Company. Both decor and food reflect their innate artistic flair and feeling. Although almost all their clients want meat or fish, Bridget is herself a vegetarian and enjoys preparing meatless meals. The vegetarian menu is five courses of imaginative, creative, delicious food (three courses, plus cheese and dessert). The meals vary enormously in content – they are strongly influenced by the season, and depend entirely on which local ingredients are currently at their best. You'll encounter vegetables from nearby villages, especially courgettes and aubergines (delicious when stuffed with pine nuts), onions from Lezignan, local fruits, and perhaps their extraordinary sorbets to finish.

Menu: 200F. Wine: excellent choice of local growers, minimum 70F/bottle. Daily for lunch and dinner except Mon, Tues lunch, and 2 Jan–23 Feb.

St Pardoux (Haute-Vienne)

CHÂTEAU DE VAUGUENIGE *87250 St Pardoux, tel. 55 76 58 55*
Guesthouse. Mainly vegetarian.
Proprietor: Marick Claude. English spoken.

To find Vauguenige if you're at St Pardoux, get on to nearby D27 (the road from Bessines to St Symphorien), and turn towards St Symphorien. After about 500 metres there's a lane on the right with a sign, 'Chambres d'Hôte Vauguenige' – go slowly or you could easily miss it. Not so much a château as a handsome manor house, Vauguenige stands in its own spacious grounds which are surrounded by a typical Limousin landscape of woodlands, rivers and lakes. There's tennis, riding (from stables next door) and lovely forest walks, while indoors rooms are calm and spacious. There's a library and separate TV and music lounges. For those who want it (and most guests have come especially for this), there are organised sessions of keep fit, jogging and yoga. The house is three km from a huge lake (330 ha./810 acres) with watersports. 35 km to the south is Limoges, the capital of the Limousin, a big town famous for its ceramics and for its fine cathedral. Marick Claude's cooking is 'dietetic' and shows strong macrobiotic influences too, but more imaginative than average, less austere, and with generous portions. An example – though the meals are completely different every day – might be gazpacho, leeks vinaigrette, courgettes with garlic, cheese, and finally baked bananas. Meals are almost entirely vegetarian, but with occasional fish dishes unless these are not wanted (Marick will even cook meat if a guest specifically requests it). Breakfast is bread, cereal, fromage blanc, coffee or tea.

Open all year. Nine rooms (which can accommodate one, two or three persons). Prices are for full board: 280F for single person, 235F per person for two sharing. Organic wine with meal: 35F/litre. No credit cards.

St Paterne-Racan (Indre-et-Loire)

CHEZ BOUCHET *1 pl de la Gare et du 8-mai, St Paterne-Racan 37370, tel. 47 29 21 67*
Guesthouse. 100% vegetarian.
Proprietor: Renée Bouchet.
Herself retired, Madame Bouchet inherited this former hotel which belonged to her parents-in-law and now runs it as a modest guesthouse. It stands in 3000 square metres of ground on the edge of this small town (opposite the railway station), and she cultivates organic vegetables and keeps a few hens. Madame Bouchet does all the cooking herself, offering simple but tasty evening meals. A typical dinner might start with a generous *crudités*, have a main course of, say, stuffed tomatoes, followed by locally made goats' cheese. Desserts could be tart, clafoutis, or fruit. Breakfasts are of cereals, eggs, bread and coffee/tea/herb tea. Although Renée Bouchet does not speak English, 90% of her guests are from Britain.
Open all year (but sometimes closed for brief periods in winter – check first). Three or four rooms are let (maximum eight guests at any one time): there are double/triple rooms, and a family room.
Half-board: 170F per night for single, 240F for two sharing.
B&B: 120F for single person, 140F for two. Dinner only: 50F.
Wine: organic wine included. No credit cards.

Ste Croix Vallée Française (Lozère)

CHÂTEAU DE LA ROUVIÈRE *Molezon 48110, tel. 66 45 06 19*
Guesthouse.
For brochure in UK, tel. (0953) 606370.
English proprietors: Tony and Jean Matthews. Jean is vègetarian.
Standing above a climbing road (about ten km from the village of Ste Croix Vallée Française on D983 in the direction of Barre-des-Cevennes), on a ridge overlooking the thickly wooded hills of the southern Cevennes, this is not so much a château – at least, to English eyes – as a large, historic country house of unfaced rough stone. The setting is superb, and the building stands within the borders of the Cevennes National Park, at the northern limits of Languedoc. The oldest part of the house dates from 1540, when it was the castle of the local Count. Later parts of the house date from the eighteenth century. Thanks to National Park regulations, the château must retain its bare stone walls and roof of rough slates. The interior has been converted into simple but comfortable,

pleasingly unadorned rooms with white walls. There is almost no outdoor space available for guests apart from a tiny terrace (with magnificent view), although Jean and Tony grow organic vegetables and keep a few hens. There's an enjoyable family atmosphere, and decent vegetarian meals familiar to the English are well prepared; I enjoyed a four-course set meal of salad, baked stuffed marrow, cheeses, and fruit pudding. Perhaps things are a little too English; there's almost no feeling of being in France. Breakfast, though, is French style: bread and butter, home-made jam, and good coffee. The surrounding country has much to see, and is marvellous for ramblers. For less active days, you can relax by the riverbank nearby. Tony and Jean can provide self-catering accommodation if you prefer, and under the name Downhill Walking Co., Tony organises inclusive walking tours in the Cevennes, and can also arrange hire of bikes, canoes and horses.

Open Apr–Nov. Six double rooms, all with shower/WC.
Room: 190F (whether for one, two or three people).
Breakfast: 25F. Dinner: 55F menu. Wine: 22F/bottle house wine.
Credit cards accepted.

Sauveterre-de-Comminges (Haute-Garonne)

Le Clos St Michel *Sauveterre-de-Comminges 31510, tel. 61 88 32 28*
Guesthouse. 100% vegetarian.
Proprietor: Michel Jourdain.
On a map, Sauveterre looks like one small village, but in fact it is divided into no fewer than eleven sections, each a separate hamlet: this guesthouse is in Hameau de Bruncan. But get to anywhere in Sauveterre, and you'll find Le Clos signposted. This is a large and rambling three-storey house within walled grounds on the edge of the village. It's a quiet, restful location and Michel is a relaxed and good-humoured host who does all the cooking himself. Meals are simple and healthy, but not austere, and always follow the same structure: salad; cooked vegetables with a whole grain, or stuffed vegetables; cheese course; home-made cakes or pastries or fruit. Dinner is a lighter meal than lunch. All guests eat together at plain wooden tables in the dining room. Breakfast is coffee or tea, wholemeal bread, butter, jam or honey. Broad wooden stairs lead up to bedrooms which are wallpapered, carpeted, reminiscent of the typical two-star country hotel, clean and calm if a little dingy. There's a family room available. While most guests stay for two weeks, overnight B&B guests are welcome.
Open Apr–Sep. Nine rooms (eight double) all with shower/WC.
Full board per night: 225F single person, 395F for two; half-board: 185F single person, 315F for two. Reductions for children.
Wine: 30F/bottle organic. No credit cards.

Thiézac (Cantal)

Le Clou *Thiézac 15450, tel. 71 47 01 45*
Guesthouse.
Dutch proprietors: Frank and Hennie van Buuren. English spoken.
Enquiries in UK: 60 Spirit Quay, London E1 9UT, tel. (071) 481 4317
On a country lane high above the pretty village of Thiézac, within the borders of the vast Parc Régional des Volcans d'Auvergne (Auvergne Volcano Park), you'll find this restored traditional Auvergne farmhouse. All around are magnificent upland landscapes, unspoiled and peaceful, a perfect setting for walking or cycling in summer, skiing in winter, or lazing around listening to the quietness at any time of year. The terrain is distinctive for its

puys – former volcanic peaks. Those in this area are bigger and older than further north. There are many curious natural rock formations, as well as fascinating wildlife, and a tremendously old-fashioned way of life. Just nine miles away are important ski resorts, including Super-Lioran: you can ski from right outside the door of Le Clou. For more sedate pleasures, there are châteaux to visit, old villages to explore, fairs and festivals to chance upon.

Accommodation at Le Clou is in ultra simple rooms or dormitories, and you must bring a sleeping bag – though if you prefer you can hire bedding. Hennie does all the cooking, everything is home-made, almost everything is organic, and much of the produce is from their own garden. The meals are different every day. Although they had no intention of running a vegetarian house, it turns out that a third to a half of their guests are vegetarian. The sort of thing Hennie makes for them is soup; crudités; main courses of brown rice with vegetables and tofu; and scrumptious desserts of things like clafoutis, chocolate mousse, or apple pie. Any dietary preference is catered for. Breakfasts are more Dutch than French, with organic bread, cheese, eggs, yoghurt, muesli, fruit, and coffee, tea or tisanes. Frank and Hennie insist on silence after 11pm, and no radios or recorded music are allowed, though if you can play a musical instrument you are urged to bring it!

Open all year. Five rooms. Half-board prices per person (payable in sterling): summer – in bedroom £16, dormitory £13; rest of year – bedroom £14, dormitory £12. Hire of bedding: £6. Picnic lunch: £2. Advance booking essential.

Thonon-les-Bains (Haute-Savoie)

Le Belvédère *3 rue des Ursules, Thonon-les-Bains 74200, tel. 50 71 75 64*
Restaurant.

A simple but attractive restaurant in the middle of this pleasant little resort on the shore of Lake Léman (or 'Lake Geneva'), Le Belvédère serves mainly feuilletés – light, flaky pastries filled with either meat or vegetables – as well as certain other dishes. Whether vegetarians can eat the Plat du Jour depends on the day, but they can always find something suitable on the *carte*. In the morning, breakfasts are served, and in the afternoon, tea and cakes.

50F for plat du jour. Wine from about 25F/half-litre.
7.30am–midnight.

Toulouse (Haute-Garonne)

Le Concierge Est Dans L'escalier *42 rue de Blinchers, Toulouse 31000, tel 61 21 24 20*
Restaurant.
Popular and lively eating place in the little district near the St Pierre bridge over the Garonne. It's not vegetarian, but has a daily Assiette du Marché – literally, market plate – which offers plenty to eat without any meat or fish.
Assiette du Marché 55F. Wine from about 38F/bottle for decent local wines. Daily 11–2, 8–12 (closed lunchtime on Sat and Sun).

Tourette-sur-Loup (Alpes-Maritimes)

La Colle Du Moulin (Chez Guerrault) *131 Chemin de la Colle du Moulin, Tourette-sur-Loup 06140, tel. 93 24 18 37*
Guesthouse. 100% vegetarian.
Proprietors: Jean and Vicky Guerrault.
It's not immediately obvious how to find this vegetarian guesthouse. It's about 2½km out of Tourette on the south side, near Camping la Cammassade (off Route de l'Ancienne Gare), which is signposted. La Colle du Moulin is the home of the Guerrault family, who are themselves vegetarians with a leaning to the French dietetic style, but flexible and accommodating in their attitude to their guests.

The cooking is uncomplicated but good and tasty. Dinner during my visit was green salad, followed by Swiss chard in a white sauce, with barley (Swiss chard is a delicious leaf vegetable rarely seen in Britain). We finished with Tarte Corinthienne (which had almonds, raisins, and eggs in it). Everything is organic. Breakfast is on typical French lines: bread, butter, honey, with coffee, tea or other hot drinks. The place itself is very pleasing – a big house, with outdoor terraces, standing among fragrant Mediterranean pines. The rooms have tile floors, and there's a big light dining room where everyone eats together at plain wooden tables. Bedrooms are simple, with plain white walls, carpeted, and functionally furnished. Enjoyable family atmosphere, with guests of all ages – but very few British ever come here.
Open 1 Mar–1 Oct. Seven double rooms, three single (all with shower/WC). Full board only, per night (minimum stay one week): 230F for one person, 420F for two persons (if you want to go out during the day, a picnic lunch will be supplied). Wine: 32F/bottle, organic. No credit cards.

La Nouvelle Aurore *306 route des Virettes, Tourette-sur-Loup 06140, tel. 93 59 30 73*
Guesthouse. 100% vegetarian.
Proprietors: Madame Serandou. English spoken.
This big country house (1½km from Tourette in the Vence direction) among the southern pines stands in 1½ hectares (around four acres) with a wide view of the Mediterranean. About twelve people live here permanently, working a vegetable garden and keeping hens. This has been a vegetarian guesthouse for 32 years. It's very moderately priced. The food is simple, family-style, and wholesome. Most of the ingredients are organic. A typical meal would be crudités, rice and vegetables, with a dessert of fruit tart. Breakfast is cereals and home-made bread with coffee or other drinks. Rooms are simple, and there's a dormitory for those who do not mind even more basic accommodation. Camping in the grounds is also available.
Open all year. Eighteen double rooms, two single (four have own bathroom/WC). Prices per night: in room without own facilities, full-board 190F single, 360F double, half-board 160F single, 290F double; in room with private facilities, full-board 250F single, 460F double, half-board 210F single, 390F double. In dormitory (sleeps ten): 155F per person full-board, 120F half-board. Camping: 140F full board, 105 half-board. Wine: 28F/bottle organic. No credit cards.

La Val Dieu (Aude)

La Val Dieu *11190 Rennes-le-Château, tel. 68 74 23 21*
Farm-guesthouse. 100% vegetarian.
English run.
All bookings and enquiries to John Minor, 11 Meadow Green, Welwyn Garden City, Herts, tel. (0707) 324631
At a remote Templar farm in the Pyrenean foothills, in a hidden fertile valley reached by a long track from the historic hilltop village of Rennes-le-Château, you can join a Circle Dancing holiday, or go on a variety of other courses geared to yoga, self-discovery, massage, and the mystical. All around are wild woods and meadows, while nearby are Cathar castles, standing stones, hot springs – all setting the mood for this exuberant, inspiring place. You don't have to take part in any of the courses: you're welcome to come simply to enjoy the air, the scenery, and the magnificent walks in every direction. Any help with haymaking is also much appre-

ciated! Rooms are simple but comfortable, or you could opt for camping. Food too, is simple and wholesome.

Open Apr–Oct. Courses last about ten days and cost from £225 for full board. No credit cards.

Germany, Austria & Switzerland

Dialling code from abroad: Switzerland – 010 41 (omit initial 0 from Swiss area code). Germany – 010 49 (omit initial 0 from German area code). Austria – 010 43 (omit initial 0 from Austrian area code).
Currency: Swiss Francs (SF, SFr, Sfr), approx 2½ SF = £1; German Deutschmarks (DM), approx 3DM = £1; Austrian Schillings (S, AS, ÖS), about 20S = £1.

The German-speaking nations of Europe constitute a single area in several ways, and especially from the vegetarian point of view. The culture and character of the populations of Germany, Austria and Switzerland, including their diet, is broadly the same – although there is some difference between the southern and northern types of cuisine – and vegetarian publications in German are intended for readers in all three countries. There's an active vegetarian movement, as well as a large number of people who, while not being part of that movement, simply try to refrain from eating much meat. There's no shortage of facilities catering for this health-conscious market, so the German-speaking countries are not difficult for vegetarian visitors.

Of the three, Switzerland claims the largest number of tourists and understandably so: stunningly beautiful in summer and winter, the Alps of course dominate the whole country. They rise dramatically, draped in white, within sight of busy city centres. Nature always feels close at hand – but it's an austere nature, largely uninhabitable, much of it untouched by man. Lakes, clean rivers, high pastures and picturesque farmhouses add to the attraction. Like Austria, it has a huge skiing industry, and that country too has much to offer in scenery and character. By contrast, only limited parts of Germany have much rural charm, but it's worth looking for them: even the cheapest accommodation is exceptionally clean and comfortable, and the welcome hearty.

The German-speaking vegetarian tradition is an old one, and

with a similar history to that in Britain. It stems from the mid-nineteenth-century German 'reform' movements which envisaged a more rational, healthier, more modern society. It soon became part of the German ideal of physical and mental cleanliness or purity (of which the great popularity of spas and 'cures' is perhaps another example), and nowadays not eating meat is closely allied with not drinking, not smoking and other practices promoting well-being. Indeed, among the establishments listed here are several which describe themselves not as a hotel but as a *kurhaus* – a place for people on a 'cure'.

Health food shops are still known as Reform Houses, and there's one in almost every town. There are, too, shops specialising in organic produce and hundreds of vegetarian restaurants scattered around the country, as well as a considerable number of guesthouses. A warning though: these often tend to be more interested in health than gastronomy, and the standard of cooking is not high.

Package Holidays

Canterbury Holidays, 248 Streatfield Rd, Kenton, Harrow, Mddx, tel. (081) 206 0411, see p. 13.
Inntravel, The Old Station, Helmsley, York YO6 4BZ, tel. (0439) 71111, see p. 15.
North Mymms Coaches, P.O. Box 152, Potters Bar, Herts EN6 3NR, tel. (0707) 371866, see p. 13.
Vegi Ventures, 17 Lilian Road, Burnham on Crouch, Essex CM0 8DS, tel. (0621) 784285, see p. 14.
World Wine Tours, 4 Dorchester Rd, Drayton St Leonard, Oxfordshire, tel. (0865) 891919, see p. 17.

Recommended Accommodation, Holiday Centres and Restaurants

Switzerland

Switzerland may not like to be described as German-speaking – this mountain state is a federation of four different language groups. German-speakers do comprise a large majority, but 18% of Swiss speak French, 12% Italian, and 5% use a native Swiss language, Romansh. However, these non-German areas show much less awareness of vegetarianism; German-Switzerland has just as old a vegetarian tradition as Germany itself. Nevertheless, by a curious twist resulting from Switzerland's cultural mix, some of the best vegetarian eating is found in French establishments, so I have included a number of good places in French-speaking parts of the country. Place names may have English, German and French versions: if so, they are given in that order (eg: Geneva/Genf/Genève).

Berne/Bern/Berne

TEESTÜBLI *Postgasse 49, Berne 3011, tel. (031) 22 64 84*
Restaurant-café. 100% vegetarian.
There's a friendly, relaxed youthful atmosphere at this popular eating place, attractive with polished parquet floor and plain wooden tables. You can have anything from a drink or a snack to a complete meal. And you can buy a loaf of bread at the same time. It is open for breakfast, lunch and dinner, and the food is almost all organic. Owner Gerald Aregger sums up the style of cooking as 'just normal, but vegetarian'. Main dishes are along the lines of pizza or crêpe or pasta, or you could have, for example, a bowl of home-made muesli with cream, or a feta salad. There's a huge selection of teas.
For complete meal allow about 17SF. No wine.
Tue–Sun 9am–11pm.

MENUETTO *Herrengasse 22, Berne 3011, tel. (031) 22 14 48*
Restaurant-café. 100% vegetarian.
In the midst of old Berne, not far from the river Aare, is a busy modern vegetarian restaurant noted for high quality and efficient service. The place itself is light, open, and uplifting, and light, imaginative, well-balanced dishes are served. Salads include marinated mozzarella, or steamed potato, fresh garden vegetables, or any of several other tasty and colourful ingredients. Other possible starters include a range of vegetable terrines. Main courses mostly revolve around deliciously prepared vegetables with tofu accompanied by a whole grain, usually brown rice, though there are also excellent wholemeal pasta dishes. Some of the best dishes are of distinctly oriental inspiration, for instance, Samurai's Rice: marinated tofu in a crisp crust, served with vegetables, kelp, brown rice, and spicy sauce. Finish with honey-sweetened ice cream. Two 'healthy eating for busy people' set meals feature at lunchtime. Snacks include six types of muesli, or sandwiches with fillings like honey and almonds. There's a tremendous selection of drinks, including warm elderflower, hot cider with cloves and cinnamon, several fruit and vegetable juices, a variety of unusual herb teas, and amazing things like rose hip milk drink. Organic wines and beers will be added as soon as the licence is granted.
Allow 38SF for three courses. Wine: coming soon at about 35SF–53SF/bottle organic. Mon–Sat 9am–10.30, closed on all national holidays.

Chemin-Dessus

Beau Site *Chemin (Martigny VS) 1927, tel. (026) 22 81 64*
Hotel-restaurant.
Proprietor: Uts Vuilleumier. English spoken.
Admirably situated for winter skiers and summer walkers, the hotel stands on the edge of a high village of chalets in the Valais region (altitude 3500ft), and commands superb mountain and valley views. Built in 1912, it's a popular place for locals wanting to meet, eat or drink. Accommodation is simple and unpretentious, but comfortable, and in addition to the bedrooms, there's a cheap dormitory (bring your own sleeping bag). In the café-restaurant, food is hearty but healthy. The Valais is noted for its meats, and while most of the menu reflects this, the vegetarian dishes are good. They include salads, a lentil and nut terrine with spicy sauce, tofu galettes with vegetables, meat-free pasta, and traditional fondu. Almost everything is organic.
Closed two weeks in spring, two weeks in autumn. Sixteen rooms. Room only: 62SF for double, B&B: 72SF for two, half-board: 106SF for two. Dinner only: 17SF for three-course vegetarian meal. Wine: from about 20SF/litre, organic from 26SF/bottle. No credit cards.

Geneva/Genf/Genève

Les Cinq Saveurs *22 rue du Prieuré, Genève 1202, tel. (022) 31 78 70*
Restaurant. Mainly vegetarian.
A sign in the window invites you to enjoy the macrobiotic, vegetarian and Asiatic dishes for the sake of your health and figure. I do think they should mention the possibility of eating just for pleasure's sake too, particularly as the food here, though simple, is tasty and enjoyable. This is a small, family business, not catering for large numbers in the course of a day. It has a smart, cheerful appearance, with a relaxed and friendly atmosphere, and is within an easy walk of the main railway station. Proprietor Linda Misa comes from the Philippines, and with the aid of another Filipino plus an Indian cook as well, she provides uncomplicated health-orientated macrobiotic dishes with an Oriental flavour. Start with soup or salad; main courses are often brown-rice based with seaweed, sesame, vegetables, tofu, and soya sauce; and there are little cakes to finish. Lunchtime is vegetarian, with a buffet of hot dishes, but meat and fish are included among evening choices. A speciality is the vegetarian Paella Aux Cinq Couleurs – five-colour paella. Fresh vegetable or fruit juice is made to order.
About 19SF for three courses. Wine: 5SF/glass.
Mon–Fri 12–2, 6–9.30.

Dent De Lion *25 rue des Eaux-Vives, Genève 1207, tel. (022) 736 72 98*
Restaurant. 100% vegetarian.
A likeable little city restaurant near Lake Léman (Lake Geneva), its name puns 'dandelion' and 'lion's tooth', and painted on the front window a lion lies down among dandelions. The atmosphere inside is friendly and relaxed but professional. An uncomplicated menu offers soya pâté, large and small salads, and hot dishes depending heavily on soya products – soya steak, soya sausage, tofu with tomato sauce – as well as a few other filling dishes such as wholewheat pancakes with vegetables, and of course whole grains. Desserts include home-made cakes, tarts and ice-creams. To drink, there are several kinds of mineral water, herb teas, milk drinks, coffee substitutes and fruit juices, but no alcohol.
20SF for three courses. No wine. Mon–Fri 10–2.30, 6–10.

★★HOSTELLERIE DE LA VENDÉE *28 chemin de la Vendée, Petit-Lancy 1213, tel. (022) 792 04 11*
Hotel-restaurant.
Proprietors: Annie and Joseph Righetto. English spoken.
This is far from being a vegetarian establishment, and if you eat here you must be prepared to see people at the next table having veal or foie gras. The place is a noted gastronomic restaurant, and highly praised for meat dishes. Yet, for some reason, the menu does offer meat-free dishes among both starters and main courses. I had asparagus, a main course of truffle cream noodles, cheeses from a beautiful selection, and excellent patisserie to finish. The setting is like a Kew Gardens greenhouse, with tile floors and vast amounts of greenery dotted about. The hotel is friendly and welcoming, offers all modern comforts, and is just ten minutes from Geneva.
Open all year. Restaurant 12–2, 7–10. 34 rooms, all with bath/shower. Bed and breakfast: from 195SF for a double room. Dinner only: about 60SF. Wine: from 22SF/bottle. Credit cards accepted.

Les Granges

HÔTEL BALANCE *Les Granges 1922, tel. (026) 61 15 22*
Hotel-restaurant. 100% vegetarian.
Proprietors: Lea and Roland Eberle. English spoken.
There's a friendly family atmosphere at this well-placed hotel, which stands at 1000m (3300 ft) altitude and has beautiful mountain views. Inside, all rooms are wood panelled. The bedrooms have balconies, and there's a garden, pool, and sauna, as well as morning exercises to take part in (optional!) and courses in cooking, yoga, shiatsu, etc. There's a library of books, some in English, about the macrobiotic philosophy. Children are made very welcome, with a play room, a sandpit, and lots of animals – goats, hens, cats, rabbits and a big St Bernard – to get to know. Children's portions are available at mealtimes. The food is standard macrobiotic fare, with plenty of soya products, and most ingredients are organic. The village of Les Granges is on a high plateau above the Trient valley. It's a great area for cross-country skiing in winter or for glorious walks in summer.
Open all year. 24 rooms (three with own shower). Half-board: from 62SF pp (two sharing). Big reductions for children according to age. Dinner only: 25SF for 3 courses. Wine: from 24SF/bottle, organic from 35SF/bottle. No credit cards.

Lausanne

Au Cous Cous *2 rue Enning, Lausanne 1003, tel. (021) 22 20 17*
Restaurant.
Founded in the 1950s, the Wegmüller family's restaurant at the top of Rue de Bourg – Lausanne's pedestrianised main shopping street – has become a well-known and popular eating place for all types of people (and children are made very welcome). From outside, the entrance could easily be missed; the restaurant is on the first floor. Inside it's casual and friendly, with startlingly vivid red and black decor and big oriental paper lampshades. The food is a mix of Tunisian/Middle Eastern specialities (hence the name) together with a wide vegetarian and macrobiotic choice, all well prepared. At lunchtime, there are three vegetarian set menus, while for dinner there are about a dozen *à la carte* vegetarian dishes. These range from straightforward brown rice and veg to timbale or vol-au-vent. Vegetarian cous-cous is a regular feature. Everything comes with a nice seasonal salad. There's an excellent home made muesli, or Bircher as they call it in Switzerland, served with yoghurt and accompanied by buttered rye bread. Or you can have it as a dessert.
Four-course vegetarian menu: from 12.50 SF.
Wine: from 11 SF/½ litre. Mon–Sat 11.30am–2.30pm, 6pm–1am; open till 2am Fri and Sat; Sun 6–1am.

Préverenges

Auberge Du Chasseur *10 route d'Yverdon. Préverenges 1028, tel. (021) 802 43 33*
Hotel-restaurant.
Proprietor: Hans and Hélène Stengel. English spoken.
In the agreeable village of Préverenges, on the shores of Lake Léman (alias Lake Geneva), with a lovely quiet setting, there's an appealing old *auberge*. Rooms are very attractive, in pale colours, clean, and comfortable. Some are designated for non-smokers only. There are two restaurants in the hotel, La Tonnelle and Le Français, and despite the name of the place – *chasseur* means hunter – they make a speciality of vegetarian dishes. In addition to those two dining rooms, you can eat out of doors on the shady terrace. Le Français is the more solid place, offering gourmet meals on the basis of whatever was best in the market that day. La Tonnelle goes in more for lighter, snackier dishes, but also has three set meals at

lunchtime. The sort of thing you'll have is a *crudités* to start, a main course of galettes of wheat or – unusually – millet, or perhaps vegetables in pastry, and a wide choice of desserts.
Closed Tue and two weeks in Feb. Twelve rooms,
all with bath/shower. Bed and breakfast: 145SF. Add 25SF for half board. Dinner only: about 45SF. Wine: from 30SF/bottle.
Credit cards accepted.

Thun

Hôtel Bio Pic *Bälliz 54, Thun 3601, tel. (033) 22 99 52*
Hotel-restaurant. 100% vegetarian.
Proprietors: Ulrich and Erika Jegerlehner. English spoken.
A conventional, five-storey, but health-orientated hotel on the island in the centre of town, the Bio Pic is well placed for excursions into the magnificent lake and mountain scenery all around. Bedrooms are simple; some have marvellous views. Food is straightforward vegetarian fare, rice and veg, etc, with plenty of salads, and some rather hedonistic cream cakes to finish.
Open all year. Seventeen rooms, three with bath/shower.
Restaurant open Mon–Fri 7am–8pm, Sat 7am–4pm.
Bed and breakfast: 62SF. Dinner: about 30SF. No wine.
Credit cards accepted.

Zürich

Gleich *Seefeldstrasse 9, Zürich 8008, tel. (01) 251 32 03*
Restaurant. 100% vegetarian.
The Gleich family's big vegetarian restaurant has been here since 1924. An overwhelmingly large *Speise Karte* (menu) confronts you (as it does in many Swiss restaurants). That's because not only is there a huge choice; it's in three languages – though the English versions are sometimes incomprehensible. The two pages listing the prolific selection available on that particular day are all only in German! While the translation may be questionable, the food is interesting and enjoyable. There's a huge choice of raw vegetables for salad-style starters, cooked vegetables priced by the portion, and main course 'specialities'. Over the page is an abundance of desserts, ranging from pies to fruit compote to muesli. There are also four three-course set meals (of which one is only available at lunchtime and the other only in the evening). The set meals are really more like suggestions from the ordinary *Karte*. For example,

you could start with a simple salad, move on to a main course of fresh home-made spinach ravioli, and finish with a creamy *Vacherin-Eistorte*. Generally, the lunch dishes are more snacky than the evening selection. Drinks range from ovaltine to beetroot juice. Good for breakfast, too.
About 30SF for three courses. Mon–Fri 6.30am–9pm, Sat 8–4.

HILTL VEGI *Sihlstrasse 28, Zürich 8001, tel. (01) 221 38 70 or (01) 221 38 71*
Restaurant. 100% vegetarian.
Ambros Hiltl would be gratified, perhaps amazed, that the vegetarian restaurant he opened in 1898 in the heart of central Zürich, just off Bahnhofstrasse, is still going strong and attracts an appreciative crowd throughout the day. In fact, it's doing better than ever, and is now two different restaurants on two floors. VEGETINI, on ground level, has a young, fresh atmosphere and quick lunchtime service. It's more in café style, with self-service and offers snacks, ice cream, teatime cakes, and a breakfast buffet in the mornings. VEGITABLE, on the first floor, is smarter, has table service and a more sedate atmosphere, with a larger choice of hot dishes. The cooking is geared towards health, but is tasty and enjoyable. You might start with a soup or mixed salad, follow with a main course of wholemeal gnocchi with a big plate of vegetables, or maybe savoury tofu galettes, and finish with home-made cakes or yoghurts. After 4pm there's a large salad bar with over 30 different salads to choose from. After 6pm, in Vegitable, there's an all-you-can-eat Indian buffet. To drink there are juices, mineral waters, milk drinks, and a huge selection of herb teas from around the world.
Allow 20SF to 25SF for three-course meal. No wine.
Mon–Sat 6.30am–9pm, Sun 9am–9pm.

Germany

Germany was one of the first countries in the west to develop any kind of vegetarian tradition. In the mid-nineteenth century, although Germany had yet to be united into a single country, a great wave of reform began to sweep through German life. There was a tremendous desire to throw off the irrationality of the past, and to move forward into a healthier, more modern and more rational nationhood. Unfortunately, a highly romanticised puritanism and patriotism was part of the trend, and some of its effects were to prove, in the long term, disastrous for Germany and its neighbours. But this was just one aspect of a movement which affected all parts of German life – even diet. From this period dates the Food Reform movement, which encouraged healthy eating and vegetarianism. To this day, health food shops – of which there are thousands in Germany – are called *Reformhäuser*. However, these are now devoted mainly to dietary supplements rather than food. A newer phenomenon is the rise of shops specialising in organic produce, appearing all over the country.

Most cities and large towns have at least one vegetarian eating place. These, to be frank, are generally not of a high standard. Some do rise above the general mediocrity and I have included a few which are useful or interesting. Many hotels in Germany can provide a vegetarian dish or two in their dining rooms, and there are also several vegetarian guesthouses.

Berlin

La Maskera *Koburgstrasse 5, 1000 Berlin 62.*
Restaurant. 100% vegetarian.
A relaxed '*vinoteca*' with a warm atmosphere and no fixed menu, serving down-to-earth wholefood vegetarian Italian dishes.
Allow about DM25 for three courses.
Organic wine from about DM3.80 per glass. Daily 5pm–1am.

Satyam *Goethestrasse 5, 1000 Berlin 12, tel. (030) 312 30 29*
Hotel-restaurant. 100% vegetarian.
Proprietor: Ashok Sharma. English spoken.
An Indian guesthouse is perhaps not quite where you would expect to find yourself when staying in Berlin, but if you want an inexpensive B&B with vegetarian food, it could be a good choice. The food is simple. Start with soup or samosa, with typical vegetable curry main course, and Indian sweets to finish.
Open all year. Seven rooms (two with own bath/shower).
Price: DM140 for bed and breakfast; allow DM25 for dinner.
Wine: organic at DM5.50 per glass. No credit cards.

Tuk-Tuk *Grossgörschenstrasse 2, 1000 Berlin 62,*
tel. (030) 781 15 88
Restaurant.
With Indonesian village-style décor and bamboo decoration, this Indonesian restaurant offers a lot of vegetarian dishes and a

complete vegetarian menu with a wide choice. Some are traditional meatless dishes, others are adapted by using soya.
Allow about DM30 for three courses. Wine: from DM5.
Daily 5.30–11.30.

Freiburg

BUSSE'S WALDSCHÄNKE *Waldseestrasse 77, 7800 Freiburg im Breisgau, tel. (0761) 74847*
Restaurant
In their homely and traditional-looking restaurant in a park on the edge of Freiburg (capital of the Black Forest), Christoph and Maria Busse serve some reasonable cooking using organic wholefoods including a vegetarian menu. Start, for example, with a terrine of tofu and vegetable with herb dressing; main courses include stuffed pancakes, pizzas, and several potato-based dishes, and there are several good desserts. There's a selection of French and German organic wines served by bottle or glass. They also have a campsite and a sauna, by the way.
Allow about DM27 for three courses. Organic wine from DM22/bottle. Daily (exc Sun) 6–11.30.

KOLPINGHAUS *Karlstrasse 7, 7800 Freiburg im Breisgau, tel. (0761) 31930*
Hotel-restaurant.
English spoken.
A large, conventional city-centre hotel, rather sombre in style, but with clean, comfortable rooms. The spacious dining room offers inexpensive plain German cooking, while vegetarians are catered for with a set meal at lunchtime or a choice of four *à la carte* main dishes at dinner. The sort of thing you'll find is a soup starter and a main course of baked courgettes with tomato and cheese topping.
Open all year. 90 rooms (all with bath/shower). B&B – DM88 single, DM120 double; lunch or dinner – about DM14 for two courses. Wine: DM3.50 per quarter-litre. Credit cards accepted.

SALAT GARTEN *Löwenstrasse 1, 7800 Freiburg im Breisgau, tel. (0761) 35155*
Restaurant-café. 100% vegetarian.
Good international vegetarian cuisine, seasonal and wholesome, is served in this light, bright city restaurant attractive with green

plants and modern paintings. Each day of the week has its own soup, choice of two substantial main courses, a plentiful salad buffet, and pudding. As well as finer dishes, there are simple pancakes, vegetarian burgers, and wholemeal pastries. To drink there are freshly squeezed juices and alcohol-free beers.
Three courses about DM17. No wine. Mon–Fri 11–8, Sat 11–6.

VICTORIA *Eisenbahnstrasse 54, 7800 Freiburg im Breisgau, tel. (0761) 31881*
Hotel-restaurant.
Proprietors: Späth family. English spoken.
This largish hotel in the town centre, opposite the Colombi Park, has a vegetarian menu. Typical starter might be cream of carrot soup with saffron, with a main course of cereal rissoles with hazelnut sauce, and an interesting muesli terrine for dessert.
Open all year, 65 rooms, all with bath/shower.
Price: DM185 for dinner, bed and breakfast for two.
House wine: DM10 per half-litre, or organic at DM30 per bottle.
Credit cards accepted.

Hamburg

Unfortunately the one-hundred-year-old Vegetärische Gaststätte (vegetarian restaurant) at Neuer Wall has been closed owing to fire damage.

Munich/München

JAHRESZEITEN *Sebastiansplatz 9, 8000 München 2, tel. (089) 2609578*
Restaurant (accommodation available at hotel next door). 100% vegetarian.
Located in the very centre of Munich, adjacent to St Jacobs-Platz and the ancient Viktualienmarkt, this is not only one of the best restaurants in Munich, it's probably the best vegetarian restaurant in Germany. It's a smart, attractive place, with arches, flowers, and pretty décor, and is frequented by just about every kind of person from backpackers to bankers. The owner, Peter Leimgruber, is a man with a mission – to transform German eating habits. He's got a tough job ahead of him, but this (and his other Munich restaurants) are a good start. The cooking is first class, and is 70% organic wholefoods. Menus are changed daily. There's soup, a big

salad buffet, and main courses of, for example, broccoli in a nest of carrots with a raisin and almond sauce and oatmeal 'biscuits', or tofu chips in cream with vegetables, tamari and rice. Desserts range from home-made ice-cream or sticky cakes (both sweetened with maple syrup or honey, not sugar) to crêpes with fruit. There are less ambitious dishes too, like savoury pancakes, omelettes, and muesli. In addition, every evening there's a fixed-price four-course set meal. Good range of organic French wines. If you're staying next door at the Blauer Bock hotel, Jahreszeiten do an excellent breakfast.
Three courses about DM30. Organic house wine from DM16.50/bottle. Daily 7am–11pm.

JAHRESZEITEN *Amalienstrasse 97, 8000 München 40, tel. (089) 390919*
Restaurant-café. 100% vegetarian.
Near the University, with a youthful and imaginative atmosphere, this is a popular eating place in the famous Schwabing area. It's around 50% organic, with self-service buffet.
Three courses about DM30. Organic house wine from DM16.50/bottle. Mon–Sat 11am–1am.

JAHRESZEITEN *Hertie-Schmankerlgasse, Banhofsplatz 7, 8000 München 2, tel. (089) 594873*
Restaurant-café. 100% vegetarian.
A self-service organic buffet snackbar next to the main railway station in the centre of the city.
Open Mon–Sat 9–6.30.

PRINZ MYSHKIN *Hackenstrasse 2, 8000 München 2, tel. (089) 265596*
Restaurant. 100% vegetarian.
Geared mainly to Mediterranean types of cooking, the menu of this accomplished restaurant also allows a few meat-free dishes from Japan or China. Although housed in 300-year-old rooms, it has modern stylish décor, giving a light, clear, clean effect. The food is imaginative. You could start with Italian antipasti, have a main course of oyster mushrooms with tofu fried in cream sauce, with vegetables and rice or pasta, and finish with dates filled with amaretto mascarpone cream. Mm! They also have pizzas and salads and a good choice of drinks.
Three courses about DM20–30. Organic wine from DM7. Daily 11–11.

Austria

In Austria, as in Germany and Switzerland, vegetarian eating is usually tied up with health cures and various kinds of therapy. Several of the hotels serving meat-free dishes to their guests call themselves *Gesundheitshotel* (Health Hotel) or *Gesundheitszentrum* (Health Centre). It's certainly not easy to find vegetarian establishments with a robust joie de vivre, offering first-class cuisine and good wines. But for some people, a health cure holiday may be just what the doctor ordered – especially taking into account that the real highlight of Austrian cuisine is magnificent rich cakes and wonderful strong coffee! A couple of useful resources: the nationwide ROMANTIKHOTEL chain (mostly four stars) and the excellent ROSENBERGER autobahn restaurants both offer vegetarian dishes on their menus.

Although the majority of Austrian hotels and restaurants can offer simple wholemeal vegetarian food, I have chosen just two attractive comfortable country hotels with an above-average standard of cooking.

Obermillstadt

Bio-Hotel Alpenrose *Obermillstadt A-9872, tel. (04766) 2500*
Hotel.
Proprietors: Obweger-Theuermann family. English spoken.

A lovely country hotel on a hill in the flowering meadows of Kärnten province, the Alpenrose is a typical old Austrian inn, handsome with lots of bare wood. Here you can enjoy clean air, mountain waters, good walks and beautiful scenery. There's a sauna, massage, a heated outdoor pool, and some supposedly health-promoting pleasures such as herb baths. Herbs feature strongly in the cooking too, and you can accompany the friendly proprietors Irvin and Getti when they go to gather them. They also grow their own grains, bake their own bread and provide hearty wholemeal organic food, with a complete four-course menu for vegetarians. (In the evening this is for hotel guests only, but at lunchtime the dining room is open to the public.)

Typically you might start with salad from the buffet, then a bowl of soup, a main course of say wholemeal vegetarian lasagne, and a dessert. It's filling and tasty. They go in for huge buffets, including a magnificent 'cake buffet' every afternoon. As if that's not inviting enough, they also give cooking lessons, and even sing and play music to entertain the guests. Children are made especially welcome, and some rooms are reserved for children. There are 'children's afternoons', when little ones can help feed the hens and goats.

Open all year. 38 rooms (all with own bath/shower except two children's rooms), and three apartments. Half-board: from 1015S per person in winter, 1100S per person in summer. Lunch only: about 160S for three courses. Organic wine: from 250S/bottle or house wine at 25S/glass. No credit cards.

Reith bei Kitzbühel

Gesundheitshotel Florian *Reith bei Kitzbühel A-6370, tel. (05356) 5242*
Hotel-restaurant. Mainly vegetarian.
Proprietor: Florian Pointner. Some English spoken.

Standing on a hill in the midst of fields and close to the edges of a forest, the Pointner family's quiet health-orientated hotel is a delightful place, a very model of Tyrolian charm, its wooden balconies loaded with flowers. It revels in wonderful air and scenery, with lovely views over the village of Reith bei Kitzbühel towards high mountains. Inside too, everything is made of wood, decorated with masses of plants, and has a satisfying country feel. Yet it's comfortable and civilised, with attractively-laid candlelit tables in the dining room (dominated by a superb bay window). The atmosphere is warm and friendly. The farm next door belongs to the hotel and provides much of the produce, mainly organic, for the excellent wholesome meals.

There are set four-course vegetarian menus, making ample use of fresh fruit and vegetables, whole grains, and home-made farm-fresh milk products. The only non-vegetarian food served is occasional fish. Vegans can be catered for easily. Typically a meal would start with salads from the buffet, with home-made bread, followed by a soup of say carrot purée, and the main course might be a 'steak' made of mixed vegetables and grains, served with a herb sauce. To finish, try the filled pancakes with carob sauce. Unlike many other 'health-hotels', here wine is served with the meal. Breakfast is another generous buffet.

This is a beautiful walking area, and in winter you can ski cross-country from right outside the door. The hotel has its own sauna and masseuse, and also claims to be the only non-smoking hotel in the whole of the Tyrol.

Open all year. Seventeen rooms (all with own bath/shower). Restaurant open 8–10, 12–2, 6–9. Half-board: summer – 530S per person, winter – 630S per person. Dinner only: four-course menus 180S and 210S. Wine: 80S/½-litre, organic from 90S/½-litre. No credit cards.

Greece

Dialling code from abroad: 010 30
Currency: Drachmas (Drs, Dr, Dx) – about 312 Dr = £1.

Hardly a haven of vegetarianism, yet Greece is not a difficult country in which to find tasty meals without meat. Indeed, many Greeks abstain from meat for religious reasons during much of the year. However, such people are regarded as very pious, and they are not really vegetarians – they do eat fish, and are quite happy to eat meat on non-fast days. There are few vegetarian places to eat or stay.

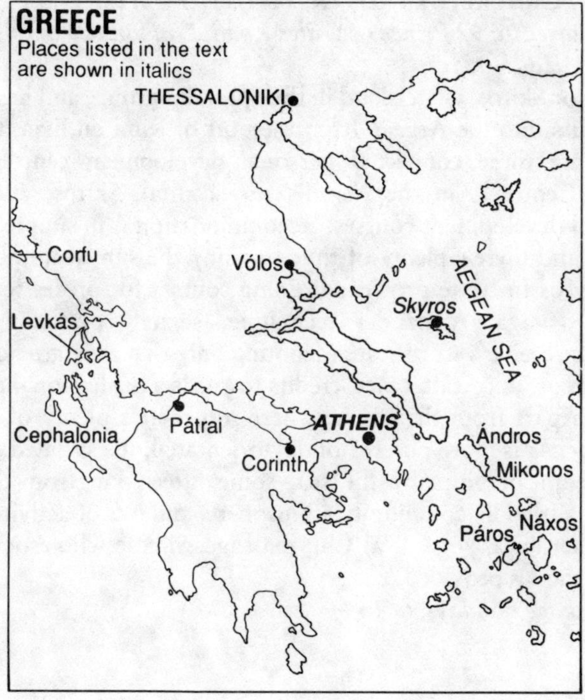

Recommended . . .

Athens

EDEN *Odos Flessa 3, Plaka, Athens*
Restaurant. 100% vegetarian.
Vegetarians who want to break the monotony of bread and salad should head for this long-established meatless restaurant in an attractive old two-storey house in the Plaka district at the foot of the Acropolis. There's a friendly atmosphere. Eat indoors or on the open-air terrace. Proprietor Timos Papadopoulos serves international and Greek food, with starters of soup or salad, a choice of around fifteen dishes for the main course, and a dessert of, say, apple pie or fruit salad, or yoghurt with nuts and honey.
Allow about 1100Dr for three courses.
Wine from 700Dr/bottle. Daily 12–12.

Skyros

SKYROS CENTRE, SKYROS INSTITUTE, ATSITSA
All enquiries to: 92 Prince of Wales Road, London NW5 3NE, tel. (071) 284 3065
Skyros (or Skiros) is an island in the Sporades group, and lies about two hours into the Aegean from the port of Kimi on Evia. On the island are three connected personal development centres. The Skyros Centre is in the island's tiny capital, Skiros, and runs personal development courses. Accommodation is in simple village rooms, and there's plenty of time to enjoy the sun, sea, and sand. The Skyros Institute provides training courses for professionals in massage, yoga, Alexander technique, sexual counselling, etc. Students receive a Certificate (denoting only that they attended the courses), or, in certain cases, credits towards a professional qualification. Apart from the courses, here too there's plenty of leisure time. Atsitsa is more purely holiday-orientated; it's situated among Mediterranean pines by the sea, some fifteen km from Skyros. There's a friendly community atmosphere, and lots of activities like dance, aerobics, yoga, T'ai Chi, massage. Simple wholesome vegetarian food is provided.
See: Package holidays, p. 13

G.A.W.F.

Cruelty to animals in Greece – in the street, on the farm and above all in the slaughterhouse – is horrific. The Greek Animal Welfare Fund is doing what it can to change things. If you'd like to help or make a donation, or would like a copy of their leaflet for visitors to Greece, contact them at 11, Lower Barn Road, Purley, Surrey CR8 1HY.

Ireland

Dialling code from Britain: Republic except Dublin – 010 353 (then dial area code, leaving out initial 0); Dublin – 0001 + Dublin number; Northern Ireland – none.
Currency: Republic – Irish pounds or punts *(I£), worth slightly less than sterling; Northern Ireland – sterling (£) is used, though sometimes on banknotes valid only in the province.*

Ireland is overwhelmingly a rural country. There are just a few important concentrations of industry, especially around the three largest towns, Dublin, Belfast and Cork, and even here you're rarely more than a fifteen-minute drive from open country. The great attractions of Ireland – both in the Republic and in the North – are its rustic simplicity, wide open landscapes, and amiable people. In the west, along the Atlantic-washed shores and the barely inhabited rock-and-water hills of the interior, you'll see some of the loveliest scenery in Europe under constantly changing skies. In almost any village you can hear foot-stomping traditional Irish folk music, still very much the music of every day in Ireland. If you have money to spend, it's worth knowing that many of Ireland's elegant Georgian country houses have become some of the most appealing hotels to be found anywhere. A few of them have acquired great reputations for luxury and civilised living, although others are all the more inviting for the unpretentious simplicity which feels so essentially Irish.

The Irish diet, too, is straightforward, uncomplicated and generous, but depends heavily on meat and potatoes. Although vegetarians are rare, many restaurants, guesthouses and hotels happily provide suitable food on request, and, surprisingly, some of the best vegetarian cooking in the world is to be found here. Vegetarianism and whole foods are better known in the six counties of Northern Ireland than in the other 26 counties.

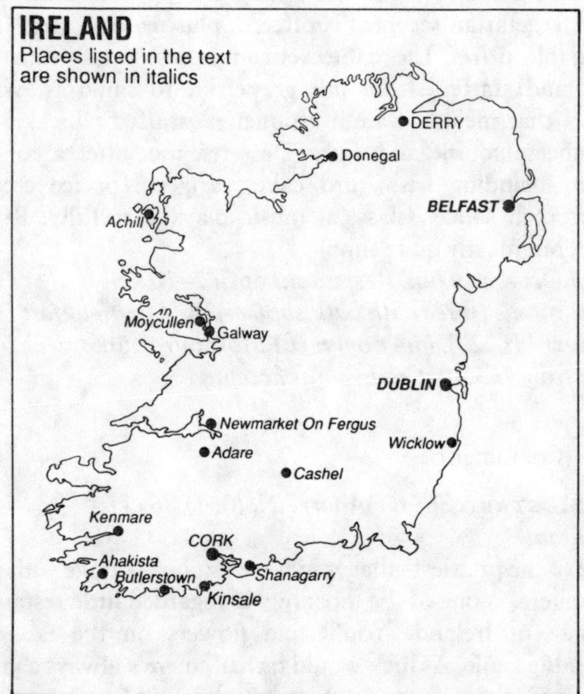

Package Holidays

Inntravel, The Old Station, Helmsley, York YO6 4BZ, tel. (0439) 71111, see p. 15
Trusthouse Forte Leisure Breaks, tel. (0345) 500 400 or (081) 567 3444, see p. 12
Vegetarian Travellers, 60 Crewys Road, London NW2 2AD, tel. (081) 201 9054, see p. 12

Recommended Hotels and Restaurants

Achill Island (Co. Mayo)

THE AMETHYST *Keel, Achill Island, tel. (098) 43104*
Guesthouse-restaurant.
Proprietors: Joan and Noel Scanlon. (Joan and Noel say that their restaurant may be closing soon, so check for the latest position.)
In Keel village, 150 paces from the beach, you can find a wide range of wholesome and well-made dishes at this spacious traditional-

style dining room, with high ceiling and exposed beams. A four-course vegetarian set meal is offered, plus tea or coffee, for a very reasonable price. The choice encompasses soups from nettle to lentil, and starters from hot grapefruit to samosas, with main courses that include walnut croquettes, stuffed pancakes, cannelloni, cheese soufflé and more. Desserts, too, offer a considerable choice, including Irish curd cake, carigeen, or ice cream with butterscotch sauce. Classical music plays peacefully. Rooms are varied, but mostly quite simple.

Closed Oct–early Jun. Restaurant open 7–10 daily.
Fifteen rooms (three with bath/shower). Bed & breakfast I£10, half-board I£22. Dinner only: I£12 for four-course meal.
Wine: from I£5.50. Credit cards accepted.

Adare (Co. Limerick)

The Mustard Seed *Adare, tel. (061) 86451*
Restaurant.

In one of the prettiest villages in the west, in a cottage with plenty of atmosphere, is one of the most highly regarded little restaurants on this side of Ireland. You'll find flowers on the tables and a welcoming smile. As luck would have it, there's always a vegetarian starter and main course on the menu. It could be a warm tartlet of spinach with pine kernels and goat's yoghurt, followed by vegetarian lasagne with marjoram sauce, and a dessert of organic strawberries with camomile cream. Delicious. But the real speciality of the house is Irish classical cooking prepared to a high standard using the best ingredients, so you must expect the other diners to be tucking into plates of meat.

Five-course meal I£19. Wine from I£9.25, organic from I£11.
Tue–Sat for dinner only, closed Feb.

Ahakista (Co. Cork)

Shiro *Ahakista, tel. (027) 67030*
Restaurant.

First-class authentic Japanese cooking in the remote south-west is surprise enough, perhaps, without also finding a separate vegetarian menu of excellent quality. Decor and atmosphere are somewhat more Japanese than Irish, with polished wood and Oriental artwork. The vegetarian meal changes frequently, but could consist of, for example, an assortment of appetisers, a little egg dish with

sushi, a 'seasonal soup', and then, as a main course, tempura (several different vegetables and noodles dipped in sauce and deep-fried, and served with Japanese pickles and rice), followed by fresh fruits. It's not cheap, but is rather special.
Set meal I£28. Wine from I£12. Daily 7–12.

Belfast (Co. Antrim)

BANANAS *4 Clarence St, tel. (0232) 339999*
Restaurant.
Next door to Restaurant 44 (see below), with not just the same owner but even the same kitchen, this wine bar/restaurant is a similar colonial-style concept but more informal, much brighter, noisier and more laid back. Not surprisingly the food is quite similar; parts of the menu are almost identical to that of its neighbour, although the list is more extensive and includes quicker, less formal items. The several dishes suitable for vegetarians are clearly so marked on the menu.
£11 for three courses. Wine from £6.25/bottle.
Mon–Fri 12–3, 5.30–11; Sat 5–11.

DUKES HOTEL *65–67 University St, tel. (0232) 236666*
Hotel-restaurant.
Proprietors: Welcome Group.
An interesting hotel in the University area on the corner of Botanic Avenue and University Street, it has grey decor throughout, relieved by the greenery of indoor plants. Rooms, some smallish, are comfortable, very well equipped, and have good views of the hills beyond the city. Health and fitness are features of the hotel: there's a small sauna, a gym, and in the dining room healthy eating is played up. Because of this, the menu lists several possible main courses in a vegetarian section. These are predictable, but none the worse for that; for example, nut cutlet, or mushroom stroganoff and rice. Starters are limited, but there's always something suitable.
Open all year. 21 rooms, all with own bath/shower.
B&B: £79 for two, £65 for one. Lunch/Dinner: allow about £15 for three courses. Wine: from £6.90/bottle. Credit cards accepted.

★RESTAURANT 44 *44 Bedford St, tel. (0232) 244844*
Restaurant.
On a corner of Bedford Street and Clarence Street in the somewhat misnamed Golden Mile area (Belfast's principal entertainments

district, but in reality a little tarnished), this is one of the best eating places in Northern Ireland. Inside there's smart colonial-style décor, a discreet, prosperous atmosphere, and expensively dressed clientele. Several items on the well-thought-out menu of surprising and imaginative dishes are suitable for vegetarians: four possible starters and a couple of main courses, as well as optional side dishes which would make a meal in themselves. There are excellent *prix fixe* three-course lunches and dinners which include at least one good vegetarian option in every course. Wines are available by glass or bottle.

I started with stilton mousse with pear in a port sauce: a delicious creamy white square of cheese mousse and a ripe, tender pear perfectly matched by the sweet sauce. My main course was a baked papaya – unexpectedly savoury – with a rich tomato sauce and crispy noodles. On the side were quite superfluous cauliflower cheese and sautéed mushrooms. Dessert was an unusual but successful version of Floating Island (Île Flottante): the meringue was topped with almonds and not floating but standing on a plate covered by two sauces – crême anglaise and fresh caramel.

Three courses: £15 lunch, £18 dinner. Wine: from £6.25/bottle (several good half-bottles). Mon–Fri 12–3, 6–11; Sat 6–11.

SAINTS & SCHOLARS *3 University St, tel. (0232) 325137*
Restaurant.

A popular eating place in the University area. Downstairs is 'The Library', with bookshelves on the walls, though the atmosphere could hardly be less studious, while upstairs is calmer, more intimate and comfortable. A very varied menu includes several vegetarian starters and three suitable main dishes, like mixed nut roast *en croûte*. An unusual touch is that none of the salads is suitable for vegetarians! Among the rich desserts are eggy crêpes or fruit salad with Greek yoghurt and honey.

Allow about £8 for three-course meal. Wine: from £5.95/bottle. Mon–Sat 12–11; Sun 12.30–2.30, 5.30–9.30.

SPICE OF LIFE *62 Donegall Street, tel. (0232) 332744*
Restaurant-café. 100% vegetarian.

Just opposite Belfast cathedral you'll see the green exterior of this small and friendly veggie eating place. Inside, it has uncovered wooden tables, a congenial atmosphere, and a noticeboard with feminist, gay, leftist items. There's good food too: wholefood hot dishes such as lasagne, salads and sandwiches.

£5 for full meal. No wine, but you can bring your own (no corkage charge). Mon–Fri 9–5.

The Strand *12 Stranmillis Rd, tel. (0232) 682266*
Restaurant.
Located in the University area, just a few paces beyond the Botanic Gardens, this cosy bistro-style restaurant tempts students and professors to sample some imaginative cooking. The menu changes every month, but there's usually a couple of vegetarian main courses, sometimes more. They're rather heavy on the cheese, and can be a little overcomplicated. For example: 'aubergine pie' – aubergine sliced, coated in sesame seeds, layered with ratatouille-type vegetables, topped with cheese and breadcrumbs, and baked; or broccoli and cashewnut flan with cheese sauce, baked potato and salad.
Allow about £8 for three-course meal. Wine: from £5.25/bottle. Mon–Sat 12–11; Sun 12–2.30, 5.30–10.

Blackrock – *See Dublin*

Butlerstown (Co. Cork)

Dunworley Cottage *Butlerstown, Clonakilty, tel. (023) 40314*
Restaurant.
In a stone cottage out in the country, beside the sea on Cork's beautiful south coast, here's high quality cooking on a long menu which is tempting for meat-eaters and vegetarians alike. Vegans are equally welcome, and indeed Dunworley makes a point of welcoming anyone with dietary restrictions – gluten free, low cholesterol, diabetic, you name it. No processed foods are used, in fact almost all the produce is organic, breads are home-made, and eggs are from their own free-range hens. You could start with nettle soup, have a main course of celeriac fritters, and finish with fresh fruit salad or apple strudel.
Around I£15 for three courses. Organic wine from I£10/bottle. Open Wed–Sun for dinner from 6.30pm (Sat & Sun open for lunch and dinner).

Cashel (Co. Tipperary)

★★Cashel Palace *Main St, Cashel, tel. (062) 61411*
Hotel-restaurant.
Proprietor: Ray Carroll.
An exceptionally grand and wonderful hotel in the former Archbishop's Palace of this historical ecclesiastical centre, one of the most dramatic locations in inland Ireland. Reception, public rooms and bedrooms are opulent, spacious, furnished with antiques. Vegetarians will have to announce themselves when booking, making clear what ingredients they won't eat, but the chef is ready to deal with this. Our dinner was a delicious avocado and walnut salad; a main course of 'ravioli with asparagus', which turned out to be a sheet of plain pasta – perfectly done – rolled up on the plate, and beside it an array of simple asparagus, carrots and other vegetables; a side dish contained more vegetable dishes, such as pommes dauphinoise – making rather a superfluity of vegetables, perhaps; a cheese course of Irish farmhouse cheeses, of which one of the best (Cashel Blue) comes from nearby; my dessert of kiwi charlotte in orange sauce was a little too creamy. Good house wine was not expensive. To finish the meal, coffee and petits fours were brought to our room. There's also another, informal eating place at the hotel – The Buttery – in which a vegetarian dish is always available.
Open all year (except Christmas Day and St Stephen's Day).
Twenty rooms, all with bath/shower. Bed & breakfast from I£70 for one, I£90 for two. Four-course vegetarian dinner: I£25.
Wine: from I£10/bottle. Credit cards accepted.

Cork (Co. Cork)

★Arbutus Lodge *Middle Glanmire Rd, Montenotte, Cork, tel. (021) 501237*
Hotel-restaurant.
Proprietor: Declan Ryan.
Montenotte is an old-established, once very prosperous suburb of Cork; it stands up on the slopes of a hill overlooking the rest of the city. Unfortunately the view is not pretty: docks, warehouses, and factories along the River Lee make their presence very obvious from this angle. But it's here that you'll find one of Ireland's best restaurants and most agreeable small hotels. It brings together polished grandeur and a relaxed friendly professionalism, while

rooms combine style, modern comforts, and antique mahogany furniture. Declan Ryan is a genial, sincere and attentive host. The sombre and elegant dining room is full every evening. Cooking is of a high standard, but sticking mainly to traditional Irish popular dishes.

However, there's also a choice of daily vegetarian dishes which may be ordered *à la carte* or substituted into the *prix fixe* dinner menu, and these do wander away from the usual Irish ideas. Bean salad with garlic croutons was almost too filling to be a starter; it was followed by an interesting char-grilled polenta served in chewy, tasty chunks with roast Mediterranean vegetables; a plate of vegetables including a tomato stuffed with lentils, grilled courgette, pommes dauphinoise, and purée of carrot; magnificent Irish farmhouse cheeses (in which Declan is very interested); and numerous tempting desserts. Much of the produce used is organic. The only 'fault' – a common one in Ireland – was that there was simply far too much of everything. But Declan says that's what the Irish customers want. Declan's special pride and joy is the wine list, which is famous and incredibly long; wines can be had by glass or bottle, including dessert wines and Champagne.

Breakfast is marvellous: delicious home-made muesli, rich and tangy 'mature farmhouse yoghurt', freshly squeezed juices, French croissants (they are brought over from France and finished in the kitchen here).

Open all year, but restaurant is closed Sun. Twenty rooms, all with bath/shower. Bed & breakfast I£68 for two, I£39 for one. Four-course vegetarian dinner I£25. Wine: from I£10/bottle. Credit cards accepted.

CRAWFORD GALLERY CAFÉ *Emmet Pl, Cork, tel. (021) 274415*

Restaurant.

Behind the Opera House in the heart of Cork, the Crawford Gallery is one of Ireland's leading art museums, with a wide collection of medieval and modern painting. Its café/dining room is smart with glass-topped tables and waitress service. It serves good quality meals and snacks, some of which are vegetarian, for example spinach and mushroom pancakes, or cheese croquettes. The bread and tea-time bakery items are excellent – they are from the Ballymaloe House bakery.

Allow about I£5 for a meal. Mon–Wed 10–5, Thu and Fri 10–9, Sat 9.30–4.30.

Quay Co-Op *24 Sullivan's Quay, Cork*
Café. 100% vegetarian.
On the quiet side of the river, very close to the tourist office, this waterside co-op is a delight. On the ground floor there's a vegetarian wholefood 'general store' whose shelves are loaded with a wide range of goods, including lots of interesting secondhand books. Upstairs is a spacious and relaxed popular cafeteria in several different rooms – it's a great meeting place with good records playing and good food available at the counter. They have sweets and savouries and it's ideal for a snack or a meal or a cup of tea. Main courses are along the lines of casseroles, crêpes, or beanburgers. There are several vegan dishes too.
Allow about I£5 for a complete meal. Daily 12–6.30.

Dublin (Co. Dublin)

Ayumi-Ya *Newpark Centre, Newtownpark Avenue, Blackrock, tel. (01) 831767*
Restaurant.
Interesting, tasty, authentic Japanese cuisine, including a vegetarian menu, can be found in the improbable setting of a small shopping complex in a Dublin suburb. The premises are intimate and traditional. The sort of food you might choose is a starter of three dishes such as noodles wrapped in seaweed, deep fried mushroom with a plum inside, deep fried aubergine with miso paste; and a main course of, say, vegetable tempura and tofu 'steak'.
Set meal of eight dishes: I£14.50. Wine: from I£8.75/bottle. Open every evening.

Café Klara *35 Dawson St, Dublin 2, tel. (01) 778611*
Restaurant.
A large popular brasserie with style and flair, the mirrored walls give tremendous appeal to this city-centre eating and drinking venue opposite the Mansion House. The menu offers good quality French *cuisine moderne* which is by no means vegetarian, and leans heavily to fish. However, vegetarians are welcome and some dishes are suitable. Start with salads, have a main course of tagliatelle, move on to Irish farmhouse cheeses and finish with fruit salad, treacle tart or chocolate marquise. Wines are good quality.
Allow I£14 for three courses. Wine from about I£10/bottle. Daily noon to midnight.

CORNUCOPIA WHOLEFOODS *19 Wickow St, Dublin 2.*
Restaurant. 100% vegetarian.

A city-centre health food shop with wholefood restaurant attached does not automatically suggest a really excellent place to go for a meal. The style is rather reminiscent of a straight caff – but with a big difference: the food here, though often simple, is creative, tasty and wholesome. Most of the produce is organic, and much use is made of tofu, tempeh, and sea vegetables. Breakfast is along the lines of freshly baked bread and muffins, coffee, and freshly squeezed orange juice; lunch dishes are all served with salad, and there's a set midday meal of soup, pie, and salad; while evening meals are all served with rice and salad, and might include, for example, broccoli and cheese strudel or vegetable stew. For pud there's apple crumble with cream or yoghurt, as well as a selection of cakes and strudels. Value for money is formidable. The restaurant has a relaxed, casual atmosphere, and it's patronised by a wide mix of clients, including artists, actors, and singers. The shop is good too, by the way.

Lunch about I£4; dinner I£6 for 3 big courses. Wine: coming soon.
Mon–Fri 8am–9pm, Sat 9–6.

PUERTO BELLA *1 Portobello Rd, off South Circular Road, Dublin 8, tel. (01) 720851 or 533536*
Restaurant.

In a rather out-of-the-way location, next to the Grand Canal, this is a relaxed, civilised place with excellent, imaginative French-style cooking. The menu includes some vegetarian options. Start with a beautiful mixed salad, or stuffed mushrooms, enjoy a main course of, say, pine-nut loaf with spicy tomato sauce. I finished with a raspberry and Drambuie bavarois with single cream. Service is friendly and efficient.

Allow about I£16 for three courses. Wine: from I£12/bottle.
Mon–Fri 12.30–2.30, 6–11.30; Sat 7–11.

Kenmare (Co. Kerry)

★★★PARK HOTEL *Kenmare, tel. (064) 41200*
Hotel-restaurant.
Proprietor: Francis Brennan

One of Ireland's best hotels, and one of its best restaurants as well, the Park is a special place to stay. The hotel stands in private parkland, looking across the tidal Kenmare River, on the edge of a

bustling village near the famous (or infamous) Ring of Kerry circular route. Outwardly austere in grey stone, inside the building is both palatial and unpretentious. Everything is of the very highest quality, yet there's a relaxed air. The moment you walk in to the entrance hall – it's too informal to be called 'Reception' – where a peat fire glows in the hearth, or the moment you walk into your beautifully equipped bedroom, or the moment you sit down in the elegant dining room, are all blissful and memorable. From the magnificent public rooms on the ground floor, an immense stairway leads up to bedrooms. Along the corridors are weighty antiques and massive old oil paintings. Bedrooms are lavishly comfortable. The dining room is distinctly grand, with big round tables not too close to each other, most attractively laid.

All guests must book in advance to stay in the Park: vegetarians should announce themselves when booking, although the chef can cope even without warning. For a three-course dinner, you will be expected to order your meal from the normal *prix fixe* menu, which has meatless and fishless possibilities, except for the main course, which will be prepared especially for you. The chef, Matthew Darcy, is as good at vegetarian dishes as at conventional Irish and French cuisine. My most recent meal started with little *amuse-gueule* of fruit and sorbet; there was a chilled cucumber and mint soup, wonderfully crisp and refreshing, and tasting mainly of cucumber, the main course was fresh tagliatelle and an 'aubergine and spinach cake' (there's no better description: the two vegetables were finely chopped, mixed, and baked together in a circular mould) in a tomato coulis, and to finish, a very reckless order of the 'chef's selection' – six different desserts beautifully presented on a plate together, all unbelievably delicious, of which the best was white chocolate in a raspberry sauce. Service is faultless, excellent home-made brown bread is served, and the wine list is superb but reasonably priced.

The breakfast menu is one of the most interesting I've seen: fresh fruit juices prepared to your order include carrot or cucumber, or you can have a plate of fresh fruit; cereals include top-quality home-made muesli with good yoghurt and fresh fruit; eggs are local free range; and the various breads are freshly made on the premises. The butter comes in little water-cooled pats. On request, there's unsalted butter, low-fat milk, decaffeinated coffee.

Open Mar–Nov. 50 rooms (all with private bathroom).
Bed & breakfast: from I£95 for one, I£79 per person for two sharing. Table d'hôte menu: I£35. Wine: from I£15/bottle.
All credit cards.

Kinsale (Co. Cork)

It seems a shame to list the best of Irish eating without mentioning pretty Kinsale on the coast of County Cork, as the village is something of a centre for Ireland's gastronomic skills. Each summer, after a Jazz Festival comes an annual Food Festival. The emphasis here though is firmly on fish and seafood; vegetarians can hardly find a sandwich. Only THE LITTLE SKILLET, 47 Main Street, tel. (021) 774202, offered a decent meal without meat. Starters include hoummous, and among the main courses there's a vegetarian shepherd's pie. Altogether about £6 for a meal.

Moycullen (Co. Galway)

⋆DRIMCONG HOUSE *Moycullen, tel. (091) 85115*
Restaurant.
The best of Irish cooking at a delightful 300-year-old lakeland house where dinner is always a festive event. Owners Gerry and Marie Galvin grow and cook the food themselves, and offer set *prix fixe* menus of a high standard. Most diners are tucking into meat and fish dishes, but there's also a complete vegetarian menu. It changes frequently, but we enjoyed baked avocado and blue cheese in filo; a vegetarian sausage and fresh vegetables; perfect Irish farmhouse cheeses; and (from among other tempting desserts) excellent home-made ice cream. Good wine list, too.

Four-course menu: I£14.95. Wine: from I£9.25.
Tue–Sat 7–10.30, closed Christmas to March.

Newmarket-On-Fergus (Co. Clare)

★★DROMOLAND CASTLE *Newmarket-on-Fergus (nr Limerick), tel. (061) 368144*
Hotel-restaurant.
Proprietor: Dowmar Securities
A real baronial castle beside a lake, standing in extensive parkland surrounded by open countryside. Inside it's thoroughly luxurious and elegant, with fine wood panelling and stonework, antique mahogany furniture, and walls hung with oil paintings. Bedrooms are of the highest standard of no-expense-spared comfort. The dining room, similarly, is opulent and beautifully laid out, with big crystal chandeliers, the candlelit tables set with charm and taste. Service is faultless. French head chef Jean-Baptiste Molinari offers a high-quality fixed-price vegetarian menu. The food is Provençale and north Italian in style, while using fresh local produce. Much use is made of vegetables, which are from the castle's own garden. The result is a great success, with a starter of, say, fresh asparagus tips in a warm olive-rich vinaigrette; followed by a cream of vegetable soup; a main course of fresh garden vegetables with individual fillings, served on a tomato coulis, or perhaps home-made spinach ravioli in vegetable sauce; a selection of the best French and Irish cheeses; followed by fabulous desserts, coffee, and petits fours. The wine list is exceptional. Breakfasts are good too.
Open all year. 73 rooms (all with own bathroom).
Room only: from I£99. Breakfast: I£12. Dinner: set vegetarian five-course meal I£33. Wine: from about I£16/bottle.
All credit cards.

Shanagarry (Co. Cork)

★★**Ballymaloe House** *Shanagarry, Midleton, tel. (021) 652531*
Hotel-restaurant.
Proprietors: Allen family.

Ballymaloe is a spacious, delightful old mansion-farmhouse surrounded by its 400 green acres. Step into the entrance hall, and you'll see the massive horns of the Irish elk dating from 12,000 BC, in a parody of the ghastly hunting trophies so often displayed at other country houses. Inside, everything is relaxed and warmly comfortable, but elegant, and all in all it's very like staying with wealthy friends. On the walls is hanging the best collection of paintings you're likely to see at any country house hotel. Bedrooms are quite simple, and not cluttered with 'luxuries': there's no TV or radio, for example. As well as being a uniquely inviting place to stay, this is, of course, a famous place to eat.

There are five dining rooms, not counting the lovely Conservatory. Myrtle Allen has long been a great ambassador of Irish cooking – she and her team make skilful, unpretentious use of fresh, high-quality local ingredients, and once ran an Irish restaurant in Paris as well as starting the highly acclaimed cookery courses now offered by her daughter-in-law Darina; one of the courses is in vegetarian cookery (call 021 646785 for details of these). Myrtle has a soft spot for vegetarians (not vegans though), and provides them with a complete dinner menu of their own. Vegetables and salads served in the evening are mostly gathered on the same day, and the excellent breads are all home made. Dinner is a set five courses along these lines: a buffet of *crudités*; blue cheese and celery millefeuille (rather too rich and creamy); a little tart filled with a ratatouille-like vegetable mixture; a selection of fine Irish farmhouse cheeses; desserts from the trolley, such as a delectable tarte tatin that was almost all apple. Coffee and petits fours are included. Ballymaloe is noted for the quality of its wine selection.

Children are made very welcome, but not in the dining room during dinner unless prepared to sit quietly: they are given their own Children's Tea at 5.30, when they can choose from a special menu (this sometimes turns into a rather riotous occasion!). Lunch is a generous buffet. Breakfasts too – the dining rooms transformed by blue gingham tablecloths – are first rate, with delicious white or wholemeal rolls just out of the oven, home-made muesli, fresh fruit salad, or porridge made of stone ground oats, and eggs from their farmyard hens.

Open all year. 30 rooms, all quite different in character and size, all with bath/shower. Prices per person: dinner, bed and breakfast I£71 winter, I£78 summer; B&B I£44 winter, I£50 summer. Dinner I£28, lunch I£14. Wine from I£12/bottle.

Wicklow (Co. Wicklow)

⋆THE OLD RECTORY *Wicklow, tel. (0404) 67048*
Hotel-restaurant.
Proprietors: Paul and Linda Saunders.

On the edge of a small harbour town, this handsome Victorian house in its attractive gardens is an agreeable small hotel with high corniced ceilings, unpretentious comfort and a country house atmosphere. There's an intimate dining room with just six tables. Though not vegetarian, Paul and Linda offer an excellent vegetarian menu which is always available. They describe their food as 'green cuisine', home-made French and Irish dishes made with fresh, organic ingredients from their vegetable, herb and flower gardens and from the wild. The range of vegetables is extraordinary – they use many which are rarely seen. Salads, for example, may include carnival lettuce, rocket, chive flowers, pak choy, salad burnett, nasturtium flowers, borage flowers, lambs lettuce, and lemon mint. Cooking is of good quality, with some interesting and unusual dishes, and everything is prepared to order (which can lead to a certain delay before your food arrives).

Starters include a sorbet of blackcurrant with red wine, or a soup of salad vegetables; among the main courses is koulibiaka, which is

layers of mushroom, aubergine, spinach and rice in brioche pastry with a sauce of wine and herbs. There are good desserts, including soya ice cream. In addition, they can provide a Special Vegetarian Menu if given advance notice of a day or so. This is a delicious, well-thought-out fixed-price set meal of five courses, followed by coffee (or tea or herb tea) and petits fours. The sort of thing you might have would be a starter of cheese in filo pastry done as little canapés, a hearty leek and oatmeal soup, a salad of mint and melon, a main course of cheese and broccoli tart with an excellent herb sauce, and a dessert of rich chocolatey 'ice cream gâteau'.
Open Easter to mid-Oct, five rooms (all with shower/bath).
B&B: I£37 per person (sharing). Half-board: I£58 per person (sharing). Evening meal only: allow about I£20 for three courses à la carte, *I£21.50 for 5 course set meal with advance notice.*
Wine: from I£10/bottle. Credit cards accepted.

IRISH ORGANIC FARM GUESTHOUSES

Ireland has a considerable number of organic farmers, mainly following old traditions rather than taking part in anything new. They have their own organisation, the Irish Organic Farmers and Growers Association. Some of its members take in paying guests, and issue a leaflet with their names and details. Standards of accommodation – and prices – vary enormously, some being simple rustic farmhouses, while others are palatial mansions standing on estates of hundreds of acres (1000 in one case). In addition to bed and a substantial breakfast, they provide evening meals largely of their own organic farm produce. All are happy to cater for vegetarians. For latest details contact Gillies Macbain, Cranagh Castle, Templemore, Co Tipperary, Ireland, tel. (0504) 53104, or any Irish Tourist Board (Bord Fáilte) office.

Israel

Dialling code from abroad: 010 972.
Currency: New Shekel (NS, sometimes NIS), about NS2=$1, NS3½ to the £. Because the shekel is not stable, many prices in Israel are given in US dollars.
Shabbat: Note that almost everything is closed on Shabbat – *the Jewish sabbath which effectively operates from late afternoon on Friday to after sunset on Saturday. There is almost no public transport on that day.*

It's not in Europe, so Israel should not, perhaps, be included in this guide. But Israel happens to be one of the best vegetarian destinations in the world and is hardly further away from the UK than, say, Spain's Canary Islands. Inexpensive charter flights leave frequently from British airports heading to Tel Aviv and Eilat. It's a fascinating country, full of energy and life. Ideas, discussion and debate fill the air – and one of the ideas which attracts a lot of support is that it is wrong to kill animals as food. Another important consideration in Israel is that Jewish dietary laws make it complicated to eat meat; nearly all restaurants are kosher, and must choose to serve either 'meat' or 'dairy' foods (note that fish is also served in 'dairy' restaurants). They can serve both only if the two are kept strictly separate and use different kitchens. An Israeli breakfast, by the way, is always 'dairy', and can come as a surprise: not many other countries start the day with a big plate of salad.

So many establishments of all kinds serve vegetarian food that it's hardly worth listing them. All kibbutz guesthouses (see box on p. 110) routinely provide a vegetarian dish on their menus, or can prepare something suitable without advance warning. Many ordinary hotels are the same. All hotels in the luxury Sheraton and Dan chains have 'dairy' restaurants. The Hyatt in Jerusalem has a 'dairy' Italian restaurant, and at the Tel Aviv Hilton the front lounge has a good 'dairy' menu.

In 'meat' restaurants (as opposed to 'dairy') you may need advice

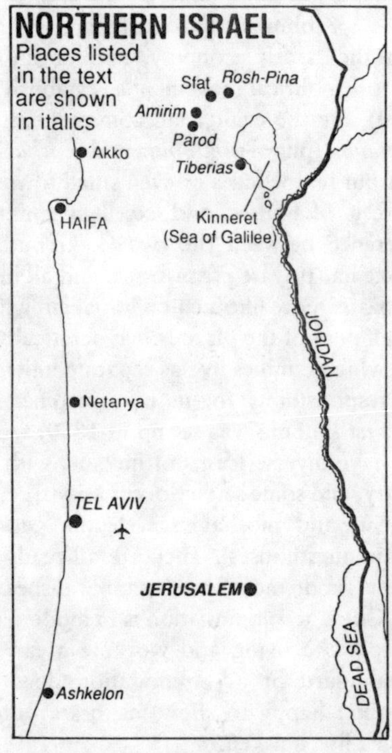

from the waiter, but there are often suitable dishes. Most are happy to make a vegetable platter. Another widely available dish is a fruit plate – usually a heap of fresh cottage cheese in the middle with chopped fresh ripe fruit piled around the edges. Among the best resources in Israel – and rarely used by tourists – are Sephardi restaurants (Sephardim are Jews from Moslem countries, while Ashkenazim come from Europe). Sephardi food, similar to Arabic, includes many suitable dishes. Israel's 'national snack' – falafel in pitta (accompanied by chopped salad and tahina) – is a typical Sephardi dish. If you're not used to Israel, at first glance you might think Sephardim and their eating places are Arabic: but look more closely and you'll see the difference. Even if you do wander into an Arab restaurant, it won't matter; and here too the food is marvellous. In the North especially, there are Lebanese restaurants, where the meat-free Arab dishes, served like a multitude of snacks all at once, are exquisite.

Kibbutzim and Moshavim

Cornerstones of the Israeli economy, and at the foundation of Zionist ideology (the political movement to establish and maintain a Jewish homeland), are the egalitarian communities known as *kibbutzim* and *moshavim* (plural of *kibbutz* and *moshav*). These are not small communes but real villages or even small towns, with perhaps 100 families, streets of houses, and excellent communal facilities. There is a difference between the two: a kibbutz is completely communal, no one has private possessions, and all income is held in common; a moshav is more like a co-operative, in which much life is shared, the overall plan of the place is democratically decided by all residents, but in which families live as separate units, eat separately, and each takes responsibility for its own income. Although early settlements (the first kibbutz was set up in 1880) were agricultural, nowadays most have diverse forms of income, with some farming, some light industry, and some service occupations.

Many kibbutzim and moshavim welcome guests in 'kibbutz hotels' or 'kibbutz guesthouses'. They are all ready and willing to provide vegetarian food; most have suitable dishes listed on their ordinary menus. Guest accommodation is in modern low-rise blocks quite separate from the living and working areas of the kibbutz residents. The standard of accommodation does vary, but not widely. All are quite happy to show visitors around and explain more about kibbutz life, if asked.

The head office of the Kibbutz Hotel Association is at 90 Ben Yehuda St, Tel Aviv 61031 Israel, tel. (03) 246161.

Some kibbutzim are open for meals only, or for guided tours with refreshments included. One which gives visitors an especially good insight into the life and work of these communities is Kibbutz Bet Haemek (Maale Hagalil 25 115, tel. (04) 960411) in the Galilee: here visitors and kibbutzniks mix freely – and the guests are required to lend a hand with the clearing up.

READ ALL ABOUT IT

In Tel Aviv, at the office of the Israeli Movement of Vegetarians and Vegans, 2 Levontin Str, Tel Aviv 65111, there is an International Vegetarian and Naturopathy Library, with books in most European languages as well as Hebrew. Librarian: Mrs Shoshana Kreisberg.

Package Holidays

El Al, 188 Regent St, London W1, tel. (071) 439 2429, see p. 15
Israel Holidays Ltd, PO Box 2045, Herzliya B, 46120 Israel, see p. 16
Vegetarian Travellers, 60 Crewys Rd, London NW2 2AD, see p. 12

Recommended Accommodation, Holiday Centres and Restaurants

Amirim

VILLAGE GUESTHOUSES *Moshav Amirim, near Carmiel, Galilee 20115, tel. (06) 989571 – ask for Sara.*
Guesthouses. 100% vegetarian.
English spoken.
Beautifully situated high in the green hills of Galilee, Amirim is a *moshav* (communal village) of about 60 families. Many take in paying guests, though only five provide meals. Perhaps the easiest with which to make advance arrangements from abroad, in English, is the CAMPBELL-LAMDAN establishment (see below). Dalia COHEN takes guests, who eat in her restaurant (see below). The other families are HAMIEL (tel. 06-989746, some English spoken, nice dining room), POKER (tel. 06-989030, some English spoken, vegan-style food), and CARMELLI (tel. 06-989316, English spoken, big family, bubbly atmosphere, home-made cheese). In addition, there are families who take guests on an accommodation-only basis, and you can eat in Dalia's Restaurant. It is also possible to turn up without a booking: just go to the office and ask for Sara.
Open all year. Room only, per night: about 100 NS for two, 70 NS for one; meals – see Dalia's Restaurant.

CAMPBELL-LAMDAN HOUSE *Moshav Amirim, near Carmiel, Galilee 20115, tel. (06) 989045*
Guesthouse. 100% vegetarian.
Proprietor: Philip Campbell. English spoken.
The Campbell-Lamdan family (ie. Philip, together with his wife's family) have a couple of comfortable, attractive little chalets to let; they stand on higher ground in the village and have tremendous views. Their guests receive half-board in the family home. I found the food plain and austere – but it's all organic and good quality,

mainly vegan. Guests come almost exclusively from Britain (as does Philip Campbell), and prices are in sterling.
Open all year. Four double rooms (all with own bath/shower).
Price calculated per day: full-board £40 for single,
£68 for two sharing; half-board £32 for single,
£52 for two sharing. No wine. No credit cards.

DALIA'S RESTAURANT *Moshav Amirim, near Carmiel, Galilee 20115, tel. (06) 989349*
Restaurant. 100% vegetarian.
Dalia Cohen's cafeteria-style dining room runs the length of a lovely house with views over to Lake Kinneret (Sea of Galilee). You pay a fixed charge to eat a complete meal with masses of good wholesome food. On the menu are, for example, stuffed peppers, vegetable soup, half-a-dozen types of salad, moussaka or blintzes with vegetables, a dessert served with a fruit salad, plus a cup of herb tea.
NS35 for complete meal. Wine from NS15/bottle. Open daily 8–8.

Ashkelon

BEIT FRUMER – NATURAL HEALTH RESORT *PO Box 9049, Ashkelon, tel. (051) 34901 or 36293*
Guesthouse. 100% vegetarian.
Temporarily closed during our research.

Jerusalem

OFF THE SQUARE *6 Yael Solomon St, Jerusalem, tel. (02) 242 549*
Restaurant. Mainly vegetarian.
In a pleasant city centre setting, this friendly 'dairy' restaurant has a wide range of simple but tempting snacks and meals. There are a few fish dishes, but everything else is vegetarian. Soups include gazpacho, yoghurt, and fruit, as well as the more usual vegetable soups. There are salads, of course, vegetable pastries, pasta, pizzas, and so on, as well as unusual options like fondue. There's a choice of over a dozen desserts, including home-made ice cream, crêpes and pies.
Allow about NS25 for a meal. Wine: NS18/bottle. Closed Shabbat.

(Near) Parod

★**Ein Kamonim** *Highway 85 near Parod, tel. (06) 989894 or (06) 989680*
Restaurant. 100% vegetarian.
Hard to find, but worth the effort, this must be the most unusual restaurant that ever was – a restaurant where they don't do any cooking. It lies just off route 85, the main road which runs across Galilee from Akko (or Acre) to Lake Kinneret (or the Sea of Galilee), separating Upper Galilee from Lower Galilee. You pass the junction with route 866 which heads off left towards Sfat (skirting Parod and Amirim): stay on 85. Soon after passing a smaller turning (806), on the right, to Maghar, you reach the inconspicuous sign at the end of the rough track which leads to Ein Kamonim, a 80-acre goat farm.

Up here stands a converted barn, where diners sit on benches at rough wooden tables. The server (usually the farmer himself) brings a succession of types of exquisite goats' cheeses of every variety, some of which the French have yet to even dream of – soft, hard, dry, moist, strong, mild. Some you scoop on to your plate with a spoon and douse in olive oil or sprinkle with *zaatar*, a salty green condiment on the table (I was told that this is called hyssop in English). To accompany the cheeses, he brings olives, glasses of very tart buttermilk, a basket of raw, washed vegetables and a sharp knife with which to slice them, pickled cabbage, tahina, hot fresh pitta bread, and more. When you've made good inroads into all this, he returns with more kinds of cheese, more salads, more pitta bread, and a carafe of red wine, which he urges you to drink on the grounds that without it the cheese is 'harder to absorb'. The succession of wonderful flavours is fabulous. Finally he brings a dessert – ours was chunks of delicious fresh watermelon – followed by coffee or herb tea.

When I talked to the farmer Amiram Ovrutski and his wife Drora (who makes all the cheeses herself), it turned out that they had just returned from England, 'where the goats' milk is so good', and had arranged to supplement their herd with several English goats.
32NS to eat as much as you like. Wine included.
Daily except Shabbat.

Rosh Pina

Mitzpe Hayamim Hotel or Sea View Hotel

PO Box 27, Rosh Pina, tel. (06) 937014
Hotel-restaurant. Mainly vegetarian.
Proprietor: Eliahu Jamui. English spoken.

Rosh Pina is an attractive old town in the Galilee hills. It's not far from the vegetarian village of Amirim while equally close in the other direction is the larger, picturesque historic town of Sfat (various spellings: Sefat, Zefat, etc). Out of Rosh Pina the road climbs and climbs, and there on a high wooded ridge looking for miles across green hills and fields is the hotel. The English name is earned by a splendid view down to the Sea of Galilee. It's a modern low-rise building among trees and flowers. Inside, there's a lounge where you can relax, watch TV, and make yourself a drink from a huge selection of teas. Downstairs, there's a jacuzzi, sauna, and gym which it's fun to use. You reach your room by walking through a big conservatory-style hall filled with tropical plants reaching up to the roof. The bedrooms are not large, and are quite simply furnished, but do have phone, bathroom, and TV, as well as a terrace. Mine needed smartening-up, and would have benefited from a fresh coat of paint.

Outside there are pleasant partly wooded grounds full of birdsong. There's a pool, lawns, and, up the road, a small farm which produces much of the hotel's food. The only non-vegetarian food at this hotel-restaurant is the fish option for the main course. The cooking is uncomplicated home-cooking of predictable vegetarian dishes – soups, quiche, vegetables, salads, cheeses, maybe a fruit salad to finish. The bread is fresh and home-baked. Some of the food is organic. The breakfast, as so often in Israel, is excellent: home-made soft cheeses, delicious bread, good granola, lovely yoghurt. Prices, as in many Israeli hotels, are reckoned in dollars (more stable than the shekel).

Open all year. 28 rooms, all with bath/shower.
Bed & breakfast – $60–$80; half-board – $87–$104;
dinner only – $14. Wine: from $8/bottle.
Restaurant open 7–9, 1–2, 7–8. Credit cards accepted.

Tel Aviv

ETERNITY *60 Ben Yehuda St, Tel Aviv, tel. (03) 203151*
Restaurant. 100% vegetarian.
On the corner of Ben Yehuda and Mendele Streets, this colourful macrobiotically-inclined café emblazons its window with the names of dishes. Within, in a simple setting, snacks and meals with rice, tofu, salads, and dishes like hoummous are on offer. One of the best desserts is soya ice cream.
NS14 for complete meal. No wine. 9am–11pm (closed Shabbat).

Tiberias

MILKWAY *5 Habonim St, Tiberias, tel. (06) 792724*
Café. Mainly vegetarian.
In the pedestrian mall at the centre of this very popular resort on the banks of Lake Kinneret (the Sea of Galilee), there's a simple, inexpensive Sephardi eating place which could be useful. Middle-Eastern salads, soups, one or two hot dishes, village bread, and cakes are served all day and half the night.
NS12 for a full meal. Wine: NS17/bottle.
9am–1am (closed Shabbat).

Italy

Dialling code from abroad: 010 39.
Currency: Lire (L, l or £): about 2165L=£1.

Italy is a glorious country, the epitome of an exuberant love of life. However, there is no one Italy. This is a country of regions, each province having its own character, dialect, and gastronomy. Some regions are almost too well-known to foreigners. Part of Tuscany, for example, a favourite for second homes, is known to a whole class of pretentious Brits as 'Chiantishire'. In fact, there's a great deal more to Tuscany than Chianti and holidays, even though, admittedly, there are few places more enjoyable for a vegetarian fortnight.

Italian food has become one of *the* great standbys for Europe's vegetarians. Pasta with a rich, meat-free tomato-based sauce is tasty, satisfying, and easy to prepare. Pizza, too, is one of the most widely available vegetarian meals. In Italy, the pasta is usually freshly made, sauces delicious and infinitely variable, and informal restaurants very widespread; and they are quite flexible about what you may order. There are often many other meat-free and fish-free dishes available as well, particularly in the abundant buffet of gorgeous *antipasti* (starters) from which you simply help yourself – it is often possible to have a complete meal (especially at lunchtime) from this selection, making it easier to eat out in Italy than almost anywhere else.

A large proportion of Italian hotels and restaurants are pleased to cater for vegetarians, and thousands of them can make a good job of it. I have not included them in my recommendations below because they do not satisfy the essential criterion of providing a complete meal for vegetarians as part of their *normal* service. You'll need to be aware that most Italian chefs and waiters don't know what vegetarians eat, and assume that a *little* bit of meat or fish will be all right. There are startling examples of this: one of the best, most famous restaurants in Rome, PIPERNO (Monte de' Cenci 9,

tel. 06/654 06 29), lists a *fritto vegetariano* among its specialities – but mixes it with salt cod.

Specifically vegetarian establishments are few. Curiously, a considerable proportion of them are *not* in the big cities. Because grains, rennet-free cheeses and good-quality vegetables are abundant and inexpensive, self-catering makes a sensible approach (there are many UK companies specialising in such 'villa' or 'apartment' holidays). Other interesting options include 'Agriturism' (see box).

AGRITURISM

Working farms which take paying guests are numerous, many are organic, and they often make a point of welcoming vegetarians. Write to Mariagrazia De Cola at S.A.P. (Silvicultura-Agrocultura-Paesaggio), CP/PO Box 93, I-50019 Sesto Fiorentino (Firenze) for information on some of the more suitable Agriturism holidays. She is also secretary of various ecological/environmental organisations, and is macrobiotic.

Package Holidays

Inntravel, The Old Station, Helmsley, York YO6 4BZ, tel. (0439) 71111, see p. 15.
World Wine Tours, 4 Dorchester Rd, Drayton St Leonard, Oxfordshire, tel. (0865) 891919, see p. 17

Recommended Accommodation, Holiday Centres and Restaurants

The selection is eclectic, and I have only listed places which make a special feature of vegetarian or macrobiotic food.

Where place names have English and Italian versions, I have put the Italian first and English second.

Castelnuovo Magra (Liguria)

La Cascina Dei Peri *Via Montefrancio 71,*
19030 Castelnuovo Magra, tel. (0187) 674085
Farm-guesthouse.
Proprietor: Marcoli M. Angiola. French and some English spoken.
Located in low hills in open country right on the border between Liguria and Tuscany, the farm is about one km from town and six km from the Mediterranean. They keep animals, and grow vegetables, grapes and olives, producing their own wine and olive oil organically. There are plenty of good walks, or you can take part in textile weaving or ceramic decoration. Nearby there is much to see, including some interesting archaeological sites. Accommodation is simple but comfortable, and the food, too, is simple, traditional cooking. There is a vegetarian menu, featuring, for example, vegetable soups or tarts, various types of vegetable and rice cakes, timbale of eggs, followed by cheeses, or fruit desserts.
Open all year. Six rooms all with own bath/shower.
Room: 40,000L for double. B&B 25,000L per person for two sharing. Half-board: 45,000L per person. Full-board 52,000L per person. Meal only: 25,000L for three courses.
Wine: own organic, 8,000L/litre. No credit cards.

Faugnacco Di Martignacco (Friuli-Venezia-Giulia)

OSTERIA ISTRIONE *Via Del Mulino 10, 33035 Faugnacco di Martignacco, Udine, tel. (0432) 678438*
Restaurant. 100% vegetarian.
Right over near the Yugoslav border, around 30 km from the town of Udine, you'll find this village where Bianca Pielich runs a pleasant little restaurant – quite probably the only vegetarian place in this part of Italy. Inside it's small, simple, and mainly white, and everywhere there are plants. There are smoking and non-smoking rooms. In the evening, candles cast a romantic light, or you can eat outside in the garden. The food is good, largely organic, always fresh. Bread and pasta are freshly home-made. There's quite a big choice on the menu. The sort of thing you'll have in a typical four-course meal is a starter of say, chickpea pâté or tofu and corn; a first course of ravioli filled with ricotta and spinach; a main course of roast seitan with mushrooms; and a hearty dessert of, perhaps, apple strudel or buckwheat cake.
Four-course meal: 25,000L. Organic wine: 9,000L/bottle.

Firenze/Florence (Toscana/Tuscany)

IL SANTOMMASO *Via Romana 80R, Firenze, tel. (055) 221166*
Restaurant. Mainly vegetarian.
A city-centre macrobiotic eating place with a menu which is almost entirely vegetarian, indeed vegan. Certain vegetarian cheeses are sometimes served but never used in cooking. Almost everything is organic. Meals follow a classic Italian pattern, but with typically macrobiotic dishes. Start with miso soup, for example. Rice, pasta or cous-cous forms the basis of most 'first dishes' (ie, after the starter), served with vegetable sauces. 'Second dishes' (ie. main courses) revolve around various soya products – such as tofu curry, or seitan scallops. Rice or tofu are used for desserts too. They also have a 'macrobiotic plate' instead of the full meal, which is a plate of rice with tofu or tempeh or seitan, vegetables, or fish, for a very moderate price.
Allow 10,000L for complete meal. No wine during my visit, licence applied for.

La Stazione Di Zima *Via Ghibellina 70R, 50122 Firenze, tel. (055) 2345318*
Restaurant. 100% vegetarian.
A relaxed informal place in one of Italy's most beautiful cities. There's a daily menu. The meal structure is traditional, and the cooking, delicious, natural and wholesome. The sort of thing you might have is a mixed salad to start, followed by brown rice and white pasta with a choice of sauces (eg. seitan ragout), then a main course of say, broccoli and mozzarella flan, or a *sformato* of mushrooms and soft stracchino cheese, and a dessert of chocolate mousse or a chocolate roll with almonds.
Allow about 18,000L for three courses. Wine: from 6,000L/litre, organic from 10,000L/bottle. 12.30–3.30, 7.30–11.30, but closed for dinner on Mon and for lunch on Sat and Sun.

Frabosa Soprana (Piemonte/Piedmont)

Albergo Miramonti *Via Roma 70, 12082 Frabosa Soprana, Cuneo, tel. (0174) 244533*
Hotel-restaurant.
Proprietor: Defilippi Ferdinando. French and some English spoken.
Frabosa Soprana (the nearest town is Mondovi) is a quiet old village in an area – the Maritime Alps close to the border with France – now lightly developed for skiing. The village, at 3000 feet, lies at the foot of Mont Moro, 5600 feet, which has some good downhill slopes ranging from easy to difficult: there are lifts direct from the village, and plenty of cross-country pistes as well. From spring to autumn, it's a region with lovely walks among flowery meadows and woods. The Miramonti is really a health hotel, offering not just comfortable and well-equipped accommodation, but also the opportunity to benefit from numerous types of therapy . . . reflexology, hydrotherapy, 'training of the nervous system', etc, etc. There's tennis, riding, a turkish bath and a gym too. Meals in the hotel's restaurant are simple, wholesome, mainly organic and largely vegetarian. There's also a separate completely vegetarian menu.
Hotel open: all year except Apr and May. Restaurant open 20/12 to Easter, and 15/6–30/9. 50 rooms (all with bath/shower).
Prices: room only – 55,000L–75,000L; breakfast – 5,000L; half-board – 45,000L–65,000L; meal only – 20,000L–25,000L for three courses. Wine: from 6,000L/bottle, organic from 10,000L/bottle. Credit cards accepted.

Genova/Genoa (Liguria)

Buona Terra *Via Teodosia 9R, 16129 Genova, tel. (010) 316744*
Restaurant. Mainly vegetarian.
A macrobiotic eating place in the centre of this busy city, it serves simple, low-fat, wholefood dishes using organic ingredients. Prices are modest. You can opt for a three-course meal of, say, miso soup, followed by a 'macroplate' of rice, beans and vegetables, finishing with carrot cake or similar. Or you could have the 'macroplate' by itself.
Allow 15,000L–20,000L for three courses. Macroplate alone is 10,000L. Wine: from 7,000L/bottle, organic from 10,000L/bottle. Mon–Sat 12.30–2.30, 7.30–9.30. Closed middle two weeks in August and one week after Christmas.

Greve In Chianti (Toscana/Tuscany)

★**La Cantinetta Di Rignana** *Loc. Rignana, 50022 Greve in Chianti, tel. (055) 852601*
Restaurant.
At a rough long table under the trees, looking across a vista of rolling vineyards in the very heart of the Chianti Classico, I had a glorious, memorable meal. However, a lot depended on chance – this is not a vegetarian restaurant, and is known above all for local rustic traditional dishes, mostly very meaty. Chef-patrone Paolo Abbarchini is a jovial, contented man who will provide whatever you want as far as he can. Once he understands that you want dishes without any meat or fish, you may have a meal like mine.

We started with a diverse assortment of antipasti – artichoke hearts, pickled onion, olives, and *crostini* (savoury pastes on little squares of toast) with vivid toppings of basil (green), mushroom (brown), olive (black), and tomato and pepper with turmeric (orange). Our pasta was ravioli filled with spinach and ricotta, served with two delicious sauces – fresh tomato and basil. A big block of parmigiano (parmesan) was placed on the table for us to grate as we wished. Then came a big mixed salad accompanied by fried battered vegetables, including potatoes, artichoke, aubergines, and most astonishing, sage leaves. Finally came a fabulous vanilla ice cream with pieces of chocolate. Then we sat back and took our pick from an amazing choice of grappas, all different colours, with various fruits or herbs.

The one snag may be finding the place. It's at the end of a four-km dirt track either from the interesting fortified village of Badia a Passignano or from the pleasant little country town of Greve. Follow the handwritten signs carefully.
30,000–35,000L for four courses, including local wine.
[The only other thing at Rignana, a few paces away from the restaurant, is the FATTORIA RIGNANA, a spacious airy old villa among the olive trees, where, as well as making their own wine and olive oil, they take in guests in simple double rooms heavy with beams and bare boards. There's a private swimming pool with superb views. Bed and breakfast: 35,000L per person for 2 sharing.]

Gúbbio (Umbria)

ALCATRAZ *Santa Cristina, 06020 Gúbbio, Perugia, tel. (075) 920052*
Holiday centre.
Proprietor: Jacopo Fo. Some English spoken.
Situated in glorious wooded country more or less midway between Gúbbio and Perugia, Alcatraz is something hard to describe in just a few words. A large estate, it contains a number of buildings scattered at a little distance from each other. One is a medieval tower, another an old stone house, while there are also purpose-built wooden bungalows: all these have simple, pleasing accommodation. There are also stables, two bars, a swimming pool, and restaurant. Although there are olives and other fruit trees being cultivated, the whole place is dedicated to enjoyment and leisure. Riding and walking are two main activities, and you can be taught about the local plants, animals and insects. Of course there's much to see in the region's old towns as well. Although some English is spoken, it helps to speak some Italian to get the best out of the experience. Every day there are two menus in the restaurant: one of good-quality vegetarian dishes influenced by *nouvelle cuisine*, the other of traditional Italian country cooking. Food is mainly organic, much of it produced on the estate.
Open spring to autumn. 30 rooms. Room only – from 20,000L; B&B – from 25,000L; three-course meal – about 15,000L. Wine: organic at 6,000L/bottle. No credit cards.

Milano/Milan (Lombardia/Lombardy)

★JOIA *Via P. Castaldi 18, 20124 Milano, tel. (02) 2049244*
Restaurant. 100% vegetarian.

Italy's most imaginative, innovative and accomplished vegetarian restaurant is Milan's Joia. It's probably fitting that it should have appeared in the centre of this fashion-conscious and food-conscious city. The premises are very modern, with a sort of austere elegance: polished wood floors, barely adorned walls, plain black tables. Diners too, tend to be young and smart. Smokers and non-smokers are kept in completely separate rooms (the smaller one is for smokers. Good idea – if smokers want to enjoy this delicious food while sitting in a cloud of fumes, I suppose that's up to them). Owners Nicola Nardi and Pietro Leemann claim to offer 'Alta Cucina Naturale' – Natural Haute Cuisine. Ingredients are best quality, ultra-fresh and organic.

In the evenings, as well as an extensive *carta*, there's a choice of three fixed-price menus: Il Piccolo (four courses for 40,000L), La Tradizione (five courses for 55,000L), and La Scoperta (six courses for 60,000L). From this last, you might find yourself ordering, for example, as a starter, 'foie gras' made of chickpeas and sesame served with a small salad with hazelnut oil. The next course was stuffed artichokes with raspberry vinegar dressing; followed by tagliatelle with cardoons in red wine (cardoons are almost never seen in Britain – they're cousin to the artichoke and a bit like celery); then came a 'fillet' of olives with a sauce of morel mushrooms. A small plate of cheeses followed, and finally a chocolate pudding with orange. All clever, light and delicious.

Lunch menus are conceived rather differently, with dishes listed according to whether they are 'quick and easy', 'pretty as a picture', 'for dieters' (this one tells you exactly how many calories and grams of different fats each dish contains!), and for midday gastronomes, 'for tasting'.

Cheapest menu: 40,000L for four courses. Three courses à la carte: from about 31,000L. Plus 5,000L cover. Wine: from 12,000L/litre; organic from 18,000L/bottle. Mon–Sat 12.30–2.30, 8.30–10.30, closed Sat lunch.

Montelupo Fiorentino (Toscana/Tuscany)

Podere Casanova *50056 Montelupo Fiorentino, Firenze, tel. (0571) 51411*
Self-catering.
Although this is self-catering accommodation, I have decided to include it because the experience of staying here, in this lovely Tuscan farmhouse on an organic vineyard, is exceptional. The house is a couple of kilometres from the village of Malmantile, near Montelupo Fiorentino, and around 22 km from Florence. It is set in hills of woods and vineyards, and is part of the estate of Tenuta San Vito in Fior di Selva – producers of organic Chianti wine and high quality extra-virgin olive oil. The house is spacious, traditional, with unpretentious taste and style. There are five guest apartments altogether, all of them capable of accommodating four people, and having traditional fireplace, fully-equipped kitchen, and bathroom with shower. Outside, there are four terraces from which you can enjoy the peace and the view.
Open all year. Write or phone for current prices (English spoken).

Montespertoli (Toscana/Tuscany)

La Fonte *Via Di Lucignano 15, 50025 Montespertoli, tel. (0571) 609514*
Restaurant. 100% vegetarian.
Open only at weekends, this rural family house is in the country about half-an-hour from Florence. There's no menu – dishes depend on what's available that day – and they cook simple macrobiotic-style vegetarian meals using fresh organic ingredients.
Three-course meal: around 20,000L. Organic wine: 3500L/bottle. Sat and Sun for lunch and dinner.

Montorgiali (Toscana/Tuscany)

Azienda Collefagiano *58050 Montorgiali, Grosseto.*
Farm-guesthouse.
American proprietor: Janet Hansen.
In wild and beautiful hilly country in the far south of Tuscany, Janet Hansen's organic farm is about twenty minutes from Grosseto, in the midst of an important Etruscan area, with many interesting and archaeological sites nearby. Janet has been in Italy for 25 years, and farming here since 1976. The farm produces

artichokes, sheeps' cheeses, and vegetables for canning and sauces. She also gives cookery classes for small groups of six to ten people, either in traditional regional Italian cooking or in health food and vegetarian cooking. There's some simple guest accommodation, and in addition there are plenty of visitors who come just for dinner. The food is broadly on typical Italian lines, and the evening meal is always four courses – starter, main dish with accompanying vegetables, cheese course, and dessert. Wine is included. Much of the food is vegetarian in any case, but where meat appears an alternative is offered. There's no fixed menu, and guests are unlikely to eat the same thing twice even during a long stay. In addition, there's a large barn adapted for yoga, movement, etc, used by instructors who organise their own courses. The place has an informal, friendly atmosphere, and guests are welcome to help on the farm if they like.
Open all year (advance booking only; state dietary preferences when booking). Five rooms. B&B – 25,000L; half-board – 45,000L; full-board – 60,000L; dinner only – 30,000L; light lunch – about 18,000L. Wine: included. No credit cards.

Pinarella (Emilia-Romagna)

HOTEL ANTHONY *Viale Titano 114, 48015 Pinarella di Cervia RA, tel. (0544) 987412*
Hotel-restaurant.
Proprietor: Moretti Giovanni. Some English spoken.
In the midst of the Adriatic beach resort area, the Anthony is a mid-range holiday hotel with a relaxed atmosphere, entertainment, simple traditional meals reasonably prepared with an eye on health considerations, and also a number of health-orientated facilities like massage, physiotherapy, sauna. It's close to the sea front. The hotel has been used for vegetarian conferences, and among its regular dishes are some suitable for vegetarians. These though are mostly along familiar lines, with risotto or pasta main courses. Lunch or dinner could be a starter of *bruschetta* (a chunk of grilled bread with garlic and olive oil), a main course of filled pasta *magra* (ie. meatless), and a dessert of fruit and ice cream.
Open May–Sep. 40 rooms, all with bath/shower. Minimum stay three days. Price: full board – from 50,000L; half-board – 10% reduction; meal only – 15,000–20,000L. Wine: included if on full- or half-board, otherwise from 5,000L/bottle. No credit cards.

Radicondoli (Toscana/Tuscany)

Il Casettino *Loc. Pennanino, Radicondoli, 53030 Siena, tel. (0577) 790672*
Guesthouse. Mainly vegetarian.
English proprietors: Don and Cindy (or Cinzia) Finch.
The Finches used to run a vegetarian guesthouse and cookery school in England (Beechmill, in Cheshire), and have now transferred themselves to the sunnier landscape of Tuscany. They are in the hills near Siena and within easy reach of Florence – two wonderful historic cities well worth a visit for their art and architecture. Il Casettino is an old Tuscan farmhouse, restored to a high standard and furnished with antiques, in about five acres of meadows, woods and olives. They take just a small number of guests, in the 'off-season' rather than in high summer (there's central heating, by the way). The atmosphere is relaxed and family-style. There's a swimming pool, and lots to see and do round about, and the surrounding country is glorious.

A set four-course meal is served each evening, to guests only, and there's a choice between a fish menu or a vegetarian menu. Cooking is along the UK Vegetarian Society's 'Cordon Vert' lines, and makes good use of the fresh local produce. A typical dinner would start with, say, courgette slivers with pine kernels, sultanas and garlic; the next course might be pasta with capers, basil, garlic, mustard and parmesan cheese; the main course follows, and could be risotto

with artichokes and mushroom, together with side dishes like green beans in wine; there is a cheese course; and a dessert of apricots in brandy, with quark. Filling and tasty. No smoking is allowed in the house.

Closed May–Sep (advance booking only). Two twin-bedded rooms. Price: B&B – 25,000L; half-board – 55,000L. Organic wine: from 3,500L/litre.

Rimini (Emilia-Romagna)

Il Grand Hotel Di Rimini and Residenza Grand Hotel *Piazzale Indipendenza, 47037 Rimini, tel. (0541) 56000*

Hotel-restaurant.

Proprietors: Families Arpesella and Annibali. English spoken.

Rimini, on the shore of the Adriatic, was the destination of two great Roman highways, and has been a popular resort ever since. The five-star Grand Hotel (and its four-star Residenza) on the sea front is the richest, most lavish and opulent place in town. In fact, not many other towns in the world have a hotel to match this standard. Built in 1908, from the outside it looks like a wedding cake, while indoors there's a satisfying mixture of the original grandeur coupled with all the most modern developments. Polished marble, superb oriental rugs, huge chandeliers in the public areas, are matched by air conditioning, cable TV and beautiful bathrooms in the rooms. The hotel has, of course, extensive gardens, a big swimming pool, and a large area of beach private to its guests.

Many of the people who stay here are vegetarian, or rather, they are vegetarian in the absence of a kosher menu (for which the Grand was noted until a few years ago). Places to eat and drink at the Grand are diverse, ranging from a snackbar to a beachside dining area to a gala banqueting restaurant. The food on offer is Italian cuisine, but the choice for vegetarians is actually very limited and unimaginative. Meals without meat or fish revolve around salad starters and main courses of pasta or rissotto. There's always something suitable on the menu, but you may have to settle for three courses instead of four. A typical meal started with avocado vinaigrette, main course was spaghetti with courgettes, dessert was fruit *tarte*. Vegetarians can also select from a good buffet lunch, either in the main restaurant or at the Grand's outdoor beachside restaurant L'OMBRELLONE.

Open all year. Main restaurant open 12.30–2.15, 7.30–9.15.

121 rooms at Grand Hotel, 48 at Residenza (all with private bathroom). Price: B&B – 150,000L; half-board – 200,000L; dinner only – three courses à la carte *65,000L; buffet lunch at beach – about 35,000L. Wine: from 18,000L/bottle. All credit cards accepted.*

Roma/Rome (Lazio/Latium)

IL CANESTRO *Via Luca Della Robbia 47, 00153 Roma, tel. (06) 5742800*
Restaurant.
Healthy 'natural' eating is the theme at this interesting city centre restaurant, where almost all the food is fresh and organic and most of it is vegetarian. In fact, non-organic items are indicated on the menus with a little asterisk. An array of set meals is available, with names like Verde (Green), Disintossicante (or 'The Day After'), and Slow Food. They range from two to four courses, and prices are very reasonable. There's also a long and multifarious Carta (ie. giving an *à la carte* choice). You could have, for example, a starter of artichoke hearts *sformati* (puréed and mixed with eggs, milk, and flour, and baked in a mould); a main course of seasoned vegetables with pasta or rice; and a dessert of mousse or cake. There's an extensive list of drinks, too.
Allow around 25,000L for three courses.
Organic wine: 4,000L/half bottle. Mon–Sat 12.30–3.30 (lunch), 7.30–12.30 (dinner).

⋆HOTEL HASSLER-VILLA MEDICI
Piazza Trinità dei Monti 6, 00187 Roma, tel. (06) 6792651
Hotel-restaurant.
Proprietors: Wirth family. English spoken.
Every Sunday one of Rome's grandest hotels, dramatically located at the top of the Spanish Steps, offers a wonderful buffet lunch in the top-floor dining room with a superb city view across the Tiber valley to the Vatican dome. Many of the dishes are without any meat or fish. Go back for more as often as you like. I had a tomato mousse, a multitude of delicious salad and vegetable preparations, a 'poor man's steak' – deep fried slice of aubergine, fried thick slices of onion, and artichoke and cream penne (tubes of pasta). For other meals life's not quite so simple, but the kitchen say they would be ready and willing to provide a completely vegetarian lunch or dinner on request.

Open all year. 107 rooms (all with bath/shower). Room only: from 380,000L single, 520,000L double. Breakfast: 24,000L, Sunday lunch buffet; 86,000L. Other lunch/dinner; allow about 120,000L. Wine: from 25,000L. All credit cards.

Scandinavia

Dialling code from abroad: Finland – 010 358; Norway – 010 47; Sweden – 010 46; Denmark – 010 45.
Currency: Finland – Finmarks, about 7FM to £1; Norway – kroner, about 11.3kr to £1; Sweden – kronor, about 10½ kr to £1; Denmark – kroner, about 11kr to £1.

All the Scandinavian countries are a pleasure to visit. They are cool and wild, with a clean and refreshing feel. Vast areas are densely forested and barely inhabited, but where there are towns and villages the architecture, too, tends to clean, uncluttered, satisfying lines. Some of the coastal regions are magnificently beautiful, an extraordinary interplay of land and water, especially along Norway's west coast, deeply penetrated by lovely cliff-sided fjords.

Much of Scandinavia has long looked for its livelihood towards the sea. Most people in the country districts here eat huge amounts of both fish and meat, and to some extent they have little choice. In the big towns, though, there's plenty of variety, and quite a number of macrobiotics as well as a few vegetarians. However, vegetarian restaurants are scarce indeed, and those worth recommending scarcer still.

While vegetarians are not unknown in Scandinavia, they are often motivated by an ascetic and rigorous preoccupation with health. They generally prefer extremely plain cooking, as indeed do non-vegetarians in this part of the world. Quite current among Scandinavian vegetarians is the raw food diet. Many others stick to Steiner's semi-mystical biodynamic principles of agriculture. Like many Scandinavians they rarely, if ever, drink alcohol, which in any case is usually either not available or absurdly expensive.

Recommended Restaurants

Norway

Bergen

SPISESTEDET KORNELIA *Fosswinckelsgate 18, 5007 Bergen, tel. (05) 32 34 32*
Restaurant. 100% vegetarian.
A single large room decorated in light greens, and with a closed-off smokers' section, Spisestedet Kornelia feels open and bright because of the several windows facing on to the street. It's well known in Norway, and has been established for almost twenty years. The food is not merely vegetarian and organic, but bio-dynamic, and includes salads, omelettes, tasty grains with vegetables, Italian specialities such as lasagne or tagliatelle, and Mexican tostadas. For pudding try their home-made ice cream. In summer you can eat outside in the back garden. Proprietors Anne Kristin and Bjorn Moen have put their ideas and recipes into a bio-dynamic vegetarian cookery book.
Allow 104kr for three-course meal. No alcohol.
Seasonal opening times: Mon–Fri 11–10, Sun 1–6; or Mon–Fri 12–8.30.

Oslo

VEGETA VERTHUS *Munkedamsveien 3b, v/Stortingsgate, tel. (02) 41 29 13*

Restaurant. 100% vegetarian.

Founded in 1938, the Vegeta has long been a beacon of vegetarianism for this part of the world. Close to the National Theatre and the University (at the far end of Oslo's main street, Karl Johans Gate) this warm and relaxed restaurant and café on two floors is a popular meeting point for students and professors. It's spacious and comfortable, with self-service buffet counters. There's a touch of the 'colonial' about the decor – lots of wickerwork, green-stained wood, and overhead fans. Upstairs has white tile floors and tables covered with pink cloths. Downstairs is funkier, with bare wooden tables and a noticeboard loaded with information about community activities, T'ai Chi, films, etc. Sometimes a piano player enlivens the atmosphere. The food is good, rich, wholesome classic vegetarian cooking: salads, brown rice with vegetables and beans, well-made savoury pizzas, and hearty desserts.

Buffet: as much as you can eat for about 100kr (inc. drink); or small mixed plate 50kr, large plate 55kr. No alcohol.
Daily 12–10.

Finland

Helsinki

AURINKOTUULI *Lapinlahdenkatu 25, 00140 Helsinki, tel. (90) 6942563*

Restaurant. 100% vegetarian.

A peaceful place near the city centre, this self-service eating house specialises in 'living food' – bean sprouts, wheat shoots, etc – which they have grown themselves. But they do also have simple cooked dishes of good wholesome ingredients. The main course is often a plate with three different dishes on it, for example, lasagne, rice and veg, and salad.

Allow about FM60 for three courses. No alcohol.
Mon–Fri 11–6, Sat 12–4. Closed July.

KASVISRAVINTOLA *Korkeavuorenkatu 3, 00140 Helsinki, tel. (90) 636892 or (90) 179212*
Restaurant. 100% vegetarian.
Ten minutes from the city centre, 500 yards from the sea, this cosy vegetarian-macrobiotic eating place offers simple tasty cooking. Most of the food is organic. There are salads, main courses of say, tofu pie or vegetable gratin with rice, and desserts of pies and cakes.
Allow FM42 to FM56 for a meal. No wine (but planning to offer organic wine soon). Mon–Fri 11–6, Sat–Sun 12–6.

Sweden

Stockholm

GRÖNA LINJEN *Master Samuelsgatan 10, Stockholm.*
Restaurant. 100% vegetarian.
A 50-year-old vegetarian eating place (on the second floor), it was something of a pioneer in this part of the world and is still going strong. In four different rooms, it has a pleasing interesting atmosphere. There's live piano music at lunchtime. You pay a set price to help yourself from a well-prepared buffet of Swedish and international vegetarian food. There are 25 different salads, soup of the day, three hot dishes, home-made bread, and fresh fruit.
65kr for self-service buffet. No wine. Mon–Sat 11–8.

Denmark

Although I have not discovered any restaurants serving exceptionally good vegetarian meals, there are many modest veggie snackbars and cafés, particularly in Copenhagen. These may come and go at fairly short notice. For up to date addresses and ideas, contact Vegetarisk Information, Valborg Alle 34, 2500 Valby, tel. (01) 17 99 11, or local tourist offices. Recommendations welcome.

Spain & Portugal

Dialling code from abroad: Spain – 010 34 (delete initial 9 from Spanish area code). Portugal – 010 351 (delete initial 0 from Portuguese area code).
Currency: Spain – Peseta (pta), about 179 pta to £1; Portugal – Escudos (esc), about 257 esc to £1.

Most of the Spanish interior is unknown territory to tourists. While Spanish Mediterranean coastal areas have thrown up thousands of tall concrete hotels and provide non-stop entertainment catering for millions of holiday visitors, the rest of the country remains largely rural and solidly Spanish in character. The same is true, in miniature, on the Spanish islands, where tourists flock to virtually uninhabited beach areas while inland the real life of the island continues much as always. It's even more the case in Portugal, where some inland regions are astonishingly rustic and old-fashioned, and the sight of a visitor is cause for great curiosity. Needless to say, in such places the only food available follows local tradition.

Both Portugal and Spain depend heavily on fish, and the Spanish are also very fond of hearty meat dishes. Spanish culture is curiously devoid of any concern for animals. Portugal does have some slight tradition of vegetarianism. But now, quite suddenly, there are far more restaurants in both countries offering vegetarian dishes than ever before – and the number is fast increasing. There are even a few entirely vegetarian places, though these sometimes are short-lived. In most Portuguese and Spanish vegetarian restaurants though, the emphasis is either on macrobiotic philosophy or on an austere health regime. Of course, you can find suitable things to eat in other kinds of restaurants too: pizzas and pasta, for example, are common, as well as Spanish dishes like tortillas (omelettes) and gazpacho (chilled soup). But the standard of cooking, whether in vegetarian places or in ordinary restaurants with some meatless option, tends to be undistinguished.

Package Holidays

Cortijo Romero, see *Recommended Accommodation – Mainland Spain* below
Vegetarian Travellers, 60 Crewys Road, London NW2 2AD, tel. (081) 201 9054, see p. 12
Vegi Ventures, 17 Lilian Road, Burnham on Crouch, Essex CM0 8DS, tel. (0621) 784285, see p. 14
World Wine Tours, 4 Dorchester Rd, Drayton St Leonard, Oxfordshire, tel. (0865) 891919, see p. 17

Recommended Accommodation, Holiday Centres and Restaurants

Mainland Spain

Barcelona (Prov Catalunya)

BIOCENTER *c/Pintor Fortuny 25, Barcelona.*
Restaurant. 100% vegetarian.
West of the Ramblas. This simple inexpensive eating place is at the back of a wholefood shop, and open during shopping hours. Good mix of well-prepared Spanish and foreign meatless dishes. There are salads, veggie pies, rice and veg, gazpacho, as well as a big choice of drinks, many of them organic.

GOVINDA *Plaça Via de Madrid 4, Barcelona, tel. (93) 318 7729*
Restaurant. 100% vegetarian.
East of the Ramblas. Describes itself as an Indian restaurant, but waiters are Spanish, there's classical Western music, and many of the dishes are not Indian at all! For example, cabbage leaves stuffed with cheese and nuts, and there are first rate pizzas. During the week there's a set lunch, on Saturday it's *à la carte*.
About 900pta for three courses. No alcohol. Mon–Sat 1–4, 8.30–11.45, closed festivals and national holidays.

Benamocarra (Prov Malaga)

CASA DE TIO PELUZA *c/Malaga, Benamocarra, tel. (05250) 3552*
Guesthouse.
English proprietors: John and Lynda Fagan.
Information in UK from: 56 Greenmoor Link, London N21 2NP.
Just six miles from the Mediterranean, in a magnificent part of Andalucia, here's a picturesque and unspoiled southern village with accommodation in a typical whitewashed old farmhouse (or *cortijo*). There are just a few simple rooms, and guests are taken on a half-board basis. Vegetarians are very welcome, and there's a vegetarian menu. You'll find some imaginative home-cooking, with (for example) starters of carrot soup or onion flan; main dishes like courgettes stuffed with almonds, or 'three-layer' terrine, both served with vegetables; and desserts of lemon meringue or home-made ice-cream. The price includes decent house wine and coffee. If required, John and Lynda organise guided tours to see the (many)

local places of interest, and are happy to collect you from Malaga airport.
Open all year. Three double rooms, two singles.
Half-board £160 per person per week, includes pick up from airport if required. No credit cards.

Granada (Prov Granada)

Oriente Y Occidente *c/La Cruz 2, Granada 18002, tel. (958) 266020*
Restaurant. 100% vegetarian.
Indian cuisine may not be the ideal experience of Spain, but it's good, vegetarian, and inexpensive.

Raices *c/Prof. Albareda 11, Granada 18008, tel. (958) 120103*
Restaurant. 100% vegetarian.
Decent vegetarian food, but a long way from town on the other side of the river Genil. There's a set meal daily.
Allow 650pta for three courses, or 850 on festivals and national holidays. Wine from 390pta/bottle. Jun–Sep – 1.30–4.30, 9–11.30 (closed Sun and Sat pm); rest of year – 1.30–4.30, 8.30–11 (closed Sun pm and Mon).

Madrid (Prov Castile)

El Granero De Lavapies *c/Argumoza 10, Madrid 2812, tel. (91) 467 7611*
Restaurant. 100% vegetarian.
An agreeable quiet restaurant, close to the city centre, devoted to macrobiotic and dairy eating. It's geared to locals, not tourists, so a knowledge of Spanish will be useful. The food's wholemeal and mostly organic. Every day there's a different set menu, with for example, a starter of soup or gazpacho, a main course of whole grains with vegetables and seaweed. Among the dishes we liked was raw chicory leaves filled with cream cheese. A dessert and herb tea are included in the menu price.
Set three-course meal 880pta. Wine from 715pta/bottle, organic (French) from 1400pta/bottle. Sun–Fri 1–4.

Orgiva (Prov Granada)

CORTIJO ROMERO *Aptdo. de Correos 31, Orgiva*
Guesthouse. 100% vegetarian.
Information in UK from 24 Grange Avenue, Chapeltown, Leeds LS7 4EJ, tel. (0532) 374015
Refresh yourself, study yoga, T'ai Chi, or take advantage of several other courses at a magnificent house surrounded by glorious countryside in the foothills of the snow-topped Sierra Nevada mountains. There's only one course at a time, all either a week or two weeks long – you'll need their brochure in order to choose what suits you best. Get together in a convivial atmosphere to enjoy vegetarian meals of locally grown organic produce. The house also has its own swimming pool. Accommodation is in comfortable twin-bedded rooms with private bathrooms.
Open Apr–Oct. Prices for the courses range from £230 to £630, including half-board accommodation. Travel out to Spain can also be arranged for you.

Sevilla/Seville (Prov Sevilla)

JALEA REAL *c/Sor Angela de la Cruz 37, Sevilla*
Restaurant. 100% vegetarian
Interesting and imaginative vegetarian cooking of Spanish and foreign dishes. Good value.

Balearics

Ibiza, Mallorca, Menorca are the popular trio of Balearic islands basking in the Mediterranean off Spain's Costa Blanca. Mallorca, the largest of the three, receives by far the most visitors and has some horribly developed areas, yet still has plenty of uncrowded corners. Menorca is much quieter, and family-orientated. Ibiza, closest to the mainland, has a more racy, youthful appeal.

Felantitx (Mallorca)

TALAYOT CENTRE *78 Ca's Concos, 4A Vuelta, Felantitx, Mallorca. No phone.*
Guesthouse.
English proprietors: Max Born and Sue Saunders.
Information in UK from Joyce West, 14 Orleans Rd, London SE19 3TA, tel. (081) 653 2836

A talayot is a prehistoric Balearic burial mound, so it might seem an improbable name for a place which celebrates life. The Centre, in a little valley on the edge of Ca's Concos village (S.E. Mallorca – 45 minutes' drive from Palma), consists of a 200-year-old stone farmhouse and converted barns in seven acres of land with almond, fig and carob trees. Accommodation is simple. Anyone visiting the island is welcome to enjoy the attractive and peaceful setting, lovely climate, and wholefood macrobiotic cooking, while spiritual/self-discovery groups of up to 30 people are especially encouraged. In addition, windsurfing lessons, bike hire and car hire can be arranged.

Open all year. Accommodation in dormitories or double rooms.
Example prices: B&B from £15 single, £25 couple;
one-week rental of two-bedroom barn (suitable for four adults plus young children), £225; dinner only, £7 per person. No credit cards.

Palma (Mallorca)

RAIXA *c/Zavella 8, tel. 71 17 11*
Restaurant. 100% vegetarian.
One of the most appealing little restaurants in Palma, with a charming atmosphere and good cooking. Dishes are predictable classic vegetarian favourites or more adventurous dishes. Very low prices.
Under 1000ptas (four courses). Mon 1–4 and Fri eves in Jun/Jul.

Mahón (Menorca)

HOTEL DEL ALMIRANTE *(Collingwood House)*
Puerto de Mahón, Carretera de Villacarlos, Mahón,
tel. (971) 36 27 00
Hotel-restaurant.
Proprietor: Francisco Montanari. English spoken.
Everything here has two names! This large and agreeable old country house on the edge of Mahón (or Maó) stands in attractive gardens set back from the main road to Villacarlos (or Es Castell). And the Almirante itself has a surprising alias, Collingwood House, which dates back to the eighteenth century. For this was the private residence of Admiral Lord Collingwood, friend and colleague of Nelson. It became a hotel in 1964, at which time the old building was carefully restored, but a new annexe was added in the grounds. Today, the Almirante has more character than any other hotel on

the island. In the old house, furnishings and decor are in period, and the walls are hung with masses of paintings. Bedrooms are simple, not large, but adequately comfortable, furnished with heavy antiques, and have lovely views – either into the gardens or across Mahón's famous harbour. Downstairs, there's a typical Spanish-style bar under vaulted ceilings (of what were once the stables), and a spacious restaurant – again with harbour views. In the annexe, rooms are more modern in style. The hotel has its own small swimming pool, tennis and games rooms. Luckily, this delightful place – although mainly catering for meat-eaters – has a Menú Vegetariano (which also has a fish section). The vegetarian food is reasonable, Spanish, with a choice of rice, pasta or bean dishes, salads, vegetables in sauce, soups, and of course a wide selection of *tortillas* (alias omelettes).

Open May–Oct (booked up well in advance). 40 rooms, all with own toilet and bath/shower. Prices, per person, per day: full-board (two sharing) from 3450pta; half-board (two sharing) from 2950pta; bed and breakfast (two sharing) from 2000pta.
Meals only: lunch 800pta (3 courses); dinner 1000pta (four courses). Wine: 300–800pta per bottle.

Portugal

Loulé (Algarve)

CASA PRIMAVERA *Cruz da Assumada, 8100 Loulé, tel. (089) 413791*
Farm-Guesthouse. 100% vegetarian.
English proprietors: Roger and Christine Thomas
Just outside the bustling little market town of Loulé, in the inland hills but only half an hour from the Algarve beaches, this is a typical farmhouse with an acre and a half of olives, figs, carob, almond and other trees. The atmosphere is friendly and informal. There's a small swimming pool. Accommodation is in adequately comfortable little bedrooms, and life is simple and rural – there's no TV, and nothing much in the way of 'entertainment': come here to relax and enjoy the Algarve. It's good walking country, and there's riding not far away for those who like it. The food is all vegetarian – vegan on request – and is good home cooking, with tasty main dishes like nut roast with vegetables and vegetable sauce. The starters would usually be soup, with desserts like pears in red wine. Wine and coffee are included. Good breakfast too.
Closed Dec/Jan. Two double rooms with bath (also two caravans for self-catering or B&B). Half-board for two persons: from £300 per week, or £520 per fortnight. Wine included. No credit cards.

The Best in Britain

There are tremendous opportunities for vegetarian holidays of all kinds throughout Britain. From Scottish highlands and northern lakes to the balmy southern coast, from green country lanes to historic city centres, it is possible to find good-quality food and lodging catering for vegetarians, and vegans too. Indeed Britain must be considered the centre of western vegetarianism, and has been so for 150 years (the Vegetarian Society and *The Vegetarian* magazine were founded in 1848). Britain is unique in that the principal reason for people becoming vegetarian is their concern for the welfare and dignity of animals; health is usually a secondary – even a minor – consideration.

No other European country is so well served with restaurants and hotels providing wholefood, organic, and vegetarian meals. Vegetarian restaurants number in thousands, and there are hundreds of guesthouses or hotels of all classes able to offer decent meals without meat or fish. Dozens of ads for accommodation can be seen on the classified pages of every issue of *The Vegetarian* and other magazines. A useful guidebook, *The Vegetarian Good Food Guide* (Consumers Association), lists about 1000 eating places. For Scotland, *The Vegetarian Guide to the Scottish Highlands and Islands* (2 Burnfarm Cotts., Avoch, Rossshire) is ideal for anyone wanting to get well off the beaten track.

For inclusive vegetarian holidays ranging from hiking with accommodation under canvas to B & Bs, to luxury breaks in top hotels, see the recommendations on pages 8–12.

The British and Food

There's nothing the British distrust more in food than that it be fresh and natural. The UK is alone among West European countries

in having historically pursued a food policy dedicated to cheapness instead of quality. Certainly, there have been revolutionary improvements in the last ten years. But despite patriotic protestations to the contrary, it remains true to say that the general standard of British cooking, vegetarian and non-vegetarian alike, is astonishingly low, especially in people's homes. In restaurants the increased sophistication which has resulted from travel to foreign countries expresses itself not in better food but in great complexity of dishes, higher aspirations which are not met, extravagance of table settings, and ridiculous menu descriptions.

In British kitchens there is usually little or no appreciation of the importance of using only fresh, high-quality ingredients, and handling them with delicacy, skill and understanding. The vast majority of British professional caterers are unable to prepare a delicious, digestible meal, no matter how simple. It's hard to know until too late that a restaurant does not deserve a visit. There are certain danger signs, though. Beware particularly of any establishment describing its food as 'fare' (or worse, the pretentiously misspelt, supposedly old-fashioned, 'fayre'), 'traditional', 'pub grub', or any which is immodest enough to pour adjectives like 'superb' or 'gourmet' on its own preparations.

It's no coincidence that in Britain flavourings and colourings are still permitted which have been banned in the USA and in the other European countries. In a succession of crises over foods contaminated with listeria (in cheese), salmonella (eggs) and artificially-created animal diseases like BSE (in bovines), the official British reaction has been to imply that it's the *consumers* who are in the wrong: they have been advised that the correct response is to cut out soft cheeses, or eggs which have not been hard-boiled. Instead, surely, the Government should be passing legislation to permit the prosecution of farmers for retailing produce which is not of saleable quality. Any farmer selling food infected with BSE or salmonella should be liable to imprisonment. On the contrary, farmers selling contaminated food have actually been compensated with taxpayers' money!

It has become a cliché among modern food writers that vegetarian restaurants need to shake off their 'stripped pine and hand-thrown pottery image'. How terribly British and banal seem such preoccupations. There's nothing in the least wrong with hand-thrown pottery or pine tables. The important things are that everything be spotlessly clean, service professional, and above all, that the food be skilfully prepared from high-quality ingredients.

British vegetarian food is inclined to two serious faults: it can be extremely heavy and bland, or, if not bland, tends to the opposite extreme and is over-seasoned. Mediterranean herbs are too liberally and artlessly used. Yet, paradoxically, many of the best meals I have ever eaten have been in Britain. For although the general standard is so poor, there are some outstanding British chefs – and among them a few who are exploring the potential of cooking without animal products.

Because of the exceptionally large number of eating places offering vegetarian meals in Britain, only one hundred have been listed – a personal selection from among the very best. Also recommended are some where the food is perhaps not remarkable, but which are particularly interesting or useful. However, *every* establishment can provide a full vegetarian meal as part of its normal service.

Britain's Top 100
plus 50 other 'also recommended' addresses

Aberystwyth (Dyfed)

Also recommended: TŶ MELINDWR *Hen Goginan, Aberystwyth, Dyfed tel. (097084) 350*
See: MELINDWR HOLIDAY COURSES under Package Holidays, p. 10

Ambleside (Cumbria)

ROTHAY MANOR *Rothay Bridge, tel. (05394) 33605*
Hotel-restaurant.
Proprietors: Nigel and Stephen Nixon.
A fine Regency manor house close to the centre of Ambleside, within minutes of Lake Windermere, the Manor is right in the heart of the Lake District. The house is striking for its first floor verandah with cast iron railings, and there are lovely landscaped gardens. The interior retains many of its original architectural and decorative features. Flowers and blazing fires make the comfortable lounges welcoming. Staff are discreet and correct but friendly. What nicer than a long walk followed by a return to a really superb afternoon tea in such a setting? But don't fill up too much at tea time, since the dinner will deserve plenty of appetite. The cooking combines English with French, quite successfully, though without an excess of delicacy, and vegetarians have their own fixed-price menu on which traditional preferences of the British vegetarian are dealt with skilfully. You can opt for a meal of two, three or five courses. A starter of melon with raspberry sauce was unusual and worked well. A soup followed, and then a hearty main course of brown rice risotto, containing several vegetables and hazelnuts cooked with tamari. There were several other possibilities, such as vegetable crumble, lentil and cheese bake, or herb and nut loaf. The choice is so wide that clearly some of the dishes have emerged from the freezer – but our dinner was good and tasty for all that. Desserts

included moka roulade and Normandy apple tart, both enjoyable, with a cheese selection in excellent condition. At lunchtimes, except Sunday, there's a splendid buffet lunch, on which most dishes are suitable. There are good drinkable table wines at modest prices and plenty of half bottles.

The house was comfortable, with well-furnished bedrooms. Children are made very welcome. There are inclusive prices for weekend breaks. Winter is passed with a succession of different special courses, for example five days devoted to the music of Schubert, another five days spent studying silver and antiques.

Closed three wks Jan–1 wk Feb. Eighteen rooms,
all with bath/shower. B&B: from £61 for one, £95 for two.
À la carte *buffet lunch: about £8. Dinner: two courses £18,*
three courses £21, five courses £24. Wine from £8/bottle.
Credit cards accepted.

Avebury (Wiltshire)

Also recommended: STONES *High St, tel. (06723) 514*
Café. 100% vegetarian.
Adjacent to the famous stone circle so strangely intruded upon by Avebury village, this is a simple counter service eatery where the food is mainly organic. There were five distinct salads, all carefully made – but served all mixed together on one small plate. Other straightforward, filling dishes, hot or cold, had been standing about for some time and looked their age: nothing was covered to keep it clean and fresh. Food was served in absurdly small plates and bowls. Our cutlery and table were not clean. Yet the cooking was good, and because of the location we were very glad to eat here. To drink there's organic beer from the barrel and organic wine. They should turn the place into a proper restaurant.

About £9 for full meal. Organic wine: from £5.75/bottle.
Spring–autumn: daily 10–6 (hot food 12–2.30); winter:
weekends only (closed Christmas–Feb).

Beaulieu (Hampshire)

MONTAGU ARMS *Palace Lane, Beaulieu, tel. (0590) 612324*
Hotel-restaurant.
Proprietor: John Leach.
In the main street of old Beaulieu, with ponies often standing about outside, this appealing greenery-draped inn has gorgeously com-

fortable bedrooms (several boasting the doubtful benefit of a four-poster bed), lovely gardens, and a pleasant oak-panelled restaurant. It all feels rather too carefully restored and manicured, and there's a certain excess of formality about the place, as if guests are expected to be on their best behaviour. The three-course Gourmet Dinner Menu, as it is called, studiously avoids having any vegetarian main courses, as these are listed on a separate three-course menu headed Vegetarian Selection, from which one gathers that it is certainly not for gourmets. I wonder if the demand for vegetarian dishes would be doubled or tripled if they were listed on the main menu.

Despite these irritations, the food deserves praise. We started with a salad of quail's egg and avocado; as a main course, the gateau of courgettes, leeks, carrots and nuts, served in a cream sauce, was enjoyable, as was the filo pastry filled with spinach and goats' cheese, served with a lemon butter sauce. Satisfying desserts from the trolley, plus coffee and petits fours. Good quality wines.
All year. 24 rooms, all with bath/shower. Restaurant open daily 7.30–9.30pm. B&B: from £68 for one, £96 for two.
Half-board: £119 for two. Dinner only: £21.
Wine from £11/bottle. Credit cards accepted.

Birchover (Derbyshire)

DRUID INN *Main St, Birchover, tel. (0629) 650302*
Pub-restaurant.
The 'main street' address is deceptive. Druid Inn stands in the middle of nowhere, in a wonderful rustic setting of hilly countryside. This is a land of stone walls and stone buildings. The little public house – erstwhile Pub of the Year – is an attractive old place, whose walls are hung with greenery. Inside, the day's menu is closely written on a blackboard with a wide variety of dishes. These are mostly meaty, but with several meat-free dishes. You might find mushroom and hazelnut pâté to start, and a main course of stilton and walnut tagliatelle with a salad, and finish with a local speciality like bakewell pudding.
Allow about £9 for three courses. Wine: from £7/bottle.
Daily 12–2 or 3, 7–9.30.

Birmingham (W. Midlands)

ALBANY HOTEL *Smallbrook, Queensway, tel. (021) 643 8171*
Hotel-restaurant.
Proprietors: Trusthouse Forte.
Vast, extremely comfortable modern hotel geared mainly to business visitors, close to motorways and convenient for the city centre. Masses of facilities. Vegetarians are catered for, rather inappropriately perhaps, in the Carvery Restaurant where there are both *à la carte* choices and a set vegetarian menu which changes every day. Starters can be chosen from the *hors d'oeuvres* buffet, or you could have a soup of, say, chilled cucumber and mint. As a main course you might be offered mushroom and asparagus ravioli in a cream sauce. Desserts from the trolley include enjoyable sorbets.
Open all year. Restaurant closed Sun and Bank Hols. 254 rooms, all with own bath/shower. Room only: from £55, single or double. Breakfast from £6.50. Lunch/Dinner: £12.50. Wine: £9.50/bottle. All credit cards.

CHUNG YING GARDEN *17 Thorp St, tel. (021) 666 6622*
Restaurant.
One of the city's best Chinese restaurants (and there are many in Birmingham), suitably located in the Chinese quarter, has big premises, a big following, and a big choice for vegetarians. Attractive setting and good cooking.
Allow £10. Wine: from £7/bottle. Daily 12–12.

Brighton (Sussex)

FOOD FOR FRIENDS *17a–18 Prince Albert St, The Lanes, tel. (0273) 202310*
Café. 100% vegetarian.
A relaxed, busy, likeable café (plus bakery) in the picturesque Lanes serving enjoyable wholefood breakfast, lunch and dinner in a friendly setting. Much of the food is organic. Menus constantly changing, with typical meals being quiche and salad, pasta and veg, or rice and stir-fried veg, with mixed salads, and followed by good cakes and puds. The menu is divided into easy-to-understand headings: starters, savouries, special (ie. dish of the day), salads, puddings, cakes. Ample portions, nice music, low prices and the day's newspapers to read.
About £5 for three courses. Wine: £4.75/bottle, organic £5.75/bottle. Daily 9am–10pm.

Bristol (Avon)

Bakers *3 Ninetree Hill, Stokes Croft, tel. (0272) 247242*
Restaurant.

Close to the city centre, this much-liked restaurant has three small dining rooms, one on the ground floor and two down below, with lots of mirrors and plants and an Edwardian look. A modestly priced set three-course dinner is offered, always with a suitable starter and main course. Cooking is essentially simple, but accomplished. Mushroom soup was followed by broccoli and cauliflower gratin. On other days you might encounter casseroles, pies, roasts, savoury crumbles. (It was disappointing to see another dish on the menu described as chestnut and red wine pie 'with a suet crust'. Suet adds nothing useful to pastry but makes it inedible for vegetarians.) Desserts included home-made ice cream and a scrumptious bread and butter pud.

£11 for three courses. Wine: £10.50/bottle. Tue–Sat 7–10.30.

Cherries *122 St Michael's Hill, tel. (0272) 293675*
Restaurant. 100% vegetarian.

A friendly, good-humoured place in the University area. It's small, intimate, candlelit, usually filled to capacity. Music playing in the background takes in vintage jazz, swing, and show tunes. A set three-course dinner is offered at a very reasonable price, though you can if preferred order *à la carte*. The menu clearly indicates which dishes are vegan – a lot are. Some of the comment on the menu is perhaps tongue-in-cheek, for example that the garlic bread is 'spoken of world wide'. The food's all well prepared and enjoyable, and combines the predictable with the imaginative. You could start with a pâté of roasted cashews with mint, or garlic mushrooms in a red wine sauce of which the menu boasts 'too much garlic'! Main courses (all served with spiced rice, hot vegetables and salad) include cheese and lentil bake, or nut roast containing fruit and sherry and served with an apple and ginger sauce. For dessert, chocolate mousse with cointreau is rich and delicious, or for something fresh and tasty try a sorbet with fresh fruit salad. The wine list is unusually good for organics. Plenty of other drinks are on offer, including a full range of quality beers, and carafes of refreshing house blends of wine, water, juices and herbs. Viennese coffee is 75% decaffeinated.

£13 for three courses. Wine from £8.65/litre, £6.55/bottle, organic from £6.95/bottle. Mon–Sat 7–11 (last orders).

MILLWARDS *40 Alfred Pl, Kingsdown, tel. (0272) 245026*
Restaurant. 100% vegetarian.
An informal, friendly candlelit restaurant, with comfortable atmosphere and imaginative vegetarian cooking using organic produce 'whenever possible'. The kitchen's on view to diners. A well-thought-out fixed-price menu of two or three courses is offered, with a limited choice of rich, delicious dishes. Anything suitable for vegans is marked with a V on the menu. You could start with pear, stilton and mint filo served with watercress yoghurt. Or fresh herb roulade filled with cashew nuts and curd cheese, with a tomato coulis. For a main course, spiced aubergines and baby sweetcorn with cous-cous, apricots and almonds is tempting, as is a filo strudel of tofu, ginger, mushrooms, bamboo shoots and water chestnuts. Finish with, for example, a clever terrine of sorbets with mango purée, or a chocolate roulade. Coffee and liqueurs could round off an enjoyable dinner.
£11 for two courses, £14 for three. Wine from £7/bottle, organic from £8/bottle. Tue–Sat 7–10.30.

Broadway (Hereford & Worcester)

★★★**THE LYGON ARMS** *Broadway, Worcestershire, tel. (0386) 852255*
Hotel-restaurant.
Proprietors: Savoy Hotel Group.
Standing grandly in the long High Street of this superbly picturesque (although rather too popular) old Cotswold market village in the midst of lovely countryside is this former coaching inn, now one of Britain's most luxurious country hotels. It's been taking guests since at least 1532. Public areas keep their historic appearance and are full of charm and interest. Bedrooms are supremely comfortable and welcoming, attractively decorated and furnished, while bathrooms are abundantly supplied with big white towels and lovely bathrobes.

The Lygon's smart restaurant in the barrel-vaulted Great Hall is well known: chef Clive Howe trained under Anton Mosimann at the Dorchester, and has continued to develop the light 'modern English' style – generous servings, delicious sauces, traditional puddings, but always with a light, fresh touch. He ardently wishes to see vegetarian cooking become part of mainstream gastronomy, and to that end he offers a delicious four-course set vegetarian menu. We had asparagus in delicate pastry, with a wonderful sauce

of ginger, mint and lime; our main course was delicious freshly-made ravioli filled with vegetables in season, and served with a basil sauce; there was a side dish with a selection of vegetables perfectly prepared – spinach, oyster mushrooms, artichoke, and rösti potatoes; the cheese board was of excellent farm-made British and Irish cheeses served with walnut bread; and finally a plate of different desserts – crême brûlée, ice cream, brandy snap, fresh summer berries. There's a good selection of wines, and with the coffee (decaf. in a cafetière) came some delicious little pastries.
Open all year. 62 rooms, all with bath/shower. Bed and breakfast: £98 for one, £138 for two. Lunch/dinner only: £28 for set four courses. Wine: from £10/bottle, organic from £12.75/bottle. All credit cards.

Brockenhurst (Hampshire)

★LE POUSSIN *behind Brookley Rd, tel. (0590) 23063*
Restaurant.
At the time of writing, the restaurant was being rebuilt behind its original premises, which fronted on to the main street of this delightful New Forest village. Now, the entrance is reached down a side entry. During our visit (to the former premises), this was a stylish and accomplished restaurant specialising in the gastronomy of south-western France. Vegetarians are welcome, and should

announce themselves when booking – the restaurant is fully booked every night so you'll have to reserve ahead in any case. We were offered a five-course set meal, but discovered that we could also eat *à la carte*. We began with 'royal of vegetables', which turned out to be an asparagus soufflé wrapped in leeks. Our main course was feuilleté of mushrooms, resembling a large *vol au vent* stuffed with an interesting selection of mushrooms with a mushroom sauce. This was followed by a selection of French and English cheeses, some unusual, including local varieties. Ambitious desserts were potentially good, but served with sauces which were far too sweet: a terrine of chocolate with orange sauce was based on *marquise au chocolat* but with a syrup almost without any taste of orange. Decaffeinated coffee was then brought to us in a pleasant separate lounge. Service was attentive but discreet, and a good wine list had an unusual leaning to Gascony and the French south-west.
Four courses: £25. Wine from £9/bottle. Tue–Sun 12–2, 7–10, except Sun evening; closed two weeks Jan, one week Jun.

Cardiff (S. Glamorgan)

★QUAYLES *8 Romilly Cres, Canton, tel. (0222) 341264*
Restaurant.
Formerly Gibsons, this smart but informal brasserie-style restaurant offers a surprising menu with a wide range of dishes. It's odd to find 'vegan tortellini with sun-dried tomatoes and olives' right next to 'foie gras and mushroom omelette'. The majority of the cooking is far from vegetarian, yet there is a good selection of suitable dishes, tasty and well-prepared. There's also a full vegetarian menu, on which vegan dishes are marked with a V. Altogether there are eight starters and eleven main courses for veggies. You could start with polenta with wild mushroom ragout, have a main course of aubergine stuffed with caerphilly cheese and walnuts, and finish with white chocolate truffle cake.
About £11 for three courses. Wine: from £8.75/litre.
12–2.30, 7.30–10.30 (closed Sun evening).

Chester (Cheshire)

ABBEY GREEN *2 Abbey Gn, Northgate St, tel. (0244) 313251*
Restaurant. 100% vegetarian (meat dishes are served in a separate restaurant).
Down an inconspicuous turn in the centre of the pleasant walled

city of Chester, Abbey Green is thoroughly congenial, in a lovely house, with a wonderful relaxed and civilised atmosphere, offering style without pretension. Decor seems genuinely pre-War: pink-washed walls, only the lower part papered, tables covered with attractive cloths of mottled colour. Children are made very welcome. There's classical music playing softly. Service is amiable and efficient. And there's an air of real enjoyment among the diners. There are tempting lunch and dinner menus, and decent house wine by the glass (as well as lots of other drinks, notably fruit juices). There are two small dining rooms with just seven and six tables – during my visit, only the 'larger' of them was open.

The food deserves high praise, yet does not fulfil all of its ambitions. I started with stilton and broccoli pâté, which was good, but the chunks of granary bread were not the right accompaniment; the offer of 'salad or baked potato' with all main dishes is unnecessary: what is the point of it? Are such dishes not able to stand on their own? My main course of nut loaf with a very red plum sauce was tasty, moist and crunchy, with discernible nuts. But the side salad was ordinary and unremarkable. There were several rich and filling puds. I had crackle flan – chocolate and cornflake base, topped with fruit and cream: not bad, but not brilliant. Coffee was served in a pleasant little lounge warmed by a glowing coal fire. There are several vegan dishes, and an excellent wine list, with a good selection of organic wines.

About £10 for three courses. Organic wine: from £6.50/bottle.
Mon–Sat 6.30–10.15 (closed Mon dinner; open till 11pm Sats).

Number 14 *14 Lower Bridge St, tel. (0244) 318662*
Restaurant. 100% vegetarian.
In an attractive, white-fronted old building in the city centre not far from the river, the restaurant has bare medieval stone walls and ancient beams across the ceiling. The cooking, using mainly organic ingredients, reaches a high standard. It's interesting, as a comment on British gastronomy, that chef and co-owner Helen Gibbons (the other half of the enterprise is husband David) freely admits that most of her ideas and recipes were gathered on trips abroad. Accordingly, although imaginative, there is nothing madly innovative on the menu, and that's as it should be. You could start with a pâté of stilton, oranges and walnuts, move on to a main course (nine to choose from) of crêpes, filled with chestnut purée, mushrooms, tomatoes and red wine, and covered with cheese sauce; or baked avocado filled with a stuffing of brazil nuts and wine, and topped with cheese. Home-made desserts include chocolate roulade, pecan pie, and profiteroles. Wines are organic.

It would be satisfying to see more simplicity in the approach and far fewer adjectives on the menu, which informs us that dishes are 'wonderful', 'marvellous' and 'superb', sauces 'delicious' and 'fabulous', that 'creations' (ie. a salad) are 'exotic', and even that the avocado is 'tender' (so what else would it be?).
About £12 for three courses. Organic wine from £7/bottle.
Daily 12–2.30, 7–10.30 (except Sun and Mon evenings).

Cockermouth (Cumbria)

⋆**Quince & Medlar** *13 Castlegate, tel. (0900) 823579*
Restaurant. 100% vegetarian.
Next door to the old castle in this Lake District market town you'll discover a smart restaurant in an elegant Georgian town house. Décor is pretty and extremely pleasing. Tables are attractively laid with real linen, flowers and candles. Proprietors since 1988, Colin and Louisa le Voi (formerly of the distinguished Sharrow Bay Hotel) have won many awards for their fine vegetarian cooking. Every day the *à la carte* menu offers a range of imaginative, well-prepared dishes which, while following traditional vegetarian tastes and preoccupations, are always interesting and inviting without setting off on any madcap quest for novelty. There are half a dozen starters, the same number of main courses, and again six desserts to follow, in addition to the cheese course.

You could start with a soup made of carrot, orange and apricot,

or a pâté of mushrooms and hazelnuts. From the main courses we were very happy with a terrine made of lentils and vegetables and a stuffing of parsley, lemon and cheese, and served with a cardamom cream sauce and some hot vegetables on the side; and equally contented with fennel, tomato and avocado bake, wrapped in vine leaves, accompanied by freshly-made noodles and a side salad. Some hearty desserts included excellent home-made ice cream like our brown bread ice cream in an almond basket. The cheeses are a selection of Britain's best. Coffee and chocolate ended a satisfying meal – and at a remarkably reasonable price.
About £14 for three courses. Wine from £5.80
(organic from £7.20). Tue–Sun from 7pm.

Corse Lawn (Gloucestershire)

★CORSE LAWN HOUSE *Corse Lawn, tel. (0452780) 479*
Hotel-restaurant.
Proprietors: Denis and Baba Hine.
Close to the Cotswolds and within easy reach of the Forest of Dean, Corse Lawn is well located for exploring some of the most glorious parts of England. A handsome three-storey sixteenth-century mansion, with newer two-storey wings, standing in flat partly-wooded country, the house is a jewel of style in the midst of an unpolished, rustic scene. There's an oval-shaped ornamental pond in front (it was originally a 'coach wash' into which you could drive and turn a stage and four), with white tables and chairs scattered invitingly beside the water. You cross a cattle grid to reach the front door – sheep wander freely on the quiet B4211 which passes outside. All around there are twelve acres of private grounds. Inside, it's elegant, beautifully furnished and decorated with pale colours and quiet taste. Bedrooms are more lavish in style, and all have an individual character. The atmosphere is smart but relaxed and friendly, and the house is the Hine family home.

Cognac lovers will recognise the proprietor's name, and he is indeed a member of the great Hine family. Wife Baba Hine oversees the cooking, which is, however, largely in the hands of talented chef Tim Earley. Unusually, he offers a full vegetarian menu, with a good choice of starters and main courses. You could begin with a terrine of wild mushrooms, move on to a brochette of mixed vegetables with wild rice and tomato, accompanied by a generous and tasty green salad, and finish with a dessert inspired by the traditional English pud, say a butterscotch sponge with ice cream.

Excellent cheeses are all unpasteurised. Wines, of course, are a strong point, with Denis in charge of this aspect of things. Marvellous breakfasts too. There's swimming, tennis and croquet in the grounds, and plenty to see and do in the area.
All year. Nineteen rooms (all with bath/shower).
B&B: from £72.50 for two, £65 for one. Lunch: £16 for set three courses. Dinner: £23.50 for set three courses.
Wine: from £5/bottle. Restaurant open: 12–2, 7–10.
Credit cards accepted.

Delph (Greater Manchester)

Woody's *5 King St, Delph, Saddleworth, nr Oldham, tel. (0457) 871197*
Restaurant. 100% vegetarian.
Delph is that curious northern mixture of rural and industrial. Despite factory chimneys, and the proximity to Manchester, it retains a village feel. In its quiet, peaceful main street, you'll find this pleasing restaurant behind a fairly scruffy interior. There are some half-dozen tables, rather elegantly laid and candlelit, and Victorian looking décor. Among ambitious vegetarian dishes, quite

successfully executed (and several suitable for vegans), were lettuce and almond soup, followed by cauliflower mornay roulade or parsnip and sweetcorn terrine with sweetcorn sauce, and excellent puds like chocolate mousse gâteau. Decent wines too, available by the glass.
£13 for three courses. Wine from £6.25/bottle.
Tue–Sun 7.30–11 (last orders 10).

Edinburgh

Also recommended: HENDERSONS *94 Hanover St, tel. (031 225 2131)*
Restaurant. 100% vegetarian.
There's live music every evening at this busy, popular wine bar in the basement of a Georgian town house. It's also a buffet-style restaurant with hearty, tasty wholefoods. During the day there's a continuous self-service buffet of soups, salads, filling hot savouries and desserts. There are good fresh breads and cakes from their bakery. A wide range of drinks includes Scottish wine.
About £5.60 for three courses. Wine from £6.70/litre (organic from £7.50/bottle). Mon–Sat 8am–10.45pm.

KALPNA *2–3 St Patrick Sq, tel. (031) 667 9890*
Restaurant. 100% vegetarian.
Kalpna means *imagination*, a lovely name for this amiable, unpretentious Indian eating place. It has chosen the mighty elephant as a logo to symbolise the effects of a meatless diet. Typical Gujarati and some South Indian vegetarian dishes are served, including a generous thali.
Allow £10 for a full meal. Wine: £6.50/bottle.
Mon–Fri 12–2, 5.30–10.30; Sat 5.30–10.30.

KELLY'S *46 West Richmond Str, tel. (031) 668 3847*
Restaurant.
A small and friendly family affair, installed in a former bakery, this is an imaginative restaurant offering lunch and dinner fixed price three-course menus that always include vegetarian dishes. These are rich, savoury and filling, but too heavily weighted towards cheese and cream, with cheese sometimes appearing in both starter and main dish. Good desserts.
£17.50 for three courses. Wine from £7/bottle.
Tue–Sat 12–2, 6.45–9.30 (last orders).

Erpingham (Norfolk)

The Ark *The Street, tel. (0263) 761535*
Restaurant-guesthouse.
Proprietors: Mike and Sheila Kidd.
Just the place to get away from it all, be cossetted and indulged, and eat good vegetarian food. The charming cottage and garden has been likened to a French country auberge. The comparison is apt – good simple accommodation, a straightforward attitude to producing excellent meals using fresh local ingredients, offering a limited choice, generous servings, an intelligent short wine list and charging extremely modest prices. It's a family home and a family business, with Sheila in the kitchen while Mike waits at the tables (in a real French auberge, the rôles would probably be reversed). Of course most diners eat meat, but vegetarians are provided with their own menu. We were offered aubergine terrine with ratatouille to start, a main course of filo pastry with a filling of spicy mushrooms, leeks, feta cheese and nuts. Several desserts were tempting. The fresh orange and mango in a rosemary-scented juice was lovely.
Closed Oct. Three rooms (two with bath/shower).
Half-board: £65. Dinner only: £14. Wine: from £7.35/bottle.
Restaurant open: Wed–Fri 12.30–2, 7–9.30; Tue and Sat evenings only; Sun lunch only. No credit cards.

Evesham (Hereford & Worcester)

Evesham Hotel and Cedar Restaurant *Coopers Lane, tel. (0386) 765566*
Hotel-restaurant.
Proprietor: John Jenkinson.
A little out of the centre of this agreeable town, but close to the river Avon, at four and a half centuries the hotel's the oldest building in the area. From the road, its plain white exterior looks quite unconvincing, but pass into the entrance courtyard – now a car park – and it becomes more appealing. The interior is a rambling complex of comfortable lounges, staircases, corridors. John Jenkinson says he likes things which are 'daft and different', and he is determinedly de-bunking and fun-loving, with a great fondness for children and humour. There's a games chest in the reception hall, and toys in the bedrooms. Decor in the bedrooms is pale, pleasing, but some of the rooms are rather small. Children are charged for half-board at the rate of £2 for every year of their life,

while in the dining room a children's menu is headed with the words 'If you can read this you're probably too old'. The list of desserts is 'Sponsored by local dentist'. The regular menu, too, is somewhat jocular, for example boasting 'limp lettuce' (it isn't) and a final note that 'I hope none of you have a good solicitor'. Continuing in similar vein the 'wine list' is contained in three bulky photo albums (New World, Europe, Non-Europe) with details of wine from *every* wine-producing country in the world – from Algeria to Zimbabwe, via England and Wales – with the exception of just two which he has 'forgotten': France and Germany!

Underneath all this, the hotel is professional and competent. The restaurant is smartly attractive, with white cloths, a big chandelier and a fine bay window looking onto the splendid, ancient cedar (now sadly missing some lower branches) from which it gets its name. On the main menu there are several suitable starters, and on a separate card vegetarian main courses are listed. They include Nut and Watercress Cakes (fried in oil and served on sherry sauce), Cheese Pie (like puff pastry pizza), and Tobasmo Flan (filo pastry filled with sweet potato, tomato, mozzarella cheese, basil, and tomato sauce). The food's good and enjoyable. At lunchtime there's a salad buffet.

Closed Christmas. Forty rooms, all with own bath/shower.
Restaurant open 7.30–9.30, 12.30–2, 7–9.30. B&B: £61 for one, £86 for two. Half-board (minimum two nights);
from £37 per person per night. Buffet lunch: £6.35. Dinner only: about £15 for 3 courses. Wine: from £8/bottle.
Credit cards accepted.

Flitwick (Bedfordshire)

★FLITWICK MANOR *Church Rd, tel. (0525) 712242*
Hotel-restaurant.
Proprietors: Greentime Ltd.

Although out in the country, Flitwick's easily accessible. If you're arriving by train, someone from the hotel will come and collect you from the station. Car drivers will find it just three miles off the M1. Drive up the avenue of mature lime trees to the door of the grand seventeenth- and eighteenth-century manor in fine grounds. Outside there's a kitchen garden enclosed by defensive walls, an ornamental pond, tennis courts and croquet lawns. Inside there's an atmosphere of comfort, civilisation and calm. The entrance hall, with flagstone floor and blazing open fire, gives an excellent first

impression. Decor and colour schemes throughout are tasteful and pleasing. Bedroom furnishings are a little heavy, with rich fabrics, antiques, and canopied four-posters in several rooms. In the dining room the day's menu always includes some suitable starters and at least one main course for vegetarians. For example, begin with nettle soup, move on to a puff-pastry case filled with spinach and goats' cheese, with a lemon butter sauce and a selection of vegetables, and finish with rhubarb soufflé. It's excellent – but expensive. Portions, in the modern fashion, are not large. There's an agreeable element of informality while everything is done perfectly. Very good selection of New World wines.
All year. Fifteen rooms (all with bath/shower).
B&B: from £98 for two. Dinner: £35 for three courses.
Wine: from £13.80. Credit cards accepted.

Glasgow (Strathclyde)

BUTTERY *652 Argyll St, tel. (041) 221 8188*
Restaurant.
In a city which has many places serving vegetarian food, but hardly any worth mentioning, the Buttery probably provides the best meatless meals in Glasgow. The location is not one of its charms – a fragment of humanity in a motorway wasteland – but step inside this former Masonic temple to discover a charming and atmospheric old restaurant with friendly service and good food. Vegetarians have their own *à la carte* menu of imaginative dishes, sometimes startlingly so, as with our fruit platter with a thin, sweetish 'pollen dressing'. Main courses included an omelette of avocado and onion in a peanut and parsley sauce, or stir-fried broccoli, cauliflower and pine nuts with noodles. If it's hard to choose between several tempting desserts, try the Buttery Grand Dessert – that's a bit of everything.
About £16 for three courses. Wine from £9/bottle.
Mon–Sat 12–2.30, 7–10.30 (last orders), closed Sat lunchtime.

CAFÉ GANDOLFI *64 Albion St, tel. (041) 552 6813*
Bar-restaurant.
As if a symbol of the new Glasgow, this brasserie feels civilised, looks stylish, and the cooking too is modern, imaginative and accomplished. It's popular from morning till night for snacks, drinks and meals, starting with the breakfast menu, which offers good egg dishes. During the day cooked dishes are light and can be

combined to make a meal of two or more courses or eaten just as a snack. Vegetarians are offered a reasonably good choice. There's a soup of the day which is usually suitable, and gratin dauphinoise is always available. Other dishes include choux pastry filled with cheese, vegetables cooked in 'filo parcels', or quiche, and there's a range of salads. The cheese selection is good, too. Finish with something like chocolate mousse or the lovely caramel shortcake. Plenty of drinks to choose from, with good coffee, above-average house wines and interesting beers.
£9 for full meal. Wine from £7.10/bottle (sometimes organic).
Mon–Sat 9am–11.30pm.

Also recommended: COLONIAL INDIA *25 High St,*
tel. (041) 552 1923
Restaurant.
Until recently this was an old-established and highly-regarded Glasgow restaurant serving traditional British and French fare. It was taken over to become an ambitious Indian restaurant, retaining the name and furnished in British Raj style. It aims to provide the best Indian food in Scotland, and perhaps it will achieve this objective eventually. Starters include some interesting vegetarian possibilities, such as the puris piled with chick peas in a spicy tomato sauce (a bit like pizza). As a main course an assembly of other vegetable dishes include some that didn't live up to expectations, but the mushroom bhaji – lovely button mushroom halves in a tasty sauce – was good.
Allow about £10 for complete meal. Wine from £5.50/bottle.
12–12 daily.

Grasmere (Cumbria)

LANCRIGG COUNTRY HOUSE HOTEL *Easendale Rd,*
tel. (09665) 317
Hotel-restaurant. 100% vegetarian.
Proprietors: Robert and Jane Whittington.
This splendid listed building just a few minutes' drive out of Grasmere stands in its own 27 acres with fine views over Easedale. Once a farm, it became a comfortable country house long enough ago for Wordsworth and his friends to have spent time here. After 1840 it was the home of Sir John Booth-Richardson, the naturalist and Arctic explorer, who was visited here by his friend Charles Darwin. The house today retains much character despite having

been brought thoroughly up to date, and it is still possible to believe, as Richardson did, that the views from the house are among the most beautiful in the world. Bedrooms, interestingly, vary from quite simple to quite luxurious, with a corresponding difference in price. The best are spacious, have antique furnishings, colour television and other little luxuries, and very well-equipped bathrooms (some with, for example, whirlpool baths). Each of these 'superior' rooms has its own personality, and indeed each is named accordingly. Even the least expensive rooms are comfortable, homely, and perhaps truer to the original character of the house. The lounge and dining room have open log fires.

The food is a high point, wholemeal ingredients are the norm and almost everything is organic. How enjoyable it is to be presented with a set no-choice four-course *table d'hôte* menu which is cooked by and for vegetarians. Our starter was a Greek-inspired assembly of marinated vegetables with feta cheese, served with wholewheat toast. Then came a spinach and sesame soup, followed by a main course of stuffed vine leaves with a sauce of tahini and orange, served with roast potatoes and three salads. Among the 'afters' was a good toffee and date pudding. Coffee and mints are included in the price. In the morning there's a big breakfast, including (on request) pancakes, vegetarian kedgeree, and free-range eggs.
All year. Fourteen rooms (twelve with own bath/shower).
Half-board: £33–£70 per person for dinner, bed and breakfast.
Organic wine from £6.50. Credit cards accepted.

Harrogate (N. Yorkshire)

Also recommended: AMADEUS *115 Franklin Rd,*
tel. (0423) 505151
Hotel. 100% vegetarian.
Proprietors: Stephen and Sylvia Barnes.
A likeable little hotel in a three-storey Victorian semi ten minutes' walk from the town centre. There are comfortable bedrooms and lounge, and Sylvia serves a good and well-prepared if sometimes preditable three-course *table d'hôte* on five nights a week. The food's mostly organic. Start, for example, with mushroom and celery pâté, have a main course of walnut and courgette bake, pleasantly spicy, with a tomato sauce and served with brown rice and steamed broccoli, and finish with bananas baked in orange juice and cinnamon, served with homemade brown bread and honey ice cream. This is excellent home cooking, using ingredients

and ideas which vegetarians can understand and enjoy. A pot of coffee or tea afterwards is included. Generous breakfast, though they stop serving it too early.
All year. Five rooms (four with bath/shower).
B&B: £14–£26 per person. Dinner: £11.50 for three courses.
Wine: from £6/bottle. No credit cards.

TIFFINS ON THE STRAY *11a Regent Parade, tel. (0423) 504041*
Restaurant. 100% vegetarian.
Regents' Parade is slightly away from the centre of this attractive spa town of fine stone buildings, and looks across the large green which surrounds Harrogate and is called The Stray. The restaurant, with green and brown decor and rush-mat floor, has a sort of stylish simplicity. Familiar, wholesome, filling vegetarian fare is served. As a starter I had tzatziki with pitta. Among main courses, rice, lentils and nuts are much in evidence. I had lentil loaf with onion gravy and stir-fried vegetables – all nicely done. Hearty afters include toffee pudding, or dried fruit compote with yoghurt. There's a wide choice of teas, juices and milk drinks.
Allow £10 for three courses. No wine (bring your own – no corkage charge). Tue–Sat 10–2, 7–10 (9 in winter on Tue and Wed).

Inverness (Highlands)

Also recommended: DICKENS RESTAURANT
77–79 Church St, tel. (0463) 7131111
Restaurant.
A place in the Highlands with a vaguely Dickensian ambience, run by a Mauritian and with a menu spanning the world, is an oddity to say the least. It sounds like a recipe for disaster, but surprisingly works well. A vegetarian section on the menu includes vegetable curry, fried rice with vegetables, and courgettes provençale. We had a good meal there.
About £10 for three courses. Wine from £6.95/litre.
Mon–Sat 12–2, 5.30–11; Sun 12.30–2.30.

Jersey (Channel Islands)

see St Brelade
see St Saviour

Keltneyburn, Nr Aberfeldy (Tayside)

Also recommended: GARTH CASTLE *Keltneyburn, Nr Aberfeldy, PH15 2LG, Scotland, tel. (08873) 519*
See: Package Holidays, p. 9

Kendal (Cumbria)

MOON *129 Highgate, tel. (0539) 729254*
Restaurant.
A friendly, informal bistro-style eating place in a busy little Lake District tourist town, this popular eating place has good hearty wholefood cooking and a relaxed ambience with rock music playing. Much of the food is organic, grown in their own gardens. Pictures on a moon-y theme decorate the walls. The day's menu is written on a blackboard; it's half veggie, half meat, but soups are always vegetarian. Main courses could be, say, a vegetable lasagne with a sauce of yoghurt, parsnip and cream; or a nut (and mushroom) roast with a basil and tomato sauce; or perhaps asparagus and brie pancakes. Most main courses are served with a side salad. One of the best desserts from a tempting selection is the unashamedly sweet and scrumptious sticky toffee pudding. Lots of good wines, including four interesting organics.
About £10 for three courses. Wine: from £6.60/litre (organic from £6.75/bottle). Sun–Thur 6–10, Fri–Sat 6–10.30.

Kings Lynn (Norfolk)

⋆GARBO'S *7 Saturday Marketplace, tel. (0553) 773136*
Restaurant.
A small, relaxed and informal restaurant in the historic quarter at the centre of the city. The cooking is admirably unpretentious and competent. Ingredients are fresh, high-quality, and usually local. Almost everything is home made, including bread, pasta, and ice-cream. While many of the dishes are for hard-core carnivores, a surprising number are completely free of meat or fish. These are not described as vegetarian and are not on a separate menu, with excellent reason: 'We don't believe in isolating vegetarian customers nor, for that matter, vegetarian dishes. Many customers who sometimes order meat dishes will order meat-free on other occasions.' One of the proprietors (Claire Shaw) is herself vegetarian, so knows exactly what's required. No meat stock, gelatine, or animal

fat (except milk fats) are used in the meat-free dishes. The sort of meal you could enjoy here would be a starter of pressed terrine of leek and asparagus with truffle vinaigrette, followed by an unusual main course of a goats' cheese hollowed out and filled with celery and walnuts, wrapped in filo pastry, and served with a sauce of white wine and grapes. Another good main course was layers of aubergine with tofu, roasted peppers and pine nuts, with a sage butter sauce. The day's desserts are written on a blackboard, and might include, for example, the delicious chocolate marquise with coffee sauce. Vegans welcomed and catered for by arrangement.
Allow about £16 for three courses. Wine: from £7.95/litre.
Tue–Sat 7.30–10.

Kirkby Lonsdale (Cumbria)

⋆LUPTON TOWER *Lupton, tel. (05395) 67400*
Hotel-restaurant. 100% vegetarian.
Proprietors: Dorothy and Graham Smith.
From the A65, a couple of miles off the M6 (junction 36), a private driveway leads to a splendid eighteenth-century country house, with a tower rising from one side and fine grounds all around, with a south-facing garden looking across the fields to Farleton Fell. Inside, it's civilised and comfortable without being particularly grand, and there's a friendly, relaxed home-from-home atmosphere. It's lovely and quiet – there's no television. Log fires make an inviting warmth. Bedrooms are all individually furnished and well-equipped, some of the best being in the tower, with good views. In the small pink-and-white dining room tables are attractive with flowers and linen. Each evening a set four-course vegetarian dinner is served, with little or no choice. Organic wholefoods are used almost exclusively. The cooking and presentation are of a high standard, achieving a light and elegant style, although not to the exclusion of some hearty puddings.

We started with fresh herb tartlets with a sauce of tomato and red pepper, followed by a soup of cauliflower and fennel. The main course was an ingenious and tasty 'terrine verte' – green terrine – made with cabbage and courgettes and served with delicious little new vegetables. A choice is offered at the dessert stage, and we opted for lemon and raspberry roulade. Then came coffee and mints. All excellent and enjoyable, and remarkable value.
Closed Christmas. Six rooms (four with own bath/shower).
B&B: from £14.50 per person. Half-board: from

£29.50 per person. Four-course set dinner only: £15.
Wine: from £6.50/litre, organic from £9.50/bottle. No credit cards.

Ledbury (Hereford & Worcester)

★★HOPE END *Hope End, near Ledbury, tel. (0531) 3613*
Hotel-restaurant.
Proprietors: Patricia and John Hegarty.
Tucked away down a country lane which descends into a hidden corner among the green hills, Hope End is a delightful house enclosed within its courtyard. It also has a wonderful walled garden, and extensive acres of countryside to call its own. Inside the house, you'll find relaxed sophistication and everything of high quality. This used to be the home of Elizabeth Barrett Browning, the poet (and poet's wife). Our room was within the strange oriental tower which rises from one corner – comfortable and private. In the dining room, Mr Hegarty waits at table while Mrs directs affairs in the kitchen. The food is organic, wholemeal, with little fat or salt, and the cooking excellent.

The Hegartys, and their guests, are victims of both the British official attitude to wholesome fresh produce and the Euromadness which would mould us into a 'single market'. First Pat and John were denied the right to give their guests fresh unpasteurised milk from their own herd of goats, then were ordered to stop serving fresh newly laid eggs from their own hens, and now have been told that they may not grow certain uncommercial varieties of fruit and vegetables prohibited by the European Commission.

There's a set, fixed price five-course meal every evening, with a choice of three main courses, one of which is always vegetarian. Strange, therefore, that there is not always a vegetarian starter, although they will happily make (and suggest) something for you. We had a chilled cress soup; courgettes stuffed with chopped nuts, served with a rich sauce (made of prunes and Vouvray!), and excellently prepared vegetables (including unusual ruby chard) from their own garden; a lovely salad of fennel and lettuce with toasted almonds; a cheese selection with good local varieties – single Gloucester, Shropshire Blue, and Pencarrig from across the border. Dessert was a chocolate marble tart, rich but not excessively, with excellent thin pastry. Every course was satisfying and well made, and there's a good wine list too, with a lot of half-bottles. We then retired for coffee in a comfortable and elegant lounge. Altogether, a marvellous experience.

Open Mar–Nov (closed Mon & Tue). Nine rooms, all with bath/shower. Restaurant open daily but is for residents only on Mon and Tue. B&B: £90–£135 for two. Dinner only: £29. Wine: from £6. Credit cards accepted.

Liverpool (Merseyside)

ARMADILLO *Matthew St, tel. (051) 236 4123*
Restaurant.
Matthew Street is the narrow backstreet in which, at the Cavern Club, the Beatles first made their name. It's a raunchy, lively district. The restaurant is at a little meeting of lanes, called Temple Court. The interior is striking with blue, white and yellow nappery and white venetian blinds. It's often fully booked; the food is rich, hearty, and satisfying, and there are always several suitable starters and main courses. As a starter you might have twice-baked cheese and onion soufflé, among main courses there's baked marrow stuffed with nuts, rice, lentils and vegetables. On Saturdays, lunch is served until 5pm, with dinner starting at 7.30pm.
About £17 for three-course dinner, £12 for lunch.
Wine from £7.25/litre. Tue–Fri lunch 12–3, 'early supper' 5–6.30, dinner 7.30–10.30; Sat 12–5, 7.30–10.30.

Also recommended: EVERYMAN BISTRO *9–11 Hope St, tel. (051) 708 9545*
Café.
A very popular, relaxed eating place beneath the Everyman Theatre, the Bistro is open and roomy with big wooden tables. The walls of white-painted brick are decorated with vintage advertising signs. 'The Third Room' is a little smarter, though the food's the same. There are long queues for the counter service, and the food itself includes reasonable snacks and meals: vegetables and pasta in Roquefort sauce, pizzas, quiche, hoummous and bread.
About £5 for a meal. Wine £5.55/bottle. Mon–Sat 12–12.

London

In addition to the restaurants named here, there are scores of less notable establishments, and good vegetarian meals can be also found with ease all over London in many local Indian, Lebanese and Italian restaurants, including the pizza chains.

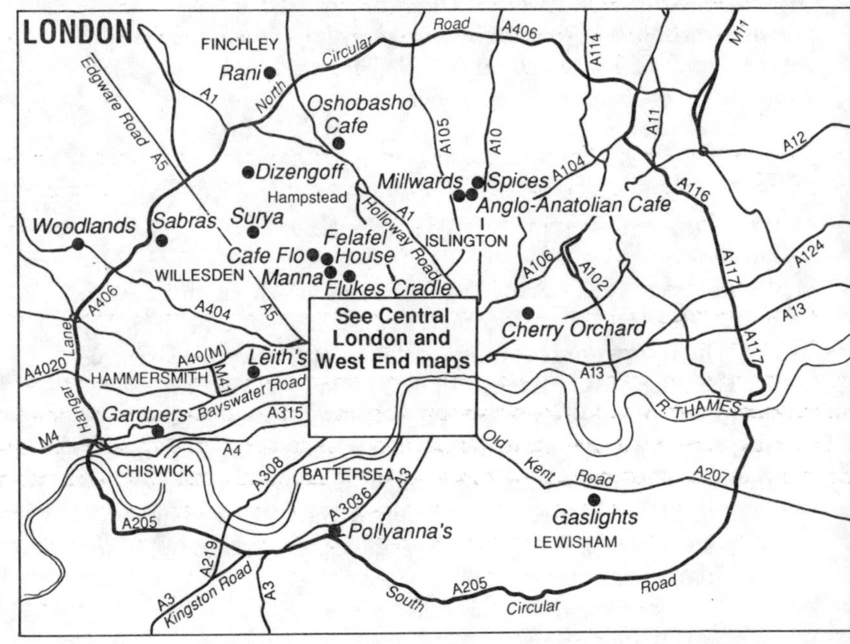

★**Alastair Little** *49 Frith St, W1, tel. (071) 734 5183 Restaurant.*

Highly praised and highly priced, leads the way in the austere new elegance. It's small and simple, with neat blue and white exterior, and plain unadorned interior with uncovered black tables, yet unmistakably luxurious. Alastair Little says some 6% of his clients are completely vegetarian, while around 25% are 'demi-veg'. It's odd, then, that no main course is suitable for vegetarians. However, several starters are free of meat or fish, and it is expected that vegetarians will ask for a starter as a main course. This makes hardly any difference to quantity in any case. The food could hardly be better prepared or more delicious. You could start with borscht, and move on to deep-fried courgette flowers. There's often pasta, and frequently 'pizzettas' – little pizzas. The speciality of the house is wild mushrooms. Other dishes could include: a warm salad of sautéed fresh cèpes; tomato soup with polenta and pesto; grilled

asparagus with machego cheese and lemon oil; or papardelle with wild mushrooms. Most of the produce used is organic, and cheeses are mainly unpasteurised. For dessert, greengage and almond tart with ice cream, dark and white chocolate truffle cake with ginger sauce, or summer pudding and crème fraîche.
About £22 for three courses. Wine: from £10/bottle.
12.30–2.30 Mon–Fri, 7.30–11.30 Mon–Sat.

Also recommended: ANGLO-ANATOLIAN CAFÉ
123 Stoke Newington Church St N16, tel. (071) 923 4349
Café-restaurant. Mainly vegetarian.
This is a budget café-style restaurant (though with waiter service), lent a touch of style by candles on the tables. On the walls hang Anatolian rugs, Anatolian music plays, and the waiters too are Anatolian, managing English only with difficulty. It's like a family front room at times, with children playing. There's a short menu, most of the dishes being suitable. The cooking is really ultra-simple, and not especially distinguished. Starters include cacik (like raita), stuffed vine leaves, imam bayildi (stuffed aubergine). Main courses are along the lines of leeks with rice, or spinach with egg, yoghurt and rice. Baklava for dessert. My coffee was instant because I failed to specify Turkish.
£7 for three courses. No wine. 1pm–11pm every day ('maybe').

CAFÉ FLO *205 Haverstock Hill NW3, tel. (071) 435 6744*
Restaurant.
An agreeable small restaurant with the look of a Parisian brasserie, often with mellow music playing, Flo is next door to the arty Screen on the Hill cinema and nearly opposite the Belsize Park tube station. It's lucky to have a wide pavement in front, with tables and cane chairs temptingly set at some distance from the Haverstock Hill traffic. I nearly didn't include this restaurant because the vegetarian choice is limited to little more than salads and omelettes. But the salads and omelettes are delicious. And there's also a starter of pasta and oyster mushrooms; and a main course of vegetable cous-cous. 'L'Idée Flo' is a set meal of soup of the day (watercress when I called) followed by omelette, chips and salad, with a cup of good strong coffee to finish. A selection of desserts includes Flo's excellent homemade 'cheesecake à l'orange'. Service is relaxed and informal, but efficient. A good wine list has several half-bottles.
About £14 for three courses. Wine: from £7.25/bottle.
10am–11pm daily.

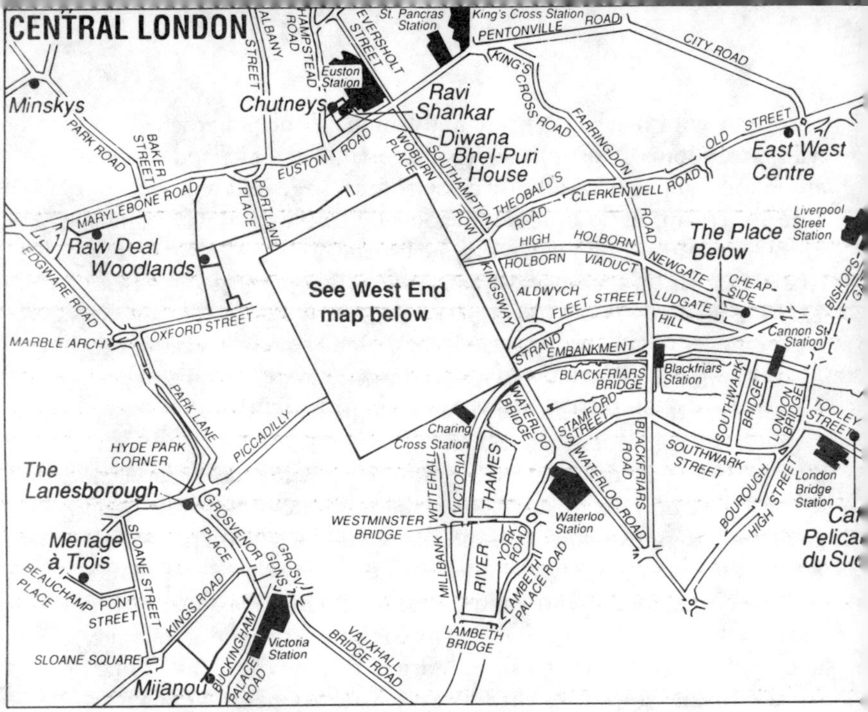

CENTRAL LONDON

Minskys
Raw Deal
Woodlands
Chutneys
Ravi Shankar
Diwana Bhel-Puri House
East West Centre
The Place Below
The Lanesborough
Menage à Trois
Mijanou
Café Pelican du Sud

ALBANY STREET
HAMPSTEAD ROAD
EVERSHOLT STREET
St. Pancras Station
King's Cross Station
PENTONVILLE ROAD
CITY ROAD
Euston Station
KING'S CROSS ROAD
FARRINGDON ROAD
OLD STREET
PARK ROAD
BAKER STREET
EUSTON ROAD
WOBURN PLACE
SOUTHAMPTON ROW
THEOBALD'S ROAD
CLERKENWELL ROAD
Liverpool Street Station
MARYLEBONE ROAD
PLACE
PORTLAND
HIGH HOLBORN
HOLBORN VIADUCT
NEWGATE
CHEAPSIDE
EDGWARE ROAD
KINGSWAY
ALDWYCH
FLEET STREET
LUDGATE HILL
BISHOPSGATE
See West End map below
MARBLE ARCH
OXFORD STREET
STRAND
EMBANKMENT
Cannon St Station
BLACKFRIARS BRIDGE
Blackfriars Station
SOUTHWARK BRIDGE
LONDON BRIDGE
TOOLEY STREET
PARK LANE
PICCADILLY
Charing Cross Station
WATERLOO BRIDGE
STAMFORD STREET
HYDE PARK CORNER
WHITEHALL
VICTORIA
THAMES
WATERLOO ROAD
BLACKFRIARS ROAD
SOUTHWARK STREET
London Bridge Station
BOUROUGH HIGH STREET
GROSVENOR PLACE
WESTMINSTER BRIDGE
Waterloo Station
SLOANE STREET
GROSV. GDNS.
MILLBANK
RIVER
YORK ROAD
LAMBETH PALACE ROAD
BEAUCHAMP PLACE
PONT STREET
KINGS ROAD
BUCKINGHAM PALACE ROAD
Victoria Station
VAUXHALL BRIDGE ROAD
LAMBETH BRIDGE
SLOANE SQUARE

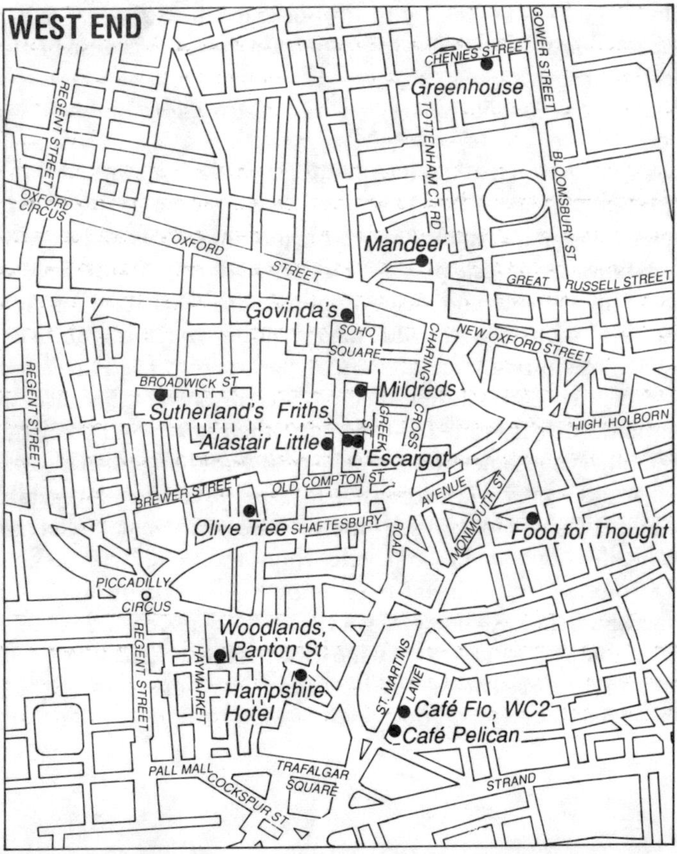

WEST END

Greenhouse
Mandeer
Govinda's
Mildreds
Sutherland's
Friths
Alastair Little
L'Escargot
Olive Tree
Food for Thought
Woodlands, Panton St
Hampshire Hotel
Café Flo, WC2
Café Pelican

CHENIES STREET
GOWER STREET
REGENT STREET
TOTTENHAM CT RD
BLOOMSBURY ST
OXFORD CIRCUS
OXFORD STREET
GREAT RUSSELL STREET
SOHO SQUARE
CHARING CROSS ROAD
NEW OXFORD STREET
BROADWICK ST
GREEK ST
HIGH HOLBORN
OLD COMPTON ST
BREWER STREET
SHAFTESBURY AVENUE
MONMOUTH ST
PICCADILLY CIRCUS
HAYMARKET
ST. MARTINS LANE
PALL MALL
TRAFALGAR SQUARE
COCKSPUR ST
STRAND

Café Flo *51 St Martins Lane WC2, tel. (071) 836 8289*
Bar-restaurant.
The long, narrow premises extending away from a busy street are really very like an urban, bohemian French brasserie, with bar, mirrors, tables not covered, tile floor, the day's papers to read, jazz playing, and posters on the wall. The difference is, of course, that it's within a few paces of Trafalgar Square and all imitation. That's as far as the replica goes, for although the menu is written partly in French, the food is a sort of anglo-franco-italian 'Continental' style. There are good salads, good omelettes, crêpe filled with ricotta and spinach, or canneloni filled with spinach and other veg and served with a tomato sauce. Have a half-carafe of house wine, and finish with a fresh fruit sorbet or white and dark chocolate cake. In the mornings there's a cooked vegetarian breakfast.
About £14 for three courses. Wine: from £7.25/bottle.
Mon–Fri 8.30am–midnight, Sat 10am–midnight, Sun 10am–11pm.

Café Pélican *45 St Martins Lane WC2, tel. (071) 379 0309*
Bar-restaurant.
A marvellous little bit of France, starting with 'Tirez' on the door; waiters, decor and food are thoroughly Gallic. One totally un-French thing, though, about this delightful Parisian-style up-market brasserie, is that it has a Menu Végétarien. This is good most of the time, but there are sometimes lapses, and some dishes are much better than others. The vegetable terrine, in a tomato sauce, is savoury, delicate, prettily served. Yet vegetable au gratin seems to be nothing but a bowl of cooked vegetables in a cheese sauce – bland, rich, uninteresting. Among desserts, one of the best is puff-pastry apple tart with raspberry sauce – freshly baked for every order. Decent wine is available by the glass, and there's a choice of coffees, including decaf. Live music every evening.
About £17 for three courses. Wine from £8/bottle.
Daily 11am–2am (last dinner orders 12.30am).

Café Pélican Du Sud *Hays Galleria, off Tooley St SE1, tel. (071) 378 0097*
Café-restaurant.
Hays Galleria, a charming converted warehouse (or something!) fronting on to the Thames' south bank riverside walk, is one of the more attractive structures in the bleak, tacky and lifeless Docklands developments. It has become a light and airy atrium-style arcade of

– needless to say – silly little shops. Café Pélican is the southern sister of the busier and better establishment of the same name in St Martin's Lane. There's a more self-conscious style and less authentic French flavour, yet the food is good, imaginative and well-prepared. There are suitable soups and salads, and a vegetarian section on the menu offers a couple of delicious dishes: poached quails' eggs on vegetables with a Muscadet sauce, or spinach and cheese ravioli with tomato and basil sauce. Nice desserts, good coffee. While you're in the area, cross over to the other side of London Bridge Road to discover the more historic and interesting backstreets of The Borough.
About £17 for three courses. Wine from £8/bottle.
Mon–Fri 10–9.45, Sun 10–6.

CHERRY ORCHARD *241 Globe Rd E2, tel. (081) 980 6678*
Restaurant. 100% vegetarian.
Hardly what you expect to find in the East End, four minutes' walk from Bethnal Green tube station: a vegetarian bistro run by a co-operative of fourteen Buddhist women. The appearance (and the menu) is Zen chic lightened with a touch of Continental flair: flowers, bentwood chairs, candles, stained glass. It's quiet and calm. The food is simple but imaginative, and reaches a good standard. There's masses of vegan choice too (all marked on the menu with a V). Vegans could have a different three-course meal every day. A typical meal could start with black olive and hazelnut pâté, and go on to a main course of 'vegetable and cashew nut plait' (the vegetables and nuts are rolled in filo pastry and served with a sauce of lemon and fresh coriander. There's also a range of salads and side vegetables. Finish with a chocolate-mad dessert like Chocaholic's Dream which includes chocolate ice cream, chocolate sauce, a chocolate wafer and a chocolate flake. Although there's no wine, a wide selection of juices and other drinks is offered, many of them organic. During the day the food is similar, but self-service and cheaper. At the beginning of the evening, from 6.30 to 7.30, a set meal is available for just £2.95.
About £10 for three courses. No wine (bring your own: £1 corkage). Tue–Fri 12–3, 6.30–10.30 (last orders), Sat 12–10.30.

CHUTNEYS *124 Drummond St NW1, tel. (071) 388 0604*
Restaurant. 100% vegetarian
The darkened glass frontage looks a little too stylish for the Asiatic squalor of Drummond Street. Within, the place has a low-budget

elegance, with pale décor and flowers on the tables. Cooking ranges across Southern and Western India, as well as offering a few European dishes. The most complete meals are the Gujarati thali and 'Chutney's de-luxe thali', equivalent to a good three-course meal, with dal, papadom, bhajias, four curries, rice, raita, chapatis, and dessert, and of course chutneys. Another good bet is the daily lunchtime buffet – all you can eat for a single low price.
£5 for full meal; lunchtime buffet £3.95. Wine: from £5.50/bottle. Daily 12–2.45, 6–11.30.

Also recommended: CRANKS *Head office: tel. (071)607 4474*
Restaurant. 100% vegetarian.
A chain of vegetarian wholefood counter-service restaurants scattered over Central London. The food is healthy and reasonably priced, but tends to be heavy, chewy and on the whole, too substantial. Yet for an acceptable vegetarian meal without fuss, Cranks is a useful institution.
About £10 for complete meal. Wine: about £6.50/bottle (not all branches are licensed). Most open Mon–Fri 8–7.

DIWANA BHEL-POORI HOUSE *121 Drummond St NW1, tel. (071) 387 5556*
Café-Restaurant. 100% vegetarian.
Very handy for Euston Station, this simple eating place has been a well-known fixture on the London vegetarian scene for a couple of decades. It's busy most of the day, with queues winding down the street occasionally. Inside there are pine tables and chairs, Indian music, stainless steel cups and jugs on the tables, and good Indian food. Despite the name, the emphasis is firmly on complete meals, and the menu divides clearly into beginning, middle and end (the bhel-poori – a spicy mix of grains, onion, potatoes, plus sweet-and-sour sauce – features as a starter). The Gujarati thali provides a substantial meal of dal, rice, two vegetable curries, one other savoury, breads, pickle, and a dessert.
About £5 for full meal. No wine. Daily 12–12.

DIZENGOFF *118 Golders Green Road NW11, tel. (081) 458 9958*
Restaurant.
One of London's leading Sephardi restaurants (Sephardim are Jews from the southern European and North African tradition; Ashkenazim are Jews from the East European tradition), with walls

decorated with big photos of Dizengoff Street in the heart of Tel Aviv, this is a popular eating place in the middle of Golders Green, one of Europe's major Jewish quarters. Tables, close together, are plain white and uncovered, but the floor is carpeted and the premises are comfortable. Most of the menu is meaty, but there's a good choice of suitable dishes, some of them listed under a 'Vegetarian' heading, while under Hors d'Oeuvres there's a 'vegetarian selection' made up according to what's available. This will stand as a main course on its own: my generous plate had tahina with olive oil and chopped herbs, and several other delicious savoury 'dip'-type cold vegetable preparations made with peppers, aubergines, and tomatoes, together with chopped beetroot, olives, and so on. Eat it with pitta bread. Or you could have excellent more substantial dishes like falafel with mixed chopped salad and pitta bread; blintzes; or vegetarian moussaka. Finish with sweet Middle Eastern desserts or Ashkenazi favourites like lokshen pudding (rather like bread and butter pudding, but made with noodles) or glorious apple strudel. The vegetarian food is in fact vegan – kosher rules dictate that as a meat restaurant, no dairy produce may be used. The coffee is (as in Israel) not brilliant; mint tea is the thing here.

About £11 for three courses. Wine from £10/bottle.
Sun–Thur: 12–12; Fri: 12–3; Sat 9pm–midnight.

Also recommended: EAST WEST CENTRE CAFÉ
188 Old St EC1, tel. (071) 608 0300
Café-restaurant. 100% vegetarian.

188 Old Street is the address of the Community Health Foundation, a Karate Centre, Genesis bookshop ('body, mind, spirit, environment') and Clearspring Natural Grocer. It's a big old building; step inside and straight away you'll catch the scent of incense. Ahead of you there are noticeboards giving details of courses in T'ai Chi, Do-in, yoga, shiatsu, etc. On the right a door leads into the café, a simple attractive counter-service macrobiotic wholefood restaurant. Decor is ultra simple, with plain white walls, polished pine tables and chairs, and bare floorboards. The windows open onto the pavements of Old Street. The staff, mainly volunteers, are pleasant and helpful and dish up salad starters and the main dish of the day. It's all hearty, heavy, filling food. Portion control is evidently determined by plate size – I found it impossible to prevent food falling on to the table from the overloaded dishes. There are some good flavours and ideas, but the cooking is not

brilliant. A typical dish of the day would be brown rice with millet and pintobean pie, carrot and pumpkin purée, greens, red cabbage and kombu. Desserts are similarly chunky: tofu cheesecake, cous-cous cake, or apple crumble.
About £7 for three courses. Wine from £5/bottle. Mon–Fri 11–8.30, Sat–Sun 11–3. Main meals served 12–3 and 5.30–8.

★L'ESCARGOT *48 Greek St W1, tel. (071) 437 2679/6828*
Restaurant.
This smart French restaurant favoured by celebrities is on three floors: 'brasserie' on the ground, and restaurant proper above. Both parts are attractive, with a touch of luxury, the tables bright with white cloths and attended by polite waiters immaculate in white aprons. The windows open on to the cosmopolitan and sometimes squalid heart of Soho. Downstairs is less expensive, and has a more relaxed air, especially in the evenings when there's often live music. Brasserie and Restaurant have separate menus, but the food is equally good in both, and on each of them there are several vegetarian options marked with a 'V'. Oddly enough, the 'V' had been omitted in a couple of cases. Cheese is (too) much used, and there's an excellent cheeseboard. Menus change fairly often, but our starters included an interesting tomato and potato soup, and a cous-cous salad with pine kernels and grapes. Among the main courses was a spinach and ricotta gnocchi baked with baby leeks, with a cheese sauce, or filo pastry filled with vegetables and mozzarella. At lunchtimes there's a useful two-course set lunch finishing with good coffee plus the house signature – chocolate snails. Many New World wines, and house wine by the glass.
About £16 for three courses. Wine: from £8.80/bottle (also Bring-Your-Own possible). 12–3, 6–11.15, Mon–Sat exc Sat lunch.

FALAFEL HOUSE *96 Haverstock Hill NW3, tel. (071) 722 6187*
Restaurant.
If you don't want to go to Golders Green to sample Israeli/Middle Eastern dishes, you could book a table at this small and simple popular eating house in the Belsize Park/Chalk Farm area. Inside, pictures of Middle Eastern scenes hang on white wooden walls; coloured light bulbs hang over the tables, which have red place settings, red napkins, red candles, red roses, even red peppermills. The menu is meaty but includes several suitable possibilities. Start with hoummous and tahina, or 'dips' like Salat Hazlim (aubergine), and enjoy one of the many good salads (Israeli, Lebanese or Greek),

latkes (like a thick pancake made of fried grated potato), boreks (filled pastries), or, of course, falafels (fried balls of savoury chick-pea mix). Desserts include baklava, halva, and 'Turkish Delight'.
£10 for full meal. Wine: from £6/bottle. Tue–Sun 6–11.

FLUKES CRADLE *273–275 Camden High St NW1, tel. (071) 284 4499.*
Bar-restaurant.
You can see without even stepping inside that this bar is not like others. If the music weren't so loud, I could live in this place. Pass the tables on the busy pavement (very close to Camden Lock) and walk into what feels and looks just like someone's sitting room – except that it has a bar along one side. It's relaxed, civilised, there's jazz playing, and real sofas and armchairs to lounge in. Pause here if all you want's a drink or light snack. If you prefer a meal, keep walking beyond the bar-room and you'll reach the restaurant. It has a down-home country-kitchen look, with tile floor, a red wash on the walls, rough uncovered wooden tables, and ordinary kitchen chairs. Service is amiable and unpretentious. And the food, from an amazing menu combining Nigerian, Moroccan, Greek and Turkish ideas, is great, and includes plenty of choice for vegetarians. Among the starters there was dolmades served with tzatziki (ie. stuffed vine leaves served with a tangy lemon-herbs-and-yoghurt mix). As a main course there was Vegetable Tajine (North African style bean casserole) or vegetarian moussaka. Desserts though were British classics like almond and apple crumble. To drink there's real Normandy cider as well as a good little selection of wines.
About £10 for three courses. Wine from £7.50/bottle, organic from £10/bottle. Daily 11–11.

Also recommended: FOOD FOR THOUGHT *31 Neal St WC2, tel. (071) 836 0239*
Café-restaurant. 100% vegetarian.
In Covent Garden, very handy for the Piazza. Cramped, crowded counter-service eating house churning out decent salads, filling hot wholemeal savouries and substantial sweets, all of somewhat variable quality, though on the whole standards are reasonably high. Long established and still with a good helping of its original late-60s atmosphere.
£6 for a meal. No wine (bring your own – no corkage charge). Mon–Sat 12–8, Sun 12–4.30.

★★**Friths** *14 Frith St W1, tel. (071) 439 3370*
Restaurant.
Stark, modern, with dark tables and plain pastel-washed walls, relaxed waiters, and a total lack of pretension, this restaurant has two menus – 'café' (completely vegetarian) and 'restaurant' (one third vegetarian). There's no real distinction between the premises, and there's also a lot of similarity between the two menus, with a strong Italian influence, and a surprising touch of the Orient too. In the 'café', apart from soup (example: courgette, green olive and lemon balm), the other dishes are all about the same price and could be either first or second course. There's a wider choice of starters in the 'restaurant', but in both you could order mozzarella fritters with a sauce of tomatoes and hazelnuts; or spring rolls of spinach, mushrooms and ricotta; or summer vegetables cous-cous. It's also possible to have a 'sampler' of several dishes. Everything was cooked and presented with flair, and it was a reminder – if any were needed – of just how good the food is in Italy. Desserts during my visit revolved around fruit – summer berries, mango, oranges – in tarts, ice creams, and parfaits. Everything is organic 'where possible', including several wines. Plenty of vegan possibilities.
About £25 for three courses. Wine: from £10/bottle, organic (Italian) from £15.50/bottle. Mon–Sat 1–2.30, 7–11 (except Sat lunch).

Gardners *156 Chiswick High Rd W4, tel. (071) 995 1656*
Restaurant.
Attractive intimate premises with pink and grey walls reflected in large mirrors, and tables laid with cream and blue nappery, make an agreeable setting in which to enjoy fine traditional French and English cooking. Quiet music plays and there's a welcoming, civilised atmosphere. You can eat either *à la carte* or from the day's unpretentious menu, written on a blackboard, which always includes a good selection of suitable dishes. Start with, for example, an interesting beetroot mould (shredded beet in vegetarian jelly) served with sour cream; follow with a main course perhaps of vegetable turnover and piquant sauce; and a dessert of 'khoshaf' – that's apricots, prunes, raisins and nuts in rosewater syrup. Most ingredients are organic, all eggs are free-range.
£11 for three-course set meal. Wine: from £7.25/bottle.
Tue–Sat 7.30–11, Sun 12.30–2.30, 7.30–10.30.
Closed Mon except Bank Holidays, following which they close on the Tue instead.

GASLIGHTS *312–314 Lewisham Rd SE13, tel. (081) 852 7978*
Restaurant. 100% vegetarian.
Formerly Veganomics, the change of name represents a change of management. This is still Britain's best vegan restaurant, arguably now better than ever. The new title does convey more of the atmosphere and appearance of premises which retain many fascinating original Victorian fixtures and fittings – including still-functioning gaslamps – dating back over a century, to when this was a village shop. The cooking is ambitious, sometimes successful, sometimes less so, but is probably as *haute* as a totally vegan eatery has ever aspired to be. It suffers at times from being too heavy and over-seasoned. For all that the place is invariably crowded with appreciative diners, especially on Saturday night. There are always five starters, five main dishes and five desserts. The sort of thing you'll be offered is a starter of aubergine and sesame pâté with pitta bread, or nori (seaweed) rolls with shoyu dip; followed by organic courgette lasagne with garlic bread, or butterbean and mushroom casserole with steamed vegetables and potatoes; and finishing with an intriguing maple and ginger cheesecake (made with tofu), or home-made ice-cream flavoured with fresh fruit in season (made with soy milk). Produce used is mainly organic, as are all the wines.
About £13 for three courses. Organic wine from £6.30/bottle.
11–11 Mon–Fri, 10am–11pm Sat–Sun, closed Tue evening.

GOVINDA'S *9 Soho St W1, tel. (071) 437 3662*
Cafe-restaurant. 100% vegetarian
Upstairs there's a Hare Krishna temple while at street level the devotees run a counter-service restaurant offering food cooked to ancient Indian recipes. There's also a strong wholefood bias, plus salads, substantial cakes and puds. In some ways this is the quintessential '60s-style vegetarian restaurant (in those days it was called Healthy, Wealthy and Wise), with wooden floor, stripped pine tables and benches, and Indian prints on the walls. But this is no ordinary veggie caff. For a start the fragrance of spices is exquisite. Secondly, the simple cooking is (on the whole) excellent. Then, the counter staff (mostly Westerners in Indian attire) are delightfully calm and friendly. The prices are heavenly too. It's wise to steer clear of peak hours: there are sometimes long queues at lunchtime, with a bizarre mix of customers ranging from street girls to office girls, shaven-headed Hindu monks to *Telegraph*-reading businessmen. There are 'salads' (with several cooked vegetables) as well as European and Indian hot dishes such as subji, pakora, bean

hotpot, lasagne, or a complete thali. Desserts are mainly cakes or fruits salads. All bread and cakes are freshly made on the premises. Food is served on Indian stainless-steel plates. There's a good range of herb teas, fruit juices and other drinks.
Small lunch for £3, full meal about £8. No wine. Mon–Sat 12–8.

Also recommended: GREENHOUSE *16 Chenies St, W1, tel. (071) 637 8038*
Café-restaurant.
Narrow steps lead through a confined basement 'area' into a dingy underground dining room with well-prepared standard vegetarian and vegan dishes – salads, pizzas, quiches and interesting vegetable bakes. Laid-back staff. Counter service. Go early, as food is cooked fresh for lunchtime and thereafter, as far as I could see, simply kept hot.
About £6 for complete meal. No wine (bring your own – no corkage). Mon–Sat 10–10 (Mon 6–10 women only).

THE HAMPSHIRE HOTEL AND CELEBRITIES RESTAURANT
48 Leicester Sq WC2, tel. (071) 839 9399
Hotel-restaurant.
Proprietors: Edwardian Hotels.
There was for many years a famous vegetarian restaurant on this site, where my parents often used to eat. It closed down in the 1960s, just missing the boom in vegetarianism which took place at the end of that decade. The Hampshire, a handsome edifice of red brick and pale stone, has since appeared here, on the south side of Leicester Square, dominating the squalor and filth of this once likeable heart of the West End. Inside, the hotel makes an unsuccessful attempt to imitate Edwardian style and luxury. Most guests seem to be American – perhaps they don't know what real Edwardian style would look like. Service is irritatingly unprofessional. At least the level of sheer material comfort is high, both in public rooms and bedrooms, as it certainly ought to be for the price.

One bright light is the restaurant, or rather, the cooking. The menu always includes four serious dishes for vegetarians. You can choose, for example, between wild mushroom soup; coconut and cabbage won ton with cherry sauce; welsh rarebit with quails' eggs and a salad dressing with hazelnut oil; and vegetarian lasagne with salad. Lunch is *à la carte*. In the evenings there's a set *prix fixe* dinner of three courses plus coffee and petits fours. This starts with a vegetarian dish – English asparagus with puff pastry and chervil butter sauce, during my visit – and for their main course vegetarians are invited to choose anything from the same *à la carte* selection.

All year. 124 rooms, all with bath/shower. Room only: ranges from £184 for single room to £475 for a suite. Continental breakfast: £10. Lunch/Dinner only: £24 for set three courses. Wine: £10/bottle, £6/half-bottle. Restaurant open: Mon–Sat 7–11, 12.30–2.30; 6–11; Sun 8–10.30, 12.30–2.30, 6–10. Credit cards accepted.

NEW

THE LANESBOROUGH *1 Lanesborough Pl SW1, tel. (071) 259 5599*

Hotel-restaurant.

Proprietors: Rosewood Hotels.

Construction work at this new luxury hotel was still continuing as I completed *The Vegetarian Guide* (December 1991). The building, on the busy junction of Knightsbridge with the Hyde Park Corner roundabout, is a superb cream-painted Regency mansion, imposing and dignified. There will be two restaurants, the formal dining room (12.30–2.30/7–10.30) and more relaxed all-day conservatory (6.30am–12 midnight). The head chef is the celebrated Paul Gayler. At his previous restaurant, Inigo Jones at Floral Street in Covent Garden, Paul Gayler affirmed his interest in vegetarian cooking by producing a magnificent five-course vegetarian set meal, the Menu Potager. The food was delicate, delicious and visually delightful, but I found myself filling-up with bread because portions were so absurdly small. When Inigo Jones closed, members of Gayler's team set up Burts, at Dean Street in Soho. Their menus did not separate vegetarian from non-vegetarian, instead offering a remarkable selection of refined dishes marked as suitable for vegetarians. Sometimes as much as half the menu, in all courses, would be suitable. The food was wonderful, imaginative and skilful; portions were a sensible size. Vegetarian epicures mourned as Burts, too, closed. At the Lanesborough, Paul Gayler again promises complete five-course vegetarian meals of the highest standard. I look forward to sampling them!

Hotel: Open all year, 95 rooms (inc 46 suites) all with own bathroom. Room only: £190–£250 plus VAT. Breakfast: £10.50. All credit cards accepted. Restaurant: table d'hôte lunch about £24, dinner about £43 (includes service).

★★LEITH'S *92 Kensington Park Rd, W11, tel. (071) 229 4481 Restaurant.*

I wish I could give the full three stars to this wonderful establishment, where all diners are offered two menus – one vegetarian and the other 'omnivorous'. This is one of London's most highly reputed eating places, owned by top caterer Prue Leith, who takes a serious interest in vegetarian cuisine. The premises themselves inspire confidence and set the right tone: three handsome houses in a prosperous North Kensington Victorian terrace have been knocked into one to accommodate this elegant establishment in a group of dining rooms. Decor is discreet and calm, with pale walls of neutral colour, a floor which appears to be of grey bricks, and intriguing lighting which creates a low light except at the tables themselves, which are all spotlit. Service is intelligent, attentive, smartly professional, though I was asked just a few too many times if I and 'everything' were all right. The diners were smartly attired too, men in suits and ties, women in expensive dresses. This is a very civilised sort of place.

The set vegetarian menu is printed twice for some reason, once in English and again in French, even though the dishes are not French. Rather, they combine English and Italian ideas. The menu consists of four courses plus tea or coffee. Only two or three courses need be taken if preferred, and you are charged accordingly. Reassuring footnotes state unambiguously that no meat stock or gelatine is used to prepare any dish or sauce on the vegetarian menu, that

much of the produce used is organic and comes from Leith's own farm, and 'if you are vegan, please tell the manager'.

Menus change by the season, and are headed Spring, Summer, etc. At any time of year starters may be taken from the tempting array on the hors d'oeuvres trolley. There are alternatives; during a previous Spring visit, there were first courses of a soup of tomato and fennel with marscapone and herbs, or red pepper mousse with grilled Mediterranean vegetables. But the trolley permits a selection of some five or six different dishes, and really could constitute a meal in itself. During an Autumn visit, my hors d'oeuvres from the trolley included a fabulous beetroot mousse; a slice from a tasty pie filled with a moist mix of chopped leek, olives and onion; a couple of pieces of asparagus, cool, crisp and perfect; and herby balls of rich soft goats' cheese with balls of juicy tomato.

For a main course, 'wild mushroom and polenta cannelloni' turned out to be like a pair of cannelloni-shaped mushroom pies, since the 'cannelloni' was apparently made of the polenta. This 'pie' mix was rather hard, and indeed a little overcooked. It was accompanied by tiny pretty pieces of delicious vegetables and mushrooms in a tasty wine and butter sauce. Next, the cheese trolley appeared, laden with a handsome selection of British cheeses in excellent condition; they were served with crisp sticks of celery. Desserts too may be chosen from a trolley, but there is also the option of a freshly-made hot pudding (there's a longish delay while this is prepared); an apple charlotte had slightly too-tangy apples in a thin light case, on a very appley sauce. Lovely petits fours, brought with the cafetière of coffee (teas or herb teas available), would have made a dessert in themselves. Very good wine list, with a number of half-bottles, and especially interesting for champagnes.
Two courses £23.50, three courses £29.50, four courses £34.50 (includes service, coffee and VAT). Wine: from £13.75/bottle (includes service and VAT). Daily 7.30–11.30 (closed during Notting Hill Carnival and at Christmas).

MANDEER *21 Hanway Pl W1, tel. (071) 323 0660*
Restaurant. 100% vegetarian.
For some twenty years the Mandeer, boasting organic wholefood Indian cooking, has been a noted fixture on London's vegetarian scene, and throughout most of that time has been making the grandest claims for itself, according to which the food is more enjoyable, healthier and more authentically Hindi than any you'll find elsewhere. These assertions are endorsed by faded old letters

and newspaper cuttings, mostly over ten years old, displayed at the entrance.

You'll find it down a narrow back street just by Centre Point, at the junction of Tottenham Court Road and Oxford Street – the location could hardly be more central. Descend from street level into a surprising oriental haven of coolness and quiet. The lighting is incredibly dim, with nothing to see by except little lamps suspended low over the round tables. There's an interesting menu, with several suggested complete meals at modest prices. For example, samosas, followed by paratha with mixed vegetables and beans, and gulab jamun to finish. The dishes are mostly classic, familiar Indian fare based on vegetables, beans, lentils, rice and Indian breads. However there are two or three oddities, such as tofu curry (rather like mattar panir), or the option of brown rice mixed with wheat grains as an alternative to the more conventional white rice. Drinks, too, include unusual offerings, such as organic lager, as well as several organic wines. Pleasant Indian classical music plays.

Set meal from about £5. Wine from about £6/bottle, organic from £7.30/bottle. Mon–Sat 12–3, 5.30–9.45.

MANNA *4 Erskine Rd NW3 tel. (071) 722 8028*
Restaurant. 100% vegetarian.

Manna's claim to be 'the oldest vegetarian restaurant in Europe – probably the world' is quite ridiculous. It was only opened in 1969, so there are several others which are twice or even three times as old. Nonetheless, this warm and relaxed Primrose Hill restaurant is a well-established vegetarian landmark, which in its early days was famous as much for its gargantuan portions as for the tasty, hearty cooking. Portions are now more restrained though still very generous and filling, but much else remains the same, including the vaguely 'communal' atmosphere generated by shared pine tables, and the good vegetarian and vegan classics such as brown rice and veg, nut loaf, and home-baked wholewheat bread. There are now some slightly less predictable dishes too, like bean pâté or feta and almond tart – everything mouthwatering and well made.

Allow £11 for three courses. Wine from £8.60/litre. Daily 6.30–11.

MÉNAGE À TROIS *15 Beauchamp Pl SW3, tel. (071) 589 4252*
Restaurant.

Tucked away among the bistros and boutiques of this smart little Knightsbridge street, an inconspicuous doorway leads down into

an unusual basement restaurant favoured by the rich, the famous, even (so I have been told) members of the royal family. Unusual mainly because of its menu, which specialises in highly-priced snacky little dishes. These are divided into half-a-dozen categories, not counting two headings just for puddings – 'Chocolate Puddings' and 'More Puddings'. Meals have neither a recognisable structure nor any particular number of courses, except for vegetarians, who won't find enough choice to have a full-scale repast here. While this is very far from being a vegetarian restaurant – even the 'Cheese and Eggs' dishes are liberal with salmon, caviar, and foie gras – there are several worthwhile possibilities. There's asparagus-filled ravioli with vegetables and wine sauce. Or the selection of hot pastries with surprising fillings – cheese, raisins and apples; ricotta, lentils and onions; and boursin with spinach. Among the cheeses is roast goats' cheese with an endive salad. The chocolate puddings are famous. There's live music in the evenings.
Allow about £25 for three courses. Wine from £8.
Mon–Sat 11.30–3.30, 6.30–11.30.

⋆MIJANOU *143 Ebury St SW1, tel. (071) 730 4099*
Restaurant.
We had to ring the doorbell to gain admission to the intimate, clubby little dining rooms (smokers upstairs, non-smokers down) of this haven of civilisation and good living in an unappealing street near Victoria. Outside, the traffic rushed by. Within, contented diners sat on comfortable expensive-looking chairs at tables handsomely laid with big glasses, big plates and thick cloths. Lunch and dinner menus both offer a fixed price meal of either two or three courses. Chef-proprietor Sonia Blech is, so I was told, 'particularly mindful of the needs of vegetarians', and although the choice is very limited they are at least willingly catered for. Vegetarian preferences for a balance of ingredients, including grain or nuts to provide a certain amount of substance (but not too much!), have been understood yet perhaps not perfectly mastered, with sometimes a little too much chewing required for complete happiness. But there is always something suitable in each course. Wild mushrooms apparently feature frequently: they were offered on three successive visits. On one occasion we started with a wonderful mousseline of wild mushrooms served with wild rice intriguingly laced with truffle oil and madeira. Texture and taste were both pleasing. Later there were crêpes filled with a fondue of strong-flavoured cheese, on a bed of endive and pecan nuts. Ravioli

stuffed with puréed vegetables and wild mushrooms made an interesting and satisfying main course. Desserts were especially imaginative and enjoyable; for example pancakes stuffed with apple mousse and flamed with Calvados – though you won't want that if you've already had crêpes. Another mouthwatering possibility was an ice cream made with white cheese, cream and wild cherries marinated in kirsch and eau de vie.

Lunch: £17 for two courses, £21 for three. Dinner: £28 for two courses, £34 for three courses. Wine from £11/bottle.
Mon–Fri 12.15–2.15, 7.15–11.

Also recommended: MILDREDS *58 Greek St W1, tel. (071) 494 1634*
Café. Mainly vegetarian.
Right next to Soho Square is this simple fish and vegetarian counter-service café with green formica tables and plain white walls hung with rather odd paintings. The food is good and wholesome, well prepared and surprisingly inexpensive. There are imaginative salads, and main courses along the lines of stir-fried vegetables and cashew nuts with rice. Gorgeous peach and strawberry cheesecake is among the best of several filling puddings.
About £5 for three courses. Wine from £6.50/bottle.
Mon–Sat 12–11.

MILLWARDS *97 Stoke Newington Church St N16, tel. (071) 254 1025*
Restaurant. 100% vegetarian.
A popular and inviting bistro-style restaurant on a corner with big windows on two sides. Inside, there's greenery and a pleasingly casual, relaxed and local atmosphere. Tables are adorned with flowers, candles and white paper tablecloths. The cooking is imaginative and generally (though not invariably) very enjoyable. Nicely prepared vegetables serve as starters, for example mange tout with fresh ginger sauce. Main courses are substantial and well made and some are imaginative: there were Armenian lentil cakes with yoghurt and tomato sauce; buckwheat pancake filled with mushrooms and walnuts and served with a cheese and wine sauce; and some interesting pasta dishes. If you don't know what to order, try Tastie Masie – that's a bit of everything! And if you're vegan, suitable dishes are marked with a V.
About £10 for three courses. Organic wine: from £6.95/bottle.
Mon–Thu 7–10, Fri–Sat 7–11, Sun 12–3, 7–10.30.

MINSKYS *Regents Park Hilton, 18 Lodge Rd NW8, tel. (071) 722 7722 Ext 4064*
Restaurant.
A copy of an old-fashioned New York deli in a plush London hotel, with a chef who used to be the kosher chef of the QEII. It's on the first floor, looking out towards Lord's Cricket Ground. A mixed menu of meat, fish and vegetarian snacks and meals is offered. There are salads or soups, including gazpacho, to start. Main courses include a tasty, spicy ravioli with ricotta filling, or aubergine charlotte filled with pasta. Several snacky side dishes are worth trying, for example potato latkes with apple sauce. A good range of desserts includes apple strudel. For a fixed price you can eat all you like (and go back as often as you want) from the buffets of hot and cold dishes, as well as having a dessert and coffee.
£7.95 for meal from cold buffet, £15.95 if from both buffets. Wine: from £13/bottle. Open 10am–midnight every day for light refreshments and with mealtimes as follows: breakfast – Mon–Sat 7–10, Sun 7.30–10.30; lunch – Mon–Sat 12–2.30, Sun 12.30–2.30, dinner – Sun–Thur 6–10.30, Fri–Sat 6–11.

Also recommended: OLIVE TREE *11 Wardour St W1, tel. (071) 734 0808*
Café-restaurant.
Just south of Shaftesbury Avenue, this small simple restaurant serves a cosmopolitan range of dishes of which a large proportion are Greek and Middle Eastern. These are mainly meat-free, and indeed the menu is divided into two sections, vegetarian and non-vegetarian. On the veggie section you'll find dolmas, falafel in pitta, imam bayeldi, stuffed peppers, and vegetarian moussaka, as well as such Arabic favourites as kushary (rice and lentils with yoghurt). The Balkan-Levantine theme is kept up with the wines too, and you can even order a bottle of Retsina; other wines come by half and quarter litres as well as by the glass. Finish with genuine 'Turkish Delight' or pistachio halva.
About £5 for a meal. Wine: from £6/bottle or £8.25/litre. Mon–Sat 11.30–11.30, Sun 12–10.30.

Also recommended: OSHOBASHO CAFÉ *Highgate Woods, Muswell Hill Rd N10, tel. (081) 444 1505*
Café-restaurant. 100% vegetarian.
This little place actually inside Highgate Woods is a marvellous spot for a snack or meal. It has its own gardens and terrace, with

tables indoors and out. The café is run by Basho (who is English but renamed himself in honour of a seventeenth-century Japanese Zen master); Osho was his Zen teacher, who died recently. The food is simple and wholesome. The regular menu features a selection ranging from a slice of toast to pasta and vegetables in a tomato sauce with parmesan cheese; there are good salads. On the blackboard are the Specials – the cuisine of a different country is represented each week. Nice breakfast too. There's a bright, celebratory air, and both staff and customers seem somewhat blissed out – must be Basho's influence. Or Osho's.
About £5 for complete meal. Wine: from £7/bottle.
8.30am–9pm (Last orders: 8pm. 8.30am–11.30am breakfast only).

Also recommended: THE PLACE BELOW *St Mary-le-Bow, Cheapside EC2, tel. (071) 329 0789*
Restaurant. 100% vegetarian.
In the unlikely setting of a barrel vaulted church crypt in the heart of the City of London. Salads, quiches, and imaginative vegetable bakes, followed by filling puddings. They'll also host a vegetarian 'do' for you – receptions, parties, etc.
Allow £8 for lunch, £16 for dinner. No wine (bring your own).
Mon–Fri 7.30am–3pm, and 6pm–9.30pm on Thu only.

POLLYANNA'S *2 Battersea Rise SW11, tel. (071) 228 0316*
Restaurant.
Pollyanna's is concealed within curtained, purple-fronted premises, a few paces from Clapham Common. There's more sober, stylish decor inside, with cream tablecloths, grey carpet, comfortable seating and well-spaced tables. While the main orientation of the menus is towards meat and fish, there are always decent vegetarian dishes. Sunday lunch is a great feature here, a plentiful and delicious meal served in convivial surroundings. Our lunch started with aubergine and artichoke mousse, followed by leek and mushroom stroganoff, and finishing with a satisfying apple pie and cream. Top quality dessert wines are available by the glass. Pollyanna's also run the wine merchants next door, as well as JUST WILLIAM'S, the wine bar round the corner, where again, there are always vegetarian dishes on the menus.
Sunday lunch £16. Weekly dinner: £21 for two courses, £27 for three courses. Wine from £11/bottle. Mon–Sat 7–12pm, Sun 12–3pm.

RANI *3 Long Lane N1, tel. (081) 349 4386*
Restaurant. 100% vegetarian
A large red frontage just off a busy High Street (Ballards Lane), with red blinds at the windows, is the eye-catching exterior of one of London's best vegetarian Indian eating houses. Inside, the premises are large, and the red woodwork theme is continued. There are red napkins on glass-covered tables, red carpet and the cane-backed chairs have red seats. The walls, though, are white and hung with photos of Indian scenes. Ceiling fans and polished brasswork add to the Indian feel. It's a family affair – the proprietor's wife and mother are in the kitchen while he and other relatives attend to the customers. The menu announces 'No egg, fish, meat or animal fat permitted on the premises.' The cooking is excellent, with an extensive selection of classic Indian dishes at very moderate prices. Most of the food is in fact vegan, with a symbol shown beside items which contain dairy products. Of special interest are a lunchtime thali for £5 (bhajia, dal, curry, two chapatis, plain rice), or a slightly larger version for £8.10 in the evenings (dal, rice, two curries, two chapatis, raita, mango chutney). Every Monday, for £10 you can eat as much as you like from a range of dishes. Finish with traditional Indian sweets or Loseley ice cream. Service is included, and a note mentions that any tips left will go to charity. Apparently that does not deter people from leaving something: Rani have so far passed on over £10,000 in this way, the largest donation being to Save The Children.
Say £9 for a full meal. Wine: from £10/litre (£5/50cl).
Mon–Tue 6–12, Wed–Sun 12.30–3, 6–12 (last orders 10.30).

Also recommended: RAVI SHANKAR *135 Drummond St NW1, tel. (071) 388 6458*
Café-restaurant. 100% vegetarian.
In the Indian quarter adjacent to Euston station, this is essentially a café: smallish premises with plain white walls, dishes displayed behind a glass counter, pine tables and chairs. Drinks are presented in traditional stainless steel tumblers, as in India. There's a big selection of snacks (samosas, bhel poori, etc) as well as good generous thalis all day long. Indian popular music plays in preference to the usual classical. A full thali includes dal, mixed veg, peas and potatoes, rice, pickles, raita, breads, and dessert.
Allow about £5 for full meal. Daily 12–11.

Also recommended: RAW DEAL *65 York St W1, tel. (071) 262 4841*
Café. 100% vegetarian.
One of the great survivors from the 'sixties veggie boom, this agreeable little counter-service café-restaurant draws in a surprising mix of people. It has homely décor, lino floor, polished wooden tables and chairs, and pictures of vegetables on the walls! A selection of well-prepared salads is on offer, properly served on decently-sized plates. A 'small' salad plate consists of five generous helpings. There's a daily soup, and a filling and enjoyable hot savoury – for example, stuffed tomatoes with rice. Finish with cakes, puddings or crème caramel.
About £7 for three courses. No wine. Mon–Sat 12–9.30.

SABRAS *263 Willesden High Rd NW10, tel. (081) 459 0340*
Restaurant. 100% vegetarian.
In the midst of an Indian neighbourhood you'll find these tiny premises, very light and bright, with formica-top tables and a posy of flowers on each. The lengthy menu is interesting and the food delicious. Among the especially inviting dishes are masala dosa with cashews, raisins and coconut. Of several thalis, one, called Laambi Thali, purports to offer a 'well-balanced meal of eight items'. Surprisingly good wine list.
About £9 for full meal. Wine from £5.50/bottle. Tue–Fri 12.30–3, 6–10 (except Mon lunch), Sat–Sun 1–10.

SPICES *30 Stoke Newington Church St N16, tel. (071) 254 0528*
Restaurant. 100% vegetarian.
Behind a distinctive Burgundy-wine exterior this South Indian and Gujarati restaurant offers excellent food in a setting of simple, inexpensive elegance; there are white paper tablecloths, candles, and lots of pictures on the walls. The menu is intelligent and offers several items not much seen here; som-tom (carrots and greens with nuts), ragara pattice (stuffed potato cakes) and malai baigan (aubergines with sour cream and spices), for example. The dosas are good, and are a house speciality. Or choose one of the tempting thalis. The establishment down the road called Spices of India, is nothing to do with the real Spices.
About £7 for full meal. Wine from £5/bottle.
Mon–Fri 12–2.30, 6–12; Sat–Sun 12–12.

Surya *59–61 Fortune Green Rd NW6, tel. (071) 435 7486*
Restaurant. 100% vegetarian
A pleasing little family-run Indian restaurant with uncluttered decor and a touch of style. Indian classical music plays softly in the background. Service is friendly and efficient, with a certain contrast between the staff, some of whom are very anglicised and fluent in English while others are less so. The food is generally quite mild, as if tempered for British tastes, but deliciously good. Each day of the week has its own 'special' starter and main vegetable dish – for example, lotus stems on Saturday.
Allow about £10 for complete meal. Wine from £6/bottle.
Daily 6–10.30, Sun also 12–2.30.

★**Sutherland's** *45 Lexington St W1, tel. (071) 434 3401*
Restaurant.
Although a leading shrine of the new gastronomy, Sutherland's seems to be not so much about taste as style, with an approach to food more cerebral than sensual. The whole place projects an image of deliberate sparseness and simplicity. The exterior resembles a shop-front, painted dark grey, with swirly patterns on the window glass reminiscent of whitewash slapped on by decorators. Indoors, the premises are narrow, almost bare of decoration, with plain pastel-washed walls. The food is expensive, but skilfully prepared, and on all lunch and dinner menus, as well as the *carte*, at least one vegetarian dish is listed in every course. The starter during our visit was a lovely salad of endive, artichoke, fennel, with a tarragon dressing. The main course was a light little feuilleté of wild mushrooms and baby turnips with a chervil and butter sauce, very enjoyable, perfect. To finish, vegetarians have as much choice as the other diners; we opted for marquise of dark chocolate with a vanilla sauce – tasting strongly of both chocolate and vanilla. Excellent wine list, with big New World selection.
£45 for three courses. Wine from £13/bottle.
Mon–Sat 12.15–2.30, 6.15–11.15 (except Sat lunch).

Woodlands *37 Panton St W1, tel. (071) 839 7258*
Restaurant. 100% vegetarian.
Peaceful, calm, tasteful setting in narrow premises just off the Haymarket. Decor is pale and fresh. There's a long and interesting menu. The food, in South Indian style, is light, delicate and delicious, with several satisfying thalis. Good desserts.
About £10 for full meal. Wine from £6.50/bottle. 12–3, 6–11.

Woodlands *77 Marylebone La W1, tel. (071) 486 3862 and 402a High Rd Wembley HA9 6AL, tel. (081) 902 9869*
Restaurant. 100% vegetarian.
Very attractive, stylish decor. Same menu and food to the same high standard as at Panton Street.
About £10 for full meal. Wine from £6.50/bottle. 12–3, 6–11.

Longhorsley, Nr Morpeth (Northumberland)

Linden Hall *Longhorsley, Morpeth, tel. (0670) 516611*
Hotel-restaurant.
Proprietors: Ian and Roy Caller.
Gorgeously comfortable, this is a fine country mansion standing in extensive grounds. It's well placed for daytime visits to Northumberland's superb countryside while enjoying luxurious evenings of relaxation. A magnificent stone staircase rises from the inner hall, there are several opulent public rooms, and bedrooms are supremely comfortable. There are also ample sports and leisure facilities. The food is not really the high point. A pompously-written menu contains an excess of adjectives and irritatingly lists prices in words rather than figures. However, vegetarians are not forgotten, and there are always a couple of vegetarian starters such as avocado and asparagus roulade with mushrooms, and a couple of vegetarian main courses, for example home-made ravioli filled with spinach and (more) mushrooms.
All year. 47 rooms, all with bath/shower. B&B: £110 for two, £89.50 for one. Dinner: £18.15. Wine: from £9.50/bottle. Restaurant open 12–2, 7–9.30. Credit cards accepted.

Lower Beeding, Nr Horsham (W. Sussex)

⋆**South Lodge** *Brighton Rd, tel. (0403) 891711*
Hotel-restaurant.
Proprietors: Laura Hotels.
A most impressive Victorian country house, mimicking some earlier periods, gabled and with greenery clinging to the stone walls, the Lodge stands in a glorious part of rural Sussex. The interior possesses tremendous style and dignity, with some original decor and furnishing, fine fabrics, chandeliers, and a great deal of dark wood panelling. Staff are formal but friendly, and the whole ambience is of cultivated good living. The dining room, again quite formal, looks out over the rolling downs. The cooking is of high

standard, yet unostentatious. Vegetarians have their own menu. It is a model of plain English and accurate description, a perfection of simplicity and common-sense. There are five dishes listed: you may order either three or five of them, at fixed prices. Five may be too much – the cooking is rich with cream, butter, eggs, cheese. A saffron broth, a hearty soup of winter vegetables with thyme, started the meal. A pasta dish followed, thin noodles cooked in cream with tomato and herbs. As a main course there was a baked cheddar cheese soufflé on a mix of globe artichokes and asparagus with butter sauce. Then came the dessert (perhaps 'sweet' in so English a meal and so English a setting) of white chocolate mousse wrapped in chocolate sponge. Finally goats' cheese roulade, rolled in walnuts, with crisp lettuce. Coffee and sweetmeats are included in the menu price.

The Lodge's bedrooms are, in keeping with all the rest, luxurious yet welcoming and relaxed. Leisure pursuits available to guests range from chess to archery, petanque to clay-pigeon shooting. The 90-acre grounds are immaculate and full of rare trees and shrubs.

All year. 39 rooms (all with own bath/shower). Restaurant open: 12–2.30, 7.30–10 (Sun lunch and Fri/Sat dinner finish half an hour later). B&B: from £110 for two. Half-board: £85 per person.
Dinner: three-course – £18, five-course – £25.
Wine from £12/bottle. All credit cards.

Lupton (Cumbria)

See Kirkby Lonsdale

Manchester

Also recommended: CORNERHOUSE *70 Oxford St, tel. (061) 228 7621*
Café. Mainly vegetarian.
At a busy junction not far from the centre of the city, this lively and popular cafeteria on the first floor of an arts complex attracts quite a lot of students from the nearby university. The food is of variable quality, and includes snacks and meals, with vegetable bakes, salads, as well as hoummous and falafels. Above all, it's inexpensive.
About £4 for 3 courses. Wine from £5/bottle. Daily 9.30–8.30

⋆THAT CAFÉ *1031-1033 Stockport Rd, Levenshulme, tel. (061) 432 4672*
Restaurant.
Although Manchester has several vegetarian restaurants, and this is not one of them, nevertheless the food here is among the best vegetarian eating the city can offer. It's a smart, comfortable place with a rather sumptuous pink and green interior, in a rather unlikely setting in one of the most unappealing districts. There's a vegetable soup daily, and among the meat and fish dishes there are always three daily vegetarian dishes (including one vegan). For example, vegetable and chestnut strudel with a tomato sauce (the veg and nuts are finely chopped and stir-fried), or broccoli and nut roast. Among interesting desserts, try the thin slices of orange in whisky syrup, or the light, flour-free passion fruit roulade.
£12 (plus service) for set three-course meal. Wine from £7/bottle.
Tue–Sat 7–10, Sun 12–2.30.

Mary Tavy, Nr Tavistock (Devon)

⋆THE STANNARY *Mary Tavy, Tavistock, tel. (0822) 810 897*
Guesthouse-restaurant. 100% vegetarian.
Proprietors: Michael Cook and Alison Fife.
In the village of Mary Tavy, within Dartmoor National Park, you'll find this partly sixteenth-century, partly Victorian house. Inside there's a comfortable and elegant restaurant serving creative and imaginative food which they describe as 'animal friendly'. High quality and unusual ingredients are used, all eggs are free-range, and almost everything is organic, including the milk. The net result is a very satisfying dining experience.

The Stannary has really set out to cater for the full range of vegetarian diets. On a lengthy menu, every dish is marked with symbols indicating whether it is gluten free, contains small amounts of gluten, could be made without gluten on request, is vegan, could be made in a vegan version on request, contains no yeast, contains a little yeast, could be yeast-free on request. If this sounds complicated, rest assured that the menu could hardly be simpler to read and understand, and the food is excellent. Choosing dishes to suit my own self-indulgent brand of lacto-vegetarianism, I started with truffle pâté (made with black and white truffles, minced vegetables and cream), served with a small salad; had as a main course the Stannary speciality of mushrooms stuffed with pine kernels, cream cheese and garlic, with a blue cheese sauce and a selection of vegetables; and an apricot, honey and sesame fool made with wild apricots and The Stannary's own honey. For a couple of pounds more you can have as much coffee or tea as you like, served with hand-made chocolates. There's an impressive wine list ranging from unpretentious and affordable *vin de pays* right up to a sought-after Meursault (a white Burgundy) at almost £50 a bottle. Many of the wines are organic, including one of the Champagnes, and those which are vegan (no animal products used in processing) are marked as such on the list. There are several half-bottles, and house wine can be had by the glass. There's also a huge range of other drinks such as mead, cordials, juices, aperitifs and spirits, and a whole page of teas and coffees (not only is there a house wine, but a house tea and a house coffee!).

Anyone staying in one of The Stannary's few rooms can enjoy a glorious breakfast either uncooked (fresh fruit, cereals, yoghurt, bread and coffee) or cooked (the choice includes 'nuteree' – rice, nuts and herbs). Before booking, it is perhaps advisable to send for the leaflet which gives an idea of the menu and the rather complicated terms (4% supplement on credit card payments, no children under twelve, no smoking in the bedrooms, etc) which might be important to some would-be guests.

All year. One twin room, two doubles (one en-suite). B&B: £37 for two, £23.50 for one. Dinner: Around £17 for three courses. Wine: organic from £6.80/bottle (except home-made fruit wine, £4.80). Restaurant open from 7pm. Credit cards accepted.

Montacute (Somerset)

MILK HOUSE *17 The Burroughs, Montacute, tel. (0935) 823823*
Restaurant-guesthouse.
Proprietors: W.R. and P.E. Dufton (Bill and Lee).

Housed in a beautiful fifteenth-century stone building in the centre of a National Trust village, this smart 'Natural Food Restaurant' offers excellent food which is low in fat, sugar and salt, and high in fibre. That doesn't mean it's vegetarian, but there are always two starters and two main courses for vegetarians (there are three for meat-eaters and one with fish) on the nightly fixed-price menu. The dishes are classic and familiar, though with a few personal or imaginative touches. You could start with 'five vegetable' soup or a crisp salad, and have a main course of sorrel crêpe filled with mushrooms in a lightly spiced sauced, or dolmades (stuffed vine leaves) baked in a tomato coulis. Desserts are rich and filling, such as baked banana with rum and a crunchy oat topping with smetana or cream. But that's not the end. There is then a course of fine traditional West Country cheeses, followed by fresh fruit, and only then do you retire to the lovely sitting room for coffee or tea and home-made chocolates. There are good wines, several organic.

There are a couple of guestrooms (no children under twelve). Outside, there's a garden which produces much of the vegetables for the kitchen (nearly everything is organic). Opposite stands Montacute House, and all around the area there are other interesting, attractive and historic buildings constructed in the local hamstone.

Two bedrooms, both with own bathroom. B&B: £58 for two people. Dinner: £18.90 for set five-course vegetarian meal. Wine from £6.70/bottle (organic from £7.10/bottle). Restaurant open: Wed–Sat from 7.30, Sun 12.30–2.30. Credit cards accepted.

New Milton (Hampshire)

★★CHEWTON GLEN *Christchurch Rd, New Milton, tel. (0425) 275341*
Hotel-restaurant.
Proprietor: Martin Skan.

A grand Georgian mansion standing in its grounds, discreetly hidden by trees, the Chewton Glen is the very picture of peace and prosperity. Outwardly it is solid, gabled and inviting, red-brick draped in greenery. The interior is opulent in a light, fresh style, with comfortable lounges furnished with antiques and reproduction pieces. It's not so much a country-house hotel as simply a hotel in the country – this is not anyone's house – but a hotel, for all that, of character and elegance. The image it projects of itself, as representing all that's best of the traditional English country house, is also not quite accurate. For it is a little *too* concerned with image. It's like a film set of a country house, appropriate enough since a good many of the guests are in show-biz. They may enjoy not only the hotel's own excellent facilities – golf, tennis, croquet lawn, snooker room, health club, etc – but equally the setting on the edge of a charming seaside village within minutes of the New Forest. Bedrooms, with pale colours, high-quality fabrics and furnishings, could hardly be more agreeable. The rooms are all named after characters in the novels of Captain Marryat, who wrote *Children of The New Forest* here in 1846.

The restaurant (The Marryat Room) offers a standard of cooking in keeping with the general air of luxury, but with an eye very much on lightness and health. The fixed price *table d'hôte* lunch and dinner are strictly for non-vegetarians. But there are always a couple of suitable *à la carte* starters and main courses. Unfortunately all but one of the veggie items were offered at both lunch and dinner, so in effect, for anyone wanting to eat both meals, the choice was actually quite limited and care would have had to be taken when ordering lunch to consider what you would want for dinner. To begin, you could have grilled vegetables in coriander dressing, or a consommé of tomato and fennel, or a leek salad with sun-dried tomatoes and cashews. Main courses for both meals were vegetarian risotto (with wild rice) or an excellent ravioli of goat cheese with lentils served with a warm tomato and parsley vinaigrette. If your appetite is not large, it would allow more choice to have just one of these courses, then move on to the magnificent cheeses from the trolley – the best of English and French varieties, served at peak condition – and one of the exquisite desserts, such as pithivier (pastry filled with almond paste and served with amaretto sauce). The wine list is something special, and wines are served at their ideal temperature.

All year. 58 rooms, all with bath/shower. Room only: £175 (for two people). Continental breakfast: £9. Lunch/dinner: say about £28 for three courses (includes service and VAT).

Wine: from £8.50/bottle lunchtime, £11/bottle dinner.
Restaurant open: 12.30–2, 7.30–9.30. Credit cards accepted.

Newton Poppleford (Devon)

JOLLY'S *The Bank, Newton Poppleford, tel. (0395) 68100*
Guesthouse-restaurant.
Proprietors: John and Lynn Davis.
Along the lines of a *restaurant avec chambres*, this comfortable, cottage-like eating place in a village near the coast offers a varied and interesting vegetarian menu. Sit in the lounge to order, be led into a dining room attractive with wall-hangings. You could enjoy mushrooms in cream and white wine to start, have a main course of brazil nut wellington with red pepper stuffing, and finish with frozen butterscotch mousse. All well-prepared, and portions generous. There are a couple of simple inexpensive bedrooms.
Rooms available Nov–Mar (restaurant all year). Two rooms.
B&B: £12.50 pp. Restaurant: summer – Tue–Sat 12–2, 7–8.30; Mon open evening only; winter – Mon–Sat 7–8.30.
Wine: from £6.15/bottle (organic £7/bottle). Credit cards accepted.

Nottingham (Nottinghamshire)

CAFÉ DES ARTISTES (AND ARTISTES GOURMANDS)
61 Wollaton Rd, Beeston, tel. (0602) 228288
Restaurant.
The café is not a café. It's a very good little French restaurant. The adjoining Artistes Gourmands (reached by walking through the Café) is a smarter place altogether – yet from the vegetarian point of view there's nothing to choose between them. Indeed the food is exactly the same. The *patron* is a Frenchman, from Burgundy. Why does he offer vegetarian food? 'Because there is a demand for it.' (Perhaps that's because Beeston is the University area, just outside Nottingham proper.) Certainly he has made a success of it. I enjoyed an unusual starter of baked avocado with stilton and walnut sauce, served with a poached egg; the main course (one of two possibilities) was tagliatelle with green vegetables: it was rather too creamy, but good; and to finish, a delicious tarte tatin with vanilla ice cream.
For three courses allow £10 for lunch, £15 for dinner.
Wine from £7/bottle. Mon–Sat 12–2, 7–10, except Sat lunch.

Oxford (Oxfordshire)

THE RANDOLPH HOTEL AND SPIRES RESTAURANT
Beaumont St, tel. (0865) 247481
Hotel-restaurant.
Proprietors: Trusthouse Forte.
Oxford is one of Britain's most handsome towns, with the fine architecture of the country's oldest university, and the Randolph is a suitably imposing place to stay or eat while you're here. Certainly its restaurant is said to be popular with Oxford dons (professors). The building, opposite the Ashmolean Museum, has an impressive Gothic grandeur. Inside, it's a smart traditional town-centre hotel, with spacious public rooms. Bedrooms are large and ornately furnished. The stylish restaurant always has several interesting vegetarian dishes. You could start, for example, with ratatouille terrine, have a main course of spring vegetable galette with carrot and coriander sauce, and finish with a dessert of sorbets and fruit in a brandy snap case.
All year. 109 rooms. Cheapest double room: £105.
Restaurant open: 12.30–2.15, 7–10. Table d'Hôte meals: lunch – £16, dinner – £21. Wine: from £10.50/bottle.
Credit cards accepted.

Plaistow (W. Sussex)

CLEMENTS *Rickmans La, tel. (040388) 246*
Restaurant. 100% vegetarian.
A converted pub in a picturesque village on the Sussex/Surrey border, this is now a most delightful vegetarian eating place. Inside it's roomy, classy, pretty. The menus are of a sensible length. For lunch, there's a good choice of *à la carte* dishes. In the evenings, intimate luxurious four-course set dinners (plus aperitif before and pot of decaf with petits fours after) are served at candlelit tables. There's a vegan option in every course, ingredients are almost all organic, smoking is not allowed, and the cooking is first rate. Meals generally begin with raw veg and dips; then follows, for example, watercress soup or falafels with yoghurt and herb dressing; a main course could be cashew *en croûte* with cranberry sauce; desserts could be rhubarb and ginger crumble or chocolate and brandy mousse. One of the most remarkable features of the place is the wine list: over twenty labels, and every one of them organic.
£18.90 for set four-course dinner. Organic wine from £7.25/bottle.
Wed–Sat 12–2, 7–11 (last orders 9.30); Sun 12–2.

Rochester, Nr Otterburn (Northumberland)

Also recommended: REDESDALE ARMS *Rochester, nr Otterburn, tel. (0830) 20668*
Hotel-restaurant.
Proprietor: Hilda P. Wright.
A sturdy 600-year-old coaching inn standing in open country within a National Park, for centuries this was the last hotel in England before travellers reached the Scottish border just twelve miles away. It still has very much the style and friendly informal atmosphere of an inn rather than a modern hotel, even though the bedrooms are equipped with colour television and phones and some have their own bathrooms. Similarly, the food is simple unpretentious home cooking which reaches a good standard. A 'vegetarian menu' – which in fact includes fish! – is available (despite hunting trophies dotted about), and on it you'll find a choice of starters such as deep fried mushroom with garlic dip, or peaches stuffed with cream cheese and walnuts, while main courses include vegetable pie or a casserole of nut, corn and cheese. Wonderful traditional puds, served with custard, number among the desserts (before ordering check which contain suet). This is a good away-from-it-all location yet within easy reach of Hadrian's Wall, Kielder Forest, Kielder Water and the Border towns. There's also a sports centre nearby.
All year. Twelve rooms (four with bath/shower).
B&B: from £16.50 per person. Dinner: about £9 for three courses.
Wine: from £4.25/bottle. Credit cards accepted.

Ryton-On-Dunsmore (W. Midlands)

Also recommended: RYTON GARDENS CAFÉ
National Centre for Organic Gardening, tel. (0203) 303517
Café. 100% vegetarian.
Ryton Gardens is the National Centre for Organic Gardening, and its café is worth a visit if only for the wide range of vegetables used – and of course nearly all of them are organically grown. The cooking is simple, straightforward and healthy. A typical meal might start with soup, have a main course of vegetable bake, and finish with home-made cheesecake. The extensive gardens show the full range of organic cultivation of herbs, vegetables, flowers and trees.
About £7 for three courses. No wine. 9–5 daily.

St Agnes (Cornwall)

Porthvean Hotel and Frins Restaurant *Churchtown, tel. (087255) 2581*
Hotel-restaurant.
Proprietors: Geoff and Frin Robinson.
St Agnes, a former tin-mining centre, is on a marvellous stretch of North Cornwall's impressive coastline with its mighty cliffs and secret coves. There are three beaches close at hand, and superb clifftop walking. This traditional old hotel – it's been in business for over 200 years – in the centre of the village is warm and attractive with stone walls, wooden beams and open log fire. Bedrooms are comfortable and well-equipped. There are two cosy dining rooms, both non-smoking, as well as a relaxing lounge bar to which you can retire for coffee after dinner. The cooking reaches a high standard. The menu, although offering mostly fairly predictable and conventional dishes, uses a V symbol to point out which are suitable for vegetarians, with a VV for vegans. A surprising number of dishes are vegetarian – eight of the starters, while for main courses there's a whole section devoted to Vegetarian Specialities, seven of them during my visit. They range from fairly simple and plain to rich and hearty. You could start with vegetarian pâté, or avocado and mushrooms in a cream and cheese sauce; have a main course of courgette bake with lemon sauce, or two 'Porthvean vol-au-vents' amply filled with vegetables and cheese; and a pudding of 'the hot sponge of the day' or a yoghurt cheesecake (with a muesli base, and sliced banana topping). For a small extra charge, have as much coffee as you want. Children are made very welcome.
Closed mid-Dec–end Jan. Six rooms (five en suite).
B&B: from £49.35 for two, £32.90 for one. Dinner: £13 for three courses. Wine: from £7/bottle. Restaurant open: Mon–Sat – from 7pm (last orders 9pm), Sun – residents' table d'hôte *only (includes vegetarian options). Credit cards accepted.*

St Brelade (Jersey, Channel Islands)

Argilston Guesthouse *Mont Nicolle, St Brelade, tel. (0534) 44027.*
Hotel-restaurant. 100% vegetarian.
Proprietors: Jack and Veronica Hall.
Go up a quiet winding lane to reach this small family-run hotel, a handsome old farmhouse in its gardens, well-known to Jerseyites as

a place for a good inexpensive dinner and live evening entertainment. This varies enormously from jazz to stand-up comics to poetry readings, though there's always music on a Saturday night (it does not go on late). Most illustrious of the regular 'performers' here is Liverpool Poet Roger McGough, a framed poem by whom, written for the Halls' young daughter, hangs in the bar. More than most veggie establishments, the Argilston is about having a good time. Certainly Jack is no ascetic. He drinks, smokes (not in the restaurant) and 'doesn't like places where things aren't allowed'. He says that he doesn't cater for vegetarians, he caters for everybody – but only vegetarian food is provided. 'Most people who come here are not vegetarians', he adds. The Halls are proud of their cooking, which is certainly a cut above the usual veggie standard. Veronica points out that the Argilston has never served an omelette. You can eat the residents' *table d'hôte* menu, or (better) choose from the *à la carte* selection. Either way, it's possible to have a completely different three-course dinner every night for fourteen nights. You eat in the conservatory, overlooking pleasant greenery.

The cooking is imaginative, and some dishes are very satisfying. Others lack finesse and sometimes fall well short of expectations. Among starters, the celeriac mousse in cream and chive sauce was good, though the sauce was too close to being pure cream. As a main course, the charlotte of courgette and carrot with tomato sauce was enjoyable, as was the cashew nut roast with red wine sauce, apple sauce, and roast potatoes. Main courses are accompanied by salad or a selection of cooked vegetables. Desserts – such as banana brûlée, apple crumble or chocolate swiss roll – are sweet and tasty, but cream is again too lavishly used sometimes. After dinner relax in the comfortable lounge with a coffee, or perhaps in the bar.

Children are made very welcome and catered for willingly. Bedrooms are comfortable, well equipped, attractively decorated, with good bathrooms. A cooked breakfast is provided; it caused a double-take when the waitress brought in plates of sausages and eggs, but of course the sausages were vegetarian and the eggs free-range – from the Argilston's own hens.

All year. Eleven rooms (eight with own bath/shower).
B&B: £22.50. Half-board: £28.50. Dinner only: allow £14 for three courses. Wine: from £7.50/bottle.

★★L'HORIZON *St Brelade's Bay, tel. (0534) 43101*
Hotel-restaurant.
Proprietors: Clipper Hotels.
The lengthy white frontage of this smart hotel along the promenade of St Brelade's immense sands is an imposing sight. Certainly for a sybaritic beachside holiday there's hardly a better location in the British Isles. The hotel itself, with grandly furnished public rooms and with staff suitably deferential, struggles to maintain a high standard of dignity, service and style despite guests wandering about in shorts, or even just towels and bathers. Many rooms have a balcony and superb sea view. Bedrooms are not luxurious, just decent and comfortable with properly equipped bathrooms. There are also Day Rooms – almost as good – available to guests who arrive too early or depart too late to occupy their bedrooms. It is bliss indeed to relax over the excellent breakfast as you idly admire the sea, sands, and immense bright sky of morning. Even more magical is a nightcap on the balcony with the moon shining over the sea.

The hotel has several dining areas: the Star Grill is the smartest and most expensive, and is noted for an *à la carte* menu with superb cooking, yet it shares a kitchen and chef with the larger Crystal Room, where there is a fixed-price four-course *table d'hôte* and evening entertainment; the poolside Brasserie is very informal, and offers pizzas, burgers, etc. While the Brasserie does have several

well-prepared vegetarian dishes, including good stir-fried vegetables (but there is nothing suitable on the Children's Menu), more interesting is to sample the choice in the Star or Crystal. Both have excellent vegetarian main courses, but for a complete meal the Star Grill (despite the name) was much easier – and vegetarian dishes were only one-third the price of meat. An interesting, extensive wine list included some grown and produced at Jersey's own vineyards. We started with delicious chilled vichyssoise, chose one main course of herb pancake filled with spinach and nuts with a saffron and cheese sauce, and another of thin strips of pasta with cèpes and morels in cream sauce; both were a great success. There was a big choice of desserts from lovely fresh fruit salad to rich cake. Some were a little oversweet. We retired contentedly to enjoy our coffee and exquisite petits fours on the beachside terrace.
All year. 104 rooms, all with bath/shower. Bed & Breakfast: £65–£85 per person (special offers in winter). Afternoon tea: £4. Table d'hôte *dinner: £21.* À la carte *lunch/dinner: allow £20. Wine: from £8/bottle. All credit cards.*

St Saviour (Jersey, Channel Islands)

★★LONGUEVILLE MANOR *tel. (0534) 25501*
Hotel-restaurant.
Proprietors: Lewis family.
One of the best hotels in the British Isles and a good restaurant too, recipient of numerous awards, and a gorgeous place to come and relax, slow down, and be looked after in the traditional manner. Pass through an unostentatious gateway into the grounds, and drive to the greenery-draped stone and brick manor house standing with splendid dignity surrounded by immaculate grounds. At the back, guests laze in civilised silence around the pool. This is a very adult place, for people who know how to enjoy life without squealing and shouting. Inside the house, although it is opulent with beautiful carpets, polished wood and comfortable furnishings, everything is similarly quietly understated. Bedrooms are large, with fireplaces and dining tables, and all individually furnished and decorated. The greater part of the rambling, fascinating building dates as far back as the thirteenth century.

The old dining room has great character, the walls darkly panelled with sides of chests seized from sixteenth-century Spanish galleons. Here vegetarians will find that for once they are properly treated. It all started just recently when a vegetarian guest com-

plained that she had been offered canapés containing fish; perhaps carnivores will take exception to such finickiness. But the Lewises were horrified by the lapse, and set about ensuring that in future vegetarians would be catered for at the same standard as the other guests. At lunchtime the set meal has something eminently suitable in each course, while in the evening, vegetarians are offered their own set menu. It started with goats' cheese pithivier (ie small light pastry filled with the cheese) and a walnut salad, then came a vegetable and noodle soup with pesto; the main course was a superb mille-feuille with a filling of mushroom and asparagus. Finally dessert from the trolley, coffee and petits fours. There's a wonderful wine list, and with dozens of half-bottles. For such dining pleasure, prices are modest.
All year. 32 rooms, all with bath/shower. Bed & Breakfast: from £68 for one, £104 for two. Half-board: add £21.50 per person per day. Three-course set lunch: £17.50. Four-course set vegetarian dinner: £25. Wine from £7/bottle. All credit cards.

Shepton Mallet (Somerset)

Bowlish House *Wells Rd, tel. (0749) 2022*
Hotel-restaurant.
Proprietors: Bob and Linda Morley.
The agreeable market town of Shepton Mallet is well-placed for West Country sightseeing. It's within half-an-hour of Wells, Bath, Cheddar Gorge and Longleat. On the outskirts of town, Bowlish House is an attractive Georgian mansion with spacious and comfortable public rooms, one of which is a large conservatory leading off the dining room. Bedrooms are comfortable and adequately equipped, while the food reaches a good standard. Surprising, since Linda is the chef and is herself a vegetarian, that so few meat-free dishes are provided. However, there's always something suitable. For example, you may be offered a starter of spinach soufflé with a provençale sauce, a main course of fresh asparagus tips with lemon cream sauce, served in a puff pastry case, and finish with a commendably rich chocolate mousse in a meringue case, served with raspberry coulis.
All year. Four double rooms (all with bath). B&B: £48 per room.
Half-board: £87 for two people, £67.50 for one.
inner only: £19.50 for three-course set vegetarian meal.
Wine: from £6.95/bottle. Restaurant open: 7–9.
Credit cards accepted.

Southampton (Hampshire)

THE TOWN HOUSE *59 Oxford St, tel. (0703) 220498*
Restaurant. 100% vegetarian.
Pink walls, bare floorboards, black bentwood chairs, pink cloths on candlelit tables combine to give simple style to this small restaurant. It's just off the High Street, within the old centre of the city (fragments of the ancient fortifications survive). Service is friendly and efficient. It was good to see on the menu the information that smoking is not permitted. Background music is a little too upbeat and the volume a little too high. The cooking reaches a good standard, with some imaginative dishes.

A starter of avocado and strawberries was unusual but delicious. Another starter was Chinese-style spring roll with a flavoursome sweet-and-sour sauce. One of our main courses was broccoli-filled crêpe baked inside a pastry case, served with a béarnaise sauce. This certainly seems a strange thing to do with a crêpe, and with all that flour the end result risked being stodgy – but wasn't; instead it was satisfying and filling. Another main course was called Aubergine Provençal – I've no idea why. It consisted of mixed vegetables – with a great deal of spinach and mushrooms as well as some aubergines – together with vegetarian cheddar, baked in two neat parcels of filo pastry, served with a tomato sauce. Perhaps the chef has never been to Provence, where spinach is rarely used, filo pastry almost never, and cheddar (vegetarian or otherwise) is virtually unobtainable, while olive oil, garlic and Provençal herbs (none of which were particularly evident in this dish) are key ingredients. Nonetheless, this course too was most enjoyable. Side dishes were of plain boiled vegetables or a substantial little bowl of salad. For dessert, wonderful Summer Pudding. A note on the menu says all dishes can be altered to suit vegans. At lunchtimes, we were told, it's a faster-moving eatery with more of a bistro atmosphere. Decent house wine at a very modest price.
£12.75 for set three-course dinner. Wine: from £5.95/bottle.
Tue–Fri 12–2, 7–9.30 (last orders); Mon – lunch only;
Sat – dinner only.

Ston Easton (Somerset)

⋆STON EASTON PARK *Ston Easton, tel. (076121) 631*
Hotel-restaurant.
Proprietor: Peter Smedley.
With austere elegance this beautifully restored eighteenth-century

Palladian mansion (listed Grade I) stands in glorious grounds. There's a river and croquet lawn and trees to sit under. Inside, the house is wonderfully opulent, with superb original architectural and decorative features – arches, plasterwork, doorways, fireplaces, porcelain, paintings. 'Downstairs' kitchens, linen room, and others, are still in use. Few other country hotels reveal so clearly the style of life which such 'great houses' enjoyed during their heyday. While most of the building is richly ornate, the main dining room is light, fresh and welcoming, with a certain modern informality despite the unmistakable air of luxury (and even though 'gentlemen are requested to wear a jacket and tie'). The cooking reflects this combination, classic English and Continental ideas with a modern touch. It's modern, too, to offer a full vegetarian three-course lunch and four-course dinner every day.

The cooking is excellent. We enjoyed mushroom and thyme soup, a main course of feuilleté of spinach and nutmeg with a nut pilaff, and pecan pie with crème anglaise (perhaps too many nuts in this meal!). The best of English cheeses are served with celery and grapes. Coffee is included in the price. The bread's good, and the wine list includes some solid clarets and burgundies at surprisingly reasonable prices.

All year. 21 rooms, all with bath/shower. Restaurant open:

daily 12.30–2, 7.30–9.30 (10 on Fri and Sat). Bed and breakfast: £135 for two people. Set lunch: £24 (inc service). Set dinner £35 (inc service). Wine: from £14.50/bottle. Credit cards accepted.

Stow-On-The-Wold (Gloucestershire)

Grape Vine Hotel *Sheep St, tel. (0451) 30344*
Hotel-restaurant.
Proprietor: Sandra Elliott.
Ideally situated close to the heart of this madly picturesque country town, itself the centre of a very 'Green' area (in the main square, The Wholemeal Shop faces The Organic Shop – with Organic Tearooms attached), the Grape Vine is a beautiful old stone building in the distinctive local style. Outside stand plants in big wooden tubs. Step inside to discover a warm, welcoming atmosphere; the building has a lot of character, with antique furniture, soothing well-considered decor, and bedroom walls partly of bare stone. Walk into the remarkably attractive pink-and-white dining room to see how the hotel gets its name. A superb grapevine grows all over the ceiling, a veritable canopy of foliage with big ripe bunches of grapes hanging down during my visit.

A different set three-course dinner is offered nightly, always with suitable starters; a note advises vegetarians to ask for their own menu, in effect a list of alternatives to the other main courses. What a strange way of doing things! Why not simply list them on the proper menu, together with the meat dishes? The food has an Italian slant. Our starter was a nice 'tricolore' salad – avocado, tomato, mozzarella and a pesto dressing. Among several tempting main courses was a vegetable strudel – layers of filo pastry and vegetables, with a tomato sauce.

Open all year except Christmas. 23 rooms (22 with bath/shower). Restaurant open 12–2, 7–9.30. Half-board: £120 for two people, £82 for one. Lunch/dinner only: £18 for three courses. Wine: from £7.25/bottle. Credit cards accepted.

Swansea (W. Glamorgan)

Roots *2 Woodville Rd, Mumbles, tel. (0792) 366006*
Café/restaurant. 100% vegetarian.
Mumbles is a seaside village on the Gower peninsula, and close to its centre (off Queens Road) you'll find this appealing and relaxed veggie café. With candlelit pine tables, plants, flowers and wall-

hangings, it has the classic vegetarian look. The food is savoury and substantial and takes its inspiration from everywhere in the world. Starters could be falafels with yoghurt and tahini, or chickpea and aubergine samosas with cucumber raita. Main courses might be, for example, hazelnut, celery and apple roast *en croûte* with a cider and onion sauce, or Moroccan-style 'Seven Vegetables Cous-Cous'. All main meals come with a decent salad. Filling cakes, crumbles and crêpes number among the desserts. Just about everything is organic, and much use is made of food gathered from the wild, especially herbs and mushrooms. Apart from that, and the local farmhouse cheeses, everything's made on the premises. The place is cheaper and snackier at lunchtime.

About £12 for three courses. No wine (bring your own: corkage £1). Mon–Tue 11–5 (Mon summer only), Wed–Sat 11–9 (last orders).

Talsarnau, Nr Harlech (Gwynedd)

Also recommended: TREMEIFION *Talsarnau, near Harlech, tel. (0766) 77091*

Guesthouse. 100% vegetarian.

Proprietors: Maureen and John Jackson.

It will be a hard act to follow the former proprietors (Andy and Glynis Rankin) who used to run this friendly, comfortable guesthouse in three acres of grounds overlooking the nearby estuary and village and with fine views of Snowdonia. Maureen has been a vegetarian caterer for several years, and guests are offered healthy, imaginative set meals. Almost everything is organic. A typical starter might be nettle soup with croutons, followed by good main courses such as nut roast with roast potatoes, or leek-filled pancakes on rice, with walnut sauce; both choices were served with a carrot salad. For dessert there was a rhubarb and orange crumble with a proper egg custard. Instead of pudding, there was a cheese selection available. At breakfast time there's cooked food together with fresh home-made breads and a home-made muesli. It's good walking country, of course, but if you'd rather stay indoors there are board games, plenty of books, and a TV room with videos. Special winter breaks are on offer, and at any time of year children under twelve pay half price.

All year. Five rooms (three with own bath/shower). B&B: £45 for two. Half-board £54 for two. Wine: all organic, from £6.95/bottle. Credit cards accepted.

Todmorden (W. Yorkshire)

Also recommended: DUMB WAITER *23 Water St, tel. (070681) 5387*
Café-restaurant.
From the outside it looks almost like the smarter type of 'caff', but calls itself a bistro, and in fact is one of the better eating places in this small town. Upturned multi-coloured umbrellas make unusual lightshades. Service is amiable, and the food simple and straightforward. About half the menu is suitable for vegetarians, with several dishes acceptable to vegans. I enjoyed carrot and nut salad with vinaigrette (too vinegary though); followed by good, simple bean casserole and rice; and finally, marvellous old-fashioned chocolate pudding with chocolate sauce.
£11 for three courses. Wine from £7.20/litre.
Wed–Sun 12–2, 7–10, except Sun lunch

Wells-Next-The-Sea (Norfolk)

★★MOORINGS *6 Freeman St, tel. (0328) 710949*
Restaurant.
A lovely, unpretentious dockside restaurant which, like the most appealing places in France, is family-run, knows what it does well, charges modest prices, and puts the greatest emphasis on using fresh local ingredients of quality. Three things, though, are not reminiscent of real French provincial restaurants in France: service is amiable and laid-back, the menu offers a flexible range of options (you could have anything from one to four courses), and there's a selection of vegetarian dishes in every course. In fact, each course is divided into meat, fish and vegetarian choices. The menu is constantly changing, so you may not encounter my excellent starter of aubergine purée (made of local aubergines), and main course of 'bean kofta' – spiced rissoles of aduki beans, bulgur and mushrooms – with a sauce of tomato, cumin and cinnamon. On the cheeseboard is a fascinating collection of outstanding British and Irish farm-made cheeses, including two or three local Norfolk varieties. Delicious 'puddings' include trifle, rice custard pudding (a family speciality), or superb home-made ice-creams. The chocolates which accompany after-dinner coffee (or decaf or tea) are home-made too. Not only is there a good wine list, but (for a hefty corkage fee) relaxed chef-proprietor Carla Phillips won't even object if you bring your own – that's something else you won't find in France!

£9.40 for one course, £12.25 for two, £15.10 for three, or £16.60 for four courses. Wine: from £6.25/bottle, organic from £6.50/bottle, or corkage £2.75. Fri–Mon lunch 12.30–2, dinner from 7.30; Thu dinner only, Tue lunch only.

York (N. Yorkshire)

BLAKE HEAD *104 Micklegate, tel. (0904) 623767*
Café-restaurant. 100% vegetarian.
At the back of an interesting bookshop, this café is smart and clean with bare wood and tile. At lunchtime it offers counter service of interesting well-prepared snacks and meals, such as cauliflower soup, broccoli and tomato quiche, and desserts like sugar-free Tassajara cake, or a delicious (and *not* sugar-free) apricot and almond cake. Vegan options are always available. Everything is freshly made on the premises, all eggs are free-range, all cheeses use non-animal rennet, and most of the produce is organic. There's a wide range of teas, and decent organic wines by the glass. On Friday and Saturday evenings it's open for table-service dinner, transformed into something more elegant, and with somewhat more ambitious dishes such as our starter of avocado and kiwi salad, and main course of spinach, mushroom and cheese in a filo pie with tomato and basil sauce, and seasonal vegetables. All well prepared.
For three courses, allow £6.50 for lunch and £9 for dinner. Organic wine: from £7/bottle. Mon–Sat 12–2.30 for lunch, 2.30–6 teas; Fri–Sat 6.30–9.30 dinner.

Also recommended: FRESHNEY'S HOTEL *54 Low Petergate, tel. (0904) 622478*
Hotel-restaurant. Proprietor: Freshney family
An old, traditional comfortable three-storey hotel in the narrow historic streets close to York's glorious Minster. The dining room always has a selection of vegetarian dishes. These are predictable – garlic mushrooms to start, main courses of curry, pasta or crêpes – but good and welcome.
All year. Eleven rooms. Double £35, with shower £50. Restaurant open 12–2.30, 6–9.30 (open till 10 Fri and Sat).
Meals: three courses for about £10. Wine: from £5.95.
Credit cards accepted.

KITES *13 Grape Lane, tel. (0904) 641750*
Restaurant.
In a narrow old lane at the heart of the Minster area, this unusual restaurant occupies intriguing premises. Push open the door and go up a narrow and unconvincing staircase which at last arrives at the toilet. Don't go in (unless you need to), but turn right into a dining room with just three tables. Go up another flight of stairs to reach the main desk and two more dining rooms with red floorboards, red chairs, red curtains, and tables laid with red gingham tablecloths – except for a few which are blue! The walls are white-painted brick with murals depicting a bizarre mix of bamboo and kites. My waitress was inept and amateurish and asked me seven times if everything was to my liking. Classical 'background' music was too loud. The menu always includes several vegetarian possibilities: three suitable starters, and five main courses (not including the salads), as well as extraordinary desserts.

The food was clever, and potentially of a high standard, but sometimes missed the mark. My starter was a local goats' cheese in filo pastry with sliced pear and sesame dressing. The filo was slightly overdone, the cheese was good, the sesame did not seem an altogether successful accompaniment. Brioche with nuts and field mushrooms followed: the brioche was an ordinary white roll, filled with a dark, crunchy, tasty nut and mushroom mix, with an enjoyable mushroomy sauce. Desserts included Rigodon – a baked mix of nuts, dried fruit, brioche crumbs, with cream, eggs, cinnamon and vanilla. There was a good selection of wines including single glasses of dessert wine.
About £14 for three courses. Wine from £6.95/bottle.
Mon–Sat 7–10.30, and Sat 12–2.

Also recommended: MILLERS YARD CAFE *Millers Yard, Gillygate, tel. (0904) 610676*
Café-restaurant. 100% vegetarian.
Small intimate premises, set back in a yard off Gillygate, very close to the city centre. Lunchtime counter service, and likeable people. The food is simple, tasty, wholesome and inexpensive. Bean pasty or tofuburger are typical dishes, with trifle pudding to follow.
About £3 for a meal. No wine (bring your own – corkage £1).
Mon–Sat 10–4, Fri–Sat 7–10pm.

Index of Holiday Companies

Index of Listed Establishments, alphabetically by country

[English names beginning *The*; French names beginning *Au, Aux, La, Le*; etc; are listed by next word in name]

CONTRIBUTORS' COMMENTS

Please complete and return this questionnaire to me at Simon & Schuster (West Garden Place, Kendal St, London W2) if you want to

- recommend a hotel or restaurant where the vegetarian food reaches **an unusually high standard**
- correct the information for an establishment already listed

---

Full name, address and phone number (inc. area code) of the establishment

Please state whether it is 100% vegetarian, has a vegetarian menu, or has vegetarian dishes on the ordinary menu:

When did you visit?

What did you eat?

What did you think of the food and service?

Describe the cooking if possible (eg health regime, *nouvelle cuisine*, simple cooking, etc, etc)

Appearance and atmosphere of the establishment

If it also has accommodation which you sampled . . .
Proprietor's name if known:

What type of establishment is it (eg guesthouse, hotel, country house)

What was the accommodation like (eg well-furnished bedroom, luxury suite, basic dormitory)

continued overleaf . . .

What facilities did you have (eg private bathroom, TV, phone in room – or bare floorboards, no heating, broken washbasin, etc!)

Any other useful information about the establishment:

YOUR NAME AND ADDRESS (Block capitals, Attach a copy of your bill if possible)